German White-Collar Workers and the Rise of Hitler

HANS SPEIER

German
White-Collar Workers
and the Rise of Hitler

YALE UNIVERSITY PRESS: NEW HAVEN AND LONDON

This book is a translation by the author of *Die
Angestellten vor dem Nationalsozialismus: Ein
Beitrag zum Verständnis der deutschen
Sozialstruktur 1918–1933* (Göttingen, 1977).
Vandenhoeck & Ruprecht, the publisher of the
German book, kindly gave permission to publish
this English-language edition, but continues to
hold the copyright for all other languages.

Designed by Sally Harris
and set in Electra type.
Printed in the United States of America by
Halliday Lithograph, West Hanover, Mass.

Library of Congress Cataloging-in-Publication Data

Speier, Hans.
    German white-collar workers and the rise of Hitler.

    Translation of: Die Angestellten vor dem
Nationalsozialismus.
    Bibliography: p.
    Includes index.
    1. White collar workers—Germany—History.   2. Clerks
—Germany—History.   3. Social classes—Germany—
History.   4. White collar workers—Germany—Political
activity—History.   I. Title.
HD8039.M4G3639413 1986   331.7′92′0943   86-9120
ISBN 0-300-03701-5

The paper in this book meets the guidelines for
permanence and durability of the Committee on
Production Guidelines for Book Longevity
of the Council on Library Resources.

10 9 8 7 6 5 4 3 2 1

For Margit

Contents

Tables

Foreword

The Weimar Republic was established in 1919 after Germany's defeat in World War I in the face of opposition from both the left and the right. It fell in 1933 because of the electoral victory of Adolf Hitler's National Socialist Party and the assault on its supporters by Nazi thugs. This republic, an experiment in democracy for Germany, has since become a critical instance used to assess the capacity of Western capitalist democracies to deal with those economic and political problems which, when unsolved, lead to violence, terrorism, and totalitarianism.

The unabated preoccupation of so much of modern social science with Hitler and his form of fascism testifies to the unease we feel about the stability of Western democratic institutions. The specter of fascism, whatever its specific possible historical forms, haunts democratic capitalistic societies as much as the image of Stalinism haunts socialist societies. Totalitarian rule in any form assumes that the exercise of naked power is the essential expression of right. It enthrones the leader in the place where law and debate, rules and procedure, mediation and compromise ought to be. Because of the significance of both the Weimar Republic and its defeat by fascism, Hans Speier's book, written in 1932, remains as important today as at the time it was written.

Is fascist governance an intrinsic possibility in the democratic West? If so, which leaders, political parties, and classes would be most attracted to such a solution? In a period of deep economic problems (inflation, budgetary deficits, unemployment, or an international banking and credit crisis) and political instability (racial tensions, protest movements, and communist threats), could the constituencies of a Western democracy conclude that their society was ungovernable except by a totalitarian leader ruling without democratic checks, civil and political liberties, and procedural restraints on power? Such questions have sustained our preoccupation with totalitarian rule long after the destruction of Nazi Germany.

Speier provides an analysis of the basic elements in Germany's social structure which made the rise of Hitler possible. His study covers the period between 1918 and 1933, between the collapse of the monarchy and the beginning of Germany's totalitarian state. Probing the social and economic psychology of individuals and groups whose life expectations were threatened by the economic and political conditions of Weimar Germany, Speier analyzes the status vulnerabilities and defenses of groups whose claims to social honor were unrecognized, leaving them with a loss of social and self-respect and making them available for the appeals of Nazism. While many groups in Weimar Germany were disposed to accept the Nazi party's appeals, Speier charts the critical role of one aggregate of these, the new middle classes—salaried white-collar administrative, supervisory, clerical, sales, and professional employees. Specifically, he analyzes them in relation to their status competition with both the older bourgeoisie and the newer industrial and blue-collar working classes, and shows how this struggle affected the structure of the state and the prospects for revolution.

This book is one of the few examples of twentieth-century post-Marxian, post-Weberian sociological analysis. Its central problem, the transformation of class and political orders in industrial society, follows in the tradition of macrostructural analysis not only pioneered by Marx and Weber but also represented by Tocqueville, Durkheim, Sombart, and Toennies, and carried forward by Lederer and Schumpeter. Speier's approach reflects the working of an innovative and synthetic intellect. Its great achievement is that it goes beyond the categories set by the earlier writers and confronts a newly emergent reality in its own terms. Impressed by the new economic, social, and political circumstances of Germany between 1918 and 1933, Speier discovered some central tendencies of the new postindustrial society. In the disorder and chaos of German social structure during the later stages of the Weimar Republic, he discovered the political and cultural significance of the new middle classes in relation to the older bourgeoisie, the proletariat, and the capitalist order as a whole. It is remarkable that Speier, while standing in the eye of the storm, was able so skillfully to disentangle the social and political roots of the Nazi ethos from the purely economic. His achievement is comparable to that of Karl Marx's in *The Eighteenth Brumaire of Louis Bonaparte*. Like Marx, he captures a truth about a society at a critical turning point in its history, providing us with insights into the interrelation of social and economic classes, with knowledge of political psychology, and with a new understanding of the sociology of the modern state.

Although it had been ready for publication in 1933, this book was not published until 1977, when it appeared in Germany under the title *Die Angestellten vor dem Nationalsozialismus: Ein Beitrag zum Verständnis der deutschen So-*

zialstruktur 1918–1933. At the moment it should have gone to press, in 1933, the Nazis came to power, new editors were assigned, and Speier's contract was canceled. Appendix B in the present edition includes the correspondence of Theodor Geiger, one of the new editors appointed by the publisher, explaining why the manuscript was rejected. Free inquiry in Germany ended abruptly, and with its end, Speier departed for New York. There he became a professor of sociology appointed by Alvin Johnson, who was recruiting a faculty of emigré scholars to staff a new graduate division at the New School for Social Research. Speier's book remained unpublished for forty-five years, until Jürgen Kocka arranged for the 1977 German edition. It appears now in its first English edition, translated by the author over fifty years after it was written.

Speier wrote his book as part of an effort to understand German society from the vantage point of his own social democratic political commitments. It was clear to him that neither doctrinaire Marxism nor Russian communism offered solutions to the political and economic problems of Germany. When he investigated the ideologies and politics of Germany's trade unions, he discovered that, except for the Afa-Bund, their own misunderstanding and misinterpretations of the new middle classes had paralyzed rational exploitation of their newly gained power. Like other organized sectors of society, the unions quickly submitted to the Nazis; by the end of 1933 they had all but disintegrated, losing all influence as an independent political force. Speier's general analysis of the unions' self-contradictory policies and loss of political direction is applicable to the Western trade union movement today. His treatment of the larger ideological and theological dimensions of labor relates types of work not only to economic survival but to self-esteem, self-fulfillment, and social status. By narrowing their moral jurisdictional concerns to the physical well-being of the worker, the unions surrendered large areas of the workers' life meanings to other agencies and institutions, including employers, capitalists, and political leaders. Not only do labor unions cope poorly with the inherent caste distinction based on color of the collar, but their leaders are too prone to search for solutions by attaching themselves and their constituencies to a political patron or, in some cases, a criminal association. Speier's treatment of such themes in this book should stimulate discussion among students of the American labor movement.

Speier writes with the disciplined passion of a committed scholar who knows he has discovered a critical problem. His insistence on understanding the real circumstances affecting middle-class ideology led him to look at his subject from every angle of refraction. For this reason the book is not only a study of white-collar workers everywhere, but also an interpretation of Germany's social structure between the years 1890 and 1933. It is because Speier responded to the actualities of his problem—and not to an a priori theoretical or ideological commitment— that his analysis is internally consistent with his conclusions, initial assumptions, and the available data; its ring is one of authenticity. Social scientific works that have this quality are rare, but it is these that survive and become part of the basic historical and hermeneutical documentation of the changing social order.

Speier must have thought that his book would make a difference, if not for the future of Germany, at least for an understanding of Weimar's social order and disintegration. His expectancies were not fulfilled: the book was not published at the time it was most needed. Hitler took power, and Speier became an exile.

The problem Speier had addressed seemed to lose salience during the Depression decade in both the United States and Germany. Except for his essay "The Salaried Employee in Modern Society," published in *Social Research* in 1934, and a published-in-mimeograph translation of the first four chapters of the original manuscript under the title "The Salaried Employee in German Society," Speier dropped his concern with the problem of the middle classes after he entered the United States. The specific historical, psychological, and institutional feeling that he had for his own society did not at first seem transferable to the new and alien country. Continuing his line of inquiry in the United States would have required extensive new research, travel, interviewing, and familiarization with American history and institutions—in short, another lifetime. The American academic and intellectual community was preoccupied less with Germany than with domestic politics, the Depression, the New Deal, and debates over social reform. By sheer force of circumstance, emigré intellectual exiles committed themselves to the survival of the United States and shifted their attention to supporting American opposition to fascism. After 1941 the defeat of fascism became more important than attempts to explain how it had come into being. I would suppose that it was for reasons such as these that Speier turned his attention to other problems. As he notes in the preface, he began to ask a new set of questions about the character and social structure of international violence, terror, war, mass communications, and propaganda. Finding himself in exile, his perspective became international and global, informed by the universal psychology of such writers as Grimmelshausen and Shakespeare. In the postwar years he became a major interpreter of Germany to the United States and of German-American relations.

Some of the themes and problems first developed by Speier in *German White-Collar Workers and the Rise of Hitler* were reopened by C. Wright Mills in *White Collar: The American Middle Classes*. Because Mills's teacher and mentor,

Hans H. Gerth, who was also a German emigré, had known Speier and shared with him an intellectual orientation informed by an understanding of both Marx and Weber, Mills had become acquainted with Speier's ideas and with the English translations of the first four chapters of this book, as well as the 1934 essay in *Social Research*. In 1945, as part of preparation for a Senate hearing, Mills had studied six middle-sized cities in the Midwest and New England for the Smaller War Plants Corporation; his research resulted in the publication of his essay "The Middle Classes in Middle-Sized Cities" in 1946. Mills's analysis of the American middle classes relies on both Speier's writings and Gerth's presentation of them, and *White Collar* represented his most explicit general statement and application of the outlook that Speier had first put forth. With the publication of Speier's book, we gain a clearer view of the genealogy of some of Mills's ideas.

To carry back this genealogy still another generation, we must recall Speier's relation to his own mentor, Emil Lederer. It was Lederer who first called attention to the new middle classes in his book *Die Privatangestellten in der modernen Wirtschaftsentwicklung*, published in Tübingen in 1912 and republished in part in English under the title *The Problem of the Modern Salaried Employee: Its Theoretical and Statistical Basis*. In 1926 Emil Lederer and Jacob Marschak had published "Der Neue Mittelstand" in *Grundriss der Sozialökonomik*, and a part of this monograph had been published in English in 1937 under the title *The New Middle Class*. It was Lederer who had advised Speier to publish some of his ideas about the middle classes; they appeared in a paper entitled "Observations on the Understanding of Social Structure" in the last issue of the *Archiv für Sozialwissenschaft und Sozialpolitik* in 1933. In the late thirties and early forties all these works formed one aspect of the social scientific milieu for the emigré scholars who had taken up residence in New York, either in the Graduate Faculty of the New School for Social Research or the Institute for Social Research on Morningside Heights.

Some of these works were also introduced to American students attending other schools where emigré scholars had found a haven. At the University of Wisconsin Hans Gerth introduced this literature to new generations of students, including, in addition to Mills, Joseph Bensman and myself. Bensman and I had known of Speier's studies through Gerth's lectures, but the original Lederer and Marschak and Speier pieces, translated by the WPA project at Columbia University, had been inaccessible to us. Certainly our orientation and perspective were guided by many of the ideas contained in this body of literature; however, our own focus was given by the substantive data we encountered in our empirical research. In *Small Town and Mass Society*, and *The New American Society: The*

*Revolution of the Middle Classes,** we analyzed American class structure, with major emphasis on the rise and the lifestyles of the new middle classes in relation to the bureaucratization and administrative centralization of American business and government and in relation to the cultural values of Protestantism. Taken collectively, all these studies constitute, along with those of other analysts, a continuing interpretation of the origins, place, and characteristics of the middle classes in the twentieth century. If there is a unity in this aggregate of studies, it is given not only by a common theoretical orientation but by the commonalities in concrete historical development of class structures in Western society. An interpretation of these studies has been made by Jürgen Kocka, "Marxist Social Analysis and the Problem of White Collar Employees,"† in vol. 1, no. 2, of *State, Culture, and Society.*

Hans Speier discerned the larger significance of the salaried white-collar employee, that seemingly insignificant worker in the European political economy's bureaucratic labyrinth. It is fitting, in both its symbolic and ironic counterpoint, that this book should make its appearance in English after the prophetic year set by Orwell for the dystopia of totalitarianism. Fascism for Speier was part of the larger phenomenon of totalitarianism, which could encompass the political extremes of left and right. Opposed to all varieties of totalitarianism, his book posed the critical questions that must be answered by all those committed to democracy in the industrial and bureaucratic worlds of both East and West.

New York 1986   Arthur J. Vidich

---

*Second enlarged edition with the title *American Society: The Welfare State and Beyond,* forthcoming, 1986, Bergin and Garvey, South Hadley, Ma.

†Published in *State, Culture, and Society:* An International Journal of the Social, Cultural, and Political Sciences, vol. 1, no. 2, p. 137–51, (1985) Associated Faculty Press, Millwood, N.Y.

Preface to the 1977 Edition

The first version of this book was written during the last years of the Weimar Republic. Only the concluding chapter was added as late as spring 1933, when I was a lecturer at the Deutsche Hochschule für Politik (German College for Political Science) in Berlin and assistant to Professor Emil Lederer at Berlin University. As early as 1932 the Ferdinand Enke publishing house announced publication of the book as number 3 in the series *Sociological Inquiries*, but for political reasons the book never appeared. After Hitler assumed power, the three editors of the series—Alfred von Martin, Sigmund Neumann, and Albert Salomon—were replaced by Theodor Geiger and Andreas Walther. Theodor Geiger agreed with the original editors and recommended publication of the work, but Professor Walther, a Nazi, objected. The background of the publisher's decision to follow Walther's advice and not publish a "politically odious" book may be gleaned from two letters by Theodor Geiger to the author, dated 21 August and 9 September 1933. These are included in the appendix. The second letter reached me in New York, where I had begun to teach as professor of sociology at the so-called University in Exile, the Graduate Faculty of Political and Social Science of the New School for Social Research.

Prior to my emigration, I had followed the advice of Emil Lederer and written a paper entitled "Observations on the Understanding of Social Structure," which presented some of the insights contained in my book. The paper was published in the *Archiv für Sozialwissenschaft und Sozialpolitik* (ASS) of August/September 1933, the last double issue of this famous journal to appear before its termination "for the time being."

The February 1934 issue of *Social Research* contained my paper "The Salaried Employee in Modern Society," in which some data from the book were summarized. In 1939 Columbia University published a translation of the first four chapters of the book under the title *The Salaried Employee in German Society*, volume 1. This mimeographed edition (which I have used in preparing the present translation), has been cited in the American literature occasionally, but it is hardly accessible. In Germany it is unknown to this day.

In the United States in the thirties I published several papers which further pursued the theoretical beginnings of my earlier work. Among these were essays on honor and social structure, on the relationship between social inequality and democracy, and on principles of social prestige.[1] Soon, however, I turned to other fields of inquiry, especially to the analysis of political propaganda and to the sociology of war. It appeared to me that, influenced by the ideology of progress and by the industrialization of the West, many social scientists came to regard economic and social risks as the greatest evils facing man and, as a result, neglected the basic phenomena of social life: *physical* hazards, that is, the danger of violent death. Both liberalism and socialism were inclined to obscure these phenomena.

The outbreak of World War II brought with it a host of more urgent problems, next to which the question of German white-collar workers in the Weimar Republic appeared to me as uninteresting. After the war the subject did acquire new significance, however, in inquiries into the origins of National Socialism in Germany. These discussions sometimes suffered because participants were not especially knowledgeable about salaried employees during the Weimar years, and even today the connections between white-collar life and National Socialism remain potentially rewarding areas of research. The present book may be useful in this regard, for it owes its origin to a political impulse to understand the widespread prejudice against democracy and manual labor held by many white-collar workers. To focus on a contemporary issue, as this book did in the twenties and thirties, is of necessity to sacrifice historical distance, but a shortened perspective sometimes sharpens one's perception of details, and in any case is a testimony of the past, which may serve later historical research.

The present text is a revision and enlargement of the original manuscript. It owes its origin to the interest and initiative of Professor Jürgen Kocka, who provided me with a conscientious criticism of the first version of my book and facilitated the revision of the original text by calling my attention to pertinent research of the past forty years. Without his encouragement I would not have resumed work on the white-collar workers in the Weimar Republic.

The original version of the book was based, among other things, on the study of sources in the archives of the following organizations, which were most helpful to me by furnishing oral and written information: Deutschnationaler Handlungsgehilfen-Verband (DHV), Gewerkschaftsbund der Angestellten (GdA), Allgemeiner freier Angestelltenbund (Afa-Bund), Bund der technischen Angestellten und Beamten (Butab), Deutscher Bankbeamten-Verein (DBV), Allgemeiner Verband der Versicherungsangestellten (AVV), and Vereinigung leitender Angestellter (Vela).

In addition, I had conversations with many trade union functionaries and politicians on the subject of my work during the last years of the Weimar Republic. Some aspects of white-collar life were known to me from personal experience. Toward the end of the Great Inflation of the early 1920s I was an apprentice in a small private bank in Berlin and later, after finishing my studies with Karl Mannheim and Emil Lederer in Heidelberg, I was employed as an editor in a large publishing house in Berlin. In the last years prior to Hitler's ascent to power, I benefited in my work from closer contacts with employed and unemployed blue- and white-collar workers. I owed these contacts to my work as lecturer at the Deutsche Hochschule für Politik in Berlin and, avocationally, in the Labor Education organization of the Social Democratic Party. Further, as a volunteer for research purposes I made home visits for the Social Service Organization of the City of Berlin. Finally, during the Great Depression I received daily reports from my first wife on the conditions in which the poorest of the poor tried to survive. My wife, who died in 1965, was at the time a municipal pediatrician in Wedding, a proletarian district of the city.

It is neither possible nor necessary to list in detail all changes in the original text which I have made for this edition. The following remarks must suffice. I have studied no additional sources. All books and articles cited with a date prior to 1934 were used in preparing the original version. In general, the organization of the material has not been changed very much, although I have made some rearrangements in the interest of clarity. I have also made a few changes and additions. In particular, I had seen the trade union policy pursued after World War I by the so-called middle-class organizations, the GdA and the DHV, merely as an adaptation to the new republican circumstances and had underestimated the significance for these organizations of representing the interests of their members vis-à-vis the entrepreneurs. Many knowledgeable people shared my views, including such trade unionists as Otto Suhr, politicians such as Carl Mierendorff, and scholars like Emil Lederer. More recent research, however, attributes greater weight to the process of radicalization, which these organizations already had entered during World War I, but this research might underestimate the process of adaptation after 1919. I have also presented the policy of the entrepreneurs with greater discrimination than I did in my youthful enthusiasm.

The data on income and unemployment, like the more precise figures on the distribution of expenditures in blue- and white-collar households, can be found only in this edition. The second section of chapter 10, "DHV and

NSDAP," was not included in the original version. The main theses on this subject could be found only between the lines.

While in the Weimar Republic I was interested in white-collar work for political as well as sociological reasons. Politically, I was closer to the Afa-Bund, the umbrella organization of the free trade unions of salaried employees, than to the less radical Allgemeiner Deutscher Gewerkschaftsbund (ADGB), in which the allied free trade unions of manual workers were organized. I still remember my feelings when I read in the last issue of *Die Arbeit* the long article by Lothar Erdmann. *Die Arbeit*, edited by Theodor Leipart, was the leading journal of the ADGB. Erdmann's article appeared to me as a stupid and shameful effort to save the free trade unions by demonstrating their affinities with National Socialism. Erdmann wrote that the German socialist workers' movement claimed the "natural right" of aggression in foreign policy, and he stressed the participation of the German workers in "the foreign policy struggle for the global reputation of their own nation."[2] He said that "the dictate of Versailles [had to] conjure up as a psychological necessity a strong nationalist movement in Germany erupting irresistibly from the will of the nation to live."[3] He saw the aim of the trade union movement in "the overcoming of the class struggle"[4] and concluded with the following admonition:

> The national organization of labor which they [the trade unions] have built up in decades of hard struggle and immeasurable effort, borne by the confidence and will to sacrifice of the German workers, is a national value, which the allied [!] forces of the national revolution must also respect and safeguard; this is especially true of the great movement which insists on the claim that its revolution is national and socialist. This great mission is an obligation.[5]

As far as I recall, no intellectual who worked for the Afa-Bund made a similar statement.

Although I was aware of the tendencies toward embourgeoisement among the workers,[6] I was convinced that Erdmann's pragmatism was based on an erroneous political estimate of the situation and that it failed to express the will of the workers. I do recall, however, that a few weeks after Hitler's ascent to power and prior to the destruction of the German trade unions, a few older and experienced Social Democratic politicians had not yet become wholly pessimistic about Germany's future. I gained this impression from a discussion at Emil Lederer's home, where I spoke about the end of Weimar. On the basis of my studies I called special attention to the appeal of National Socialism to members of the DHV and the GdA and to unorganized white-collar workers. I also stressed the DHV's contribution to disseminating the National Socialist creed. For years, the ideology of the DHV had appeared to me to be intolerably prejudiced, and politically I regarded it as no less pernicious than views that were expressed in the magazine *Die Tat* and held by other right-wing radical intellectuals.[7]

Andreas Walther had no trouble recognizing my political views in the original version of this book, for despite my effort at objectivity I had revealed these views to the attentive reader. In revising the old text I did not remove the traces of my political passion, although I am better informed today about the DHV than I was at the beginning of the thirties. In view of new research, I have modified a few statements on the DHV. However, the DHV can never be vindicated of having contributed to Hitler's electoral victories, of having shared reactionary and National Socialist views, and of having contributed to their dissemination in the Weimar Republic.

In my work I have tried to present not only the economic interests of the salaried employees but also their social and political differentiation and their relation to the manual workers. The social theory on which my investigation was based was sketched only very briefly in the original introduction. For this edition I have somewhat enlarged the conclusion of this introduction and have composed chapter 7 from remarks that were originally scattered, so as to justify more precisely my reliance on the concept of prestige, borrowed from Max Weber. Although it has become customary today to speak of social status instead of social honor, respect, or prestige, I still hold the view that investigations of this kind cannot do without the concept of social prestige. In my opinion, status can be reduced to principles of social prestige, and these principles, but not status differences as such, provide insights into the structure of a given society. The privileges of civil servants and salaried employees are indeed aspects of the status enjoyed by these strata, but these advantages guaranteed by law—longer notices given for termination of employment, separate social insurance, and so forth—are based on structural features of German society, which have their origin in claims to and validations of respect. In any event, the status of salaried employees does not result from particular labor functions, otherwise the status privileges of white-collar workers would be the same in all modern societies. Nor can the status of salaried employees be derived from their economic class position, for with respect to the necessity that they sell their labor to owners of the means of production or to owners of commercial and service capital, white-collar workers are the equals to blue-collar workers, with whom they share a structural dependency. In other respects, however, which must not be neglected, white-collar workers do not resemble their blue-collar counterparts at all.

Acknowledgments

At all stages of the production of this edition, Arthur Vidich has been very helpful and encouraging. He also arranged for Michael Hughey's painstaking editing of the English text. I am most grateful to these gentlemen. Others helped and I am indebted to them as well. My old friend Margit Leipnik had typed the original German version in Berlin in 1932–33; more than forty years later, in 1976, she also typed, now as Margit Speier, the second version in various stages of its development. Finally, she typed the first draft of this translation in 1983. Her patience and perseverance were matched only by her cheerfulness. In the long process of seeing the project through to its end, Daria Martin attended to many administrative details in her usual quiet and competent manner. Finally, I wish to thank Gladys Topkis, senior editor of Yale University Press, for her support and Michael Joyce for his consummate skill and courtesy as manuscript editor.

For work on the second German version of the book, I received financial support from the Fritz Thyssen Stiftung, which I wish to acknowledge gratefully.

Hans Speier

Hartsdale, N.Y. 1986

Acronyms

ADGB   Allgemeiner Deutscher Gewerkschaftsbund (General Association of German Trade Unions, "free," socialist)

Afa-Bund   Allgemeiner freier Angestelltenbund (General Association of Free Employees, "free," socialist)

AVV   Allgemeiner Verband der Versicherungsangestellten (General Association of Insurance Employees, liberal-national)

BdI   Bund der Industriellen (League of Industrialists)

Butab   Bund der technischen Angestellten und Beamten (Association of Technical Employees and Civil Servants, "free," socialist)

Butib   Bund der technisch-industriellen Beamten (Association of Technical-Industrial Employees)

BVP   Bayerische Volkspartei (Bavarian People's Party)

CVDI   Centralverband Deutscher Industrieller (Central Association of German Industrialists)

DAF   Deutsche Arbeitsfront (German Labor Front)

DBV   Deutscher Bankbeamtenverein e.V. (German Bank Employees Association, liberal-national)

DDP   Deutsche Demokratische Partei (German Democratic Party)

DGB   Deutscher Gewerkschaftsbund (German League of Trade Unions, Christian-national umbrella organization of blue- and white-collar workers' associations)

DHV   Deutschnationaler Handlungsgehilfen-Verband (German National Association of Commercial Clerks, Christian-national)

DNVP   Deutschnationale Volkspartei (German National People's Party)

DTV   Deutscher Techniker Verband (German Association of Technicians)

DVP   Deutsche Volkspartei (German People's Party)

DWB   Deutscher Werkmeister-Bund (German Foremen's League, Christian-national)

DWV Deutscher Werkmeisterverband (German Foremen's Association, "free," moderately socialist)

GdA Gewerkschaftsbund der Angestellten (Federation of Salaried Employees, liberal-national)

Gedag Gesamtverband der Angestelltengewerkschaften (Federation of Employees' Unions, Christian-national)

Gwr Gewerkschaftsring Deutscher Arbeiter-, Angestellten- und Beamtenverbände (Trade Union Cartel of the Associations of German Workers, Employees, and Civil Servants, liberal-national)

KPD Kommunistische Partei Deutschlands (German Communist Party)

NSBO Nationalsozialistische Betriebszellenorganization (National Socialist Organization of Factory Cells)

NSDAP Nationalsozialistische Deutsche Arbeiterpartei (National Socialist German Workers' Party)

RfW Reichskuratorium für Wirtschaftlichkeit (Reich Board for Economic Affairs)

SA Sturmabteilung (Storm Troop)

SPD Sozialdemokratische Partei Deutschlands (Social Democratic Party of Germany)

USPD Unabhängige Sozialistische Partei Deutschlands (Independent Socialist Party of Germany)

VdDI Verband deutscher Diplom-Ingenieure (Association of German Academic Engineers)

VDH Verband Deutscher Handlungsgehilfen zu Leipzig (Association of German Commercial Clerks)

Vela Vereinigung leitender Angestellter (League of Executive Employees)

VwA Verband der weiblichen Handels- und Büroangestellten (Association of Female Business and Office Employees, Christian-national)

ZdA Zentralverband der Angestellten (Central Federation of Employees, "free," socialist)

ZdH Zentralverband der Handlungsgehilfen und Handlungsgehilfinnen (Central Association of Male and Female Commercial Employees)

German White-Collar Workers and the Rise of Hitler

Introduction

After the postwar inflation in Germany the salaried employee became the subject of many statistical, sociological, sociographical, and sociopsychological inquiries. Social science had discovered him only a few years before World War I; now investigations were undertaken, fiction tried to give his life literary flavor, and periodicals, magazines, and the theater took the subject up with enthusiasm. All presented it in their own particular way to a wide audience. Public opinion in industrial society was openly partial to this motley stratum, the creature of social developments. Views of the employee differed, but they were expressed with more animation than when artisans or peasants were under discussion.

The reason for this attitude is simple: a writer on sociological problems comes into frequent contact with white-collar workers. He knows them better than manual workers and farmers, for example, because as a member of the intelligentsia he is socially closer to them than to members of other strata. Even if his sympathies are with the latter, these feelings are often derived from reading, while his opinions about white-collar workers are based upon observation and concrete experience. An indirect confirmation of the significance of this contact is the fact that those salaried employees who most closely resemble blue-collar workers have received the least attention in the literature. Less is known about foremen than about commercial employees. Moreover, almost all opinions about employees in general pertain to commercial employees in larger cities, whereas the commercial employees of small- and medium-sized towns are usually neglected because they live beyond the social horizon of the metropolitan writer.

It has often been pointed out that the largest German cities are not cities of industrial workers but of salaried employees and civil servants. The administrative and distributive functions of society are concentrated in large cities, and writers who help to mold public opinion live and practice their profession there. Intellectuals and commercial employees are thus acquainted with each other, and frequently the intellectual is himself a white-collar worker. But while this social proximity is responsible for the public's relatively accurate information on

1

salaried employees in the Weimar Republic, it does not account for the lively interest in them. This attention cannot be fully explained by the rapid and vigorous growth of the white-collar stratum during the past few decades. To be sure, social scientists had noticed that the number of gainfully employed manual workers had not even doubled between 1882 and 1925, while that of salaried employees and civil servants had grown five times, and that the total number of employees, estimated at about one-and-one-half million persons in 1907, had increased in twenty-five years to four million. But the public does not base its opinion on statistics; qualitative rather than quantitative changes in society have aroused its interest.

The living conditions of large sections of the middle and lower strata of the middle classes changed radically and extraordinarily rapidly during the inflationary period following World War I. Forced to live under deteriorated economic conditions, they were often so deprived of their economic security—considered the characteristic of their class—that the term *middle class* had dubious meaning. During the preceding generation the old self-employed middle class had lost many of its members to the salaried employees. Because their new work increased their insecurity and lack of freedom, they regarded this change as a social descent. The interest in salaried employees is grounded to a large extent in the middle-class desire for self-understanding, a desire born of the bitter experiences of inflation, office automation, and, since 1929, of the economic crisis.

This development had rendered very timely the old theory that the proletariat will expand as capitalism advances, while the middle class is necessarily destined to perish. Before World War I this theory was embraced by an orthodox group of socialist leaders, and the workers adhered to it with an enthusiasm kindled by a rationalized promise of victory. The theory did not reflect a socialist desire to destroy the middle class, but merely articulated a Marxist prediction of the course of economic development. The middle class, however, apprised so sternly of its downfall, held the socialists responsible for its future fate. Although the development was shown only in theory, the projected future of the middle class formed a dark background against which labor could stand out more brightly.

After the revolution German labor gained a certain influence in governmental affairs through one of its political parties. The unions were recognized by industry and the state alike. The social stigma which had clung to labor even throughout World War I—despite the emperor's declaration of domestic peace (Burgfriede)[1]—began to fade. In a country whose middle class jealously guarded its distance from the workers and was unaccustomed to their participation in the political life of the state, this change in the political order almost inevitably led to maladjustments.

In these maladjustments the past avenged itself. The influence of the middle class had been strong from the reactionary years following the abortive revolution of 1848, through the period of anti-socialist laws of 1878–90, up through World War I, when the class privileges of the Prussian electoral franchise remained intact. On the basis of its past experiences, the bourgeoisie connected its present social destitution with the political ascent of labor. These experiences were insignificant enough, because of the system of government. Before the war, not only had manual workers been denied social recognition and an opportunity to shoulder responsibility, but the political education of ordinary middle-class people, who differed so greatly from the economically powerful bourgeoisie, had also been neglected. Order was all that mattered in Germany, and no one asked about the price. Upon this lack of political education, and not upon its pauperization alone, rested the disorientation of the middle classes in the Weimar Republic. As has been pointedly remarked, they supported a different party at almost every election.[2]

When the middle classes were impoverished, they tried to identify the authors of their misery. In doing so, they laid the groundwork for a political counter-revolution by actively supporting those political leaders who sought to reverse unwanted changes by attributing them to "guilty" politicians and calling for their punishment. Nationalist ideas proved to be a strong propelling force in this development, not only because of Germany's international situation, but also for another, entirely different reason: these ideas were closely allied with the social conceptions of the middle class.

Because it had been victorious in the wars of the nineteenth century, the army stood as a symbol for the nation in Germany and particularly in Prussia. It would be erroneous to trace the military's influence to the economic interests of particular portions of the population, although both industry and the lower middle classes profited from the existence of the standing army. Before the outbreak of World War I, a single infantry regiment "contributed a direct yearly income of about 900,000 marks to its garrison town through the salaries of its officers, doctors, and civil service employees, the wages of noncommissioned officers and privates, and the bonuses and revenues from the commissaries, kitchen, and officers' mess halls."[3] But these economic facts were less important for the political and social order in Germany than the traditional prestige of military life and its militaristic extension to civil society. This prestige sustained the molding force of pre-industrial power and pre-capitalist values in industrial society.

The social models of the prewar middle class also had a military character. The member of the veterans' organizations, the ex-serviceman entitled to a civil service position, the reserve officer, and the dashing fraternity student were a source of pleasure to the humble citizen, as well as an object of economic interest to the lodging-house keeper and tradesman. As models, such persons also guaranteed the continuation of the social rank order, at the apex of which stood the non-bourgeois feudal class. Its members were instrumental in securing approval of the hierarchy among the middle classes; they made it appear desirable to members of the bourgeoisie to marry into the nobility or to get knighted themselves. At the same time, these social models represented the stages in a conceivable and reasonable ascent, which always carried with it an increase in social prestige and usually economic security, if not always financial gain. Similarly, in higher spheres, the titled industrial magnate or banker, with his right to be presented at court, was more highly esteemed than his colleague who had nothing but wealth.

The composition of the social hierarchy was determined by the values and notions of the nobility, while its base was formed by small townspeople and lower-level civil servants. Manual workers were not included. They stood outside the pale of society, despised or feared on account of their strong discipline. No one noticed therefore, that manual workers had created a society of their own in their clubs and organizations and that this society was generally one of proletarians aspiring to be petits bourgeois—a repetition on a large scale of the phenomenon of the would-be-gentleman, but on a lower level. The higher strata always set the patterns for styles of life, even though the lower strata might oppose the higher ones both economically and politically.

Germany's defeat in World War I did not result in internal peace, because divisions in the social hierarchy were accentuated by the weakness of the army and labor's perceptible gains in power—evident in the Social Democratic Party's gaining access to government and the legal recognition of the trade unions. The impoverished middle strata saw a connection between these two phenomena and attributed their own destitution to both of them. They believed that the politically and socially successful leaders of the working class, if not the class as such, were responsible both for the moral and physical pauperization of the middle classes and for the distress of society and the nation. Thus, the theory that the proletariat was ascending in power as the middle classes foundered was accepted by the bourgeoisie as a painful truth at the very moment when its unqualified application was beginning to be doubted by the working class itself.

In its bare outlines, at least, this proletarian-socialistic theory of society had been the main stimulus in the political awakening of the working class. Now the course of social development posed a problem that demanded thorough scrutiny of the entire doctrine. According to Marx's well-known prognosis, the proportion of labor in the population would grow absolutely and relatively. Statistics showed, however, that this had not held true in the most recent phase of capitalism. From 1895 to 1925 the number of wage laborers in industry dropped from 56.8 percent to 45.1 percent of the total workforce. This development would have presented a disquieting problem to Marxist sociologists had they not defined the concept of "proletariat" more liberally than Marx.

Socialist theorists found justification in the living and working conditions of modern white-collar workers for including them in the working class. Although salaried employees were not manual laborers, they were workers who, like blue-collar workers, had to sell their labor in order to live. But the existence of a "white-collar proletariat" meant that a fundamental "restructuring of the proletariat"[4] itself had occurred, and this change would require sociological and ideological evaluation. Because the concepts of "proletariat" and "middle class" had become vague as a result of the social development of the two classes, new definitions of the terms were necessary. In the efforts to furnish such definitions, the key position of the salaried employees became evident. According to one interpretation, their mode of living was seen as having extreme importance for the transmission, preservation, and revival of national culture. According to another interpretation, the modern employee shared the proletarian status of the worker. Thus two sociological interpretations, which will be referred to as "middle-class theory" and "lower-class theory," contended with each other in the social arena. Proponents of neither had anticipated this confrontation. The lower-class theory, derived from an analysis of the blue-collar proletariat, necessarily encountered difficulties when applied to understanding the differences between salaried employees and workers, while the middle-class theory lacked the methodological means to explain either the similarities between these groups or the consequences of those similarities.

The two theories are sharply contradictory. For example, in amplifying and extending the features of a single social group, proponents of the middle-class theory thought they were illuminating the nature of industrial society itself. Their view that the historical accent in the next epoch would be placed "on the stratum of salaried employees"[5] was exaggerated to the neglect not only of workers and farmers, but also of civil servants, and even of the more powerful social strata. The middle-class theory was, of course, hotly contested, but it and other positions all had the same effect: by focusing on white-collar workers, they tended to invalidate older sociological notions of society as a whole. Even if these notions did not always originate in a clearly defined, comprehensive conception of society, they all did assume the possibility of arriving at a general understanding of the structure of postwar German society.

This generalizing assumption was shared by every theory focusing on white-collar workers, including Schumpeter's view that the increasing number of salaried employees would produce a bureaucratized future;[6] the prediction of a brewing class struggle between white- and blue-collar workers;[7] the thesis that the "mass character" of employees cannot determine their mentality[8] and that the employees are entangled in an "artificial hierarchy";[9] Kracauer's critical contention that white-collar workers seek to escape from reality;[10] and the assertion of the Deutschnationaler Handlungsgehilfen-Verband that the commercial employee is basically an entrepreneur.[11]

It is quite unfeasible to make a sociological statement about the status or prestige of any social stratum without assuming the possibility of further sociological inferences, for the sociology of a particular stratum presupposes knowledge of the whole social structure. This is particularly true of a sociology of white-collar workers, for they form a stratum of considerable social range. It includes unskilled and semiskilled workers who operate office machines without preliminary training, who are saleswomen in one-price stores and do not require special qualifications, or who are merely pen pushers. Their income, as well as the status of their work, is therefore generally lower than that of the average worker, and is far below that of the highly skilled worker. However, certain employees who perform highly skilled work also belong to this stratum. The transition from this group to the top of the pyramid—to the genuine entrepreneurs—is almost imperceptible. Laborers' children with only elementary school education enter the ranks of salaried employees side by side with high-level civil servants' children with long academic records. The range of income between the lower and upper ranks of employees is very wide. If executives are included, it is greater than the differences in income between highly skilled workers and unskilled laborers. In short, the social structure of the salaried employees may be pictured as a pyramid comparable to that of industrial society generally. Likewise, disagreements over the sociology of salaried employees are comparable to related disputes about the sociology of industrial society waged by the intellectuals of an impoverished middle class striving for self-understanding on the one side and by a proletariat ideologically disturbed by internal shifts on the other.

Inasmuch as salaried employees are wage earners, the task of a sociology of white-collar workers is to specify how they differ from blue-collar workers and to determine how and why these differences are significant. In fact, hostility between proponents of the various theories originates with attempts to resolve these issues. Adherents of the lower-class theory made an ideological and a so-cioeconomic judgment when they described white-collar workers as a "new pro-letariat." Proponents of the opposing middle-class theory classified these employees as a "new middle class" despite their character as wage earners. They thus either considered the social and economic differences between white-collar workers and labor to be more important than those between employees and employers, or they contested the close relationship between socioeconomic and ideological factors, which was not questioned by the lower-class theory.

This book attempts an interpretation of the salaried employees in the Weimar Republic with references to the structure and character of German society. It is insufficient in such an effort to take account only of economic class structure, which in theory is identical in all capitalist societies. The difference between capitalists and labor, traceable to ownership and non-ownership of the means of production, is always present, as is the conflict of interests between the two classes played out on the labor market. Viewed exclusively in terms of their economic class position, salaried employees are proletarians. But to confine the analysis of a capitalist society to class positions is to trace all differences between capitalist societies to differences in their rates of development, that is, to degrees of "ripeness" of the system. Modern Western societies, however, do not differ *only* in their rates of modernization, for otherwise capitalist societies would display equivalent stages at comparable points in their history, and they clearly do not. For example, even though the capitalist industrialization of Germany occurred later than that of England, the structure of German society never resembled that of English society. In Germany the gentleman was never a social model, English society was free of militarism, and so forth.

Differences in the structure of capitalist societies find expression and effect in a number of areas that are not traceable exclusively to the labor market and its conflicts. These include the styles of life of their different strata; the status inequalities, sometimes buttressed by law and tradition, of people who share identical class positions; and the different ways in which social groups are able to appropriate respectability or validate its claim. To use Max Weber's words, these status factors "hinder the strict carrying through of the sheer market prin-ciple."[12] Weber defined the social differentiation of "estates" *(Stände)* as "typically utilizing positive or negative privileges in social valuation, based upon

a) style of life, hence
b) formal education . . .
c) hereditary or occupational prestige."[13]

Social order, for Weber, referred to the "distribution" of "social honor (prestige)" between "typical groups."[14] We shall follow the considerations on which these definitions are based, but use the terms "social esteem," "social prestige," or "social respect" instead of "honor" or "valuation."

It is also useful to call attention to Max Weber's remarks on the relation between power and honor. On the basis of his comparative historical studies, he taught that power conditioned economically as well as in other ways could be the foundation of social honor. In his view, however, not every kind of power entails social honor, as can be gleaned from his examples of the "typical American boss" and the "typical big speculator." Finally, Weber pointed out, not only can power be the basis of social honor, but "indeed, social honor or prestige may even be the basis of economic power, and very frequently has been. Power, as well as honor, may be guaranteed by the legal order."[15]

We shall relate the social prestige of the salaried employees to particular perceptions of social value in German society. Three different insights will result from this procedure.

First, there existed no uniform standards for evaluating and assigning social prestige by which each social stratum could locate and accept its own (and others') rank on the ladder of inequalities. Instead, a plurality of social valuations contended with one another, resulting in opposed views of the appropriate relations of subordination and superordination. Capitalist and proletarian conceptions of the "just" distribution of power and prestige were not the only protagonists in this struggle. Pre-capitalistic, military, bureaucratic, and still other conceptions of value also took part. These were not simply the expressions of historical memories and romantic longings for the past. Rather, they provided particular social strata both with the foundations of their social identity and with more or less effective means in the struggle for power and prestige.

Second, salaried employees were themselves divided over their conceptions of value and the grounds on which their claims for prestige were based. They were not a unified stratum. Other strata and classes also displayed some heterogeneity, but the differences were most strongly pronounced among white-collar workers. This can be explained by the fact that this stratum ranged from the lumpenproletariat in one direction to the strata of small businessmen and directors of medium and large enterprises in the other.

Finally, salaried employees characteristically generated no social valuations of their own, but typically adopted them from other strata. In part, they adopted the value conceptions of the workers, and in part those of the civil servants, the military, the old middle class, the "cultivated" bourgeoisie, and even, to an extent, those of the entrepreneurs. It is therefore possible to characterize the German salaried employees in the Weimar Republic as value-parasites. It is largely for this reason that many German white-collar workers were early victims of the propagandists of *Volkstum* and of national "revival": they lacked the reassuring support of a moral tradition that they could truly call their own.

I A Survey of the Stratum

The census of 1885 showed Germany to have only 90,000 unmarried and 51,000 married commercial clerks. The merchant's assistant belonged to the merchant class. Even in capitalist society he could be considered a member of this class because his economic dependence was regarded only as a stepping stone on the way to economic independence. His typical course of vocational development was from apprentice to assistant to boss. Relations between the employer and his clerk were patriarchal. Assistant and apprentice were admitted to the family circle and very often boarded with their employer. For example, Frau Jenny Treibel, the heroine of Theodor Fontane's novel of the same name (1893), recalls that as a young girl she had helped her father in his shop by pasting together small and large paper bags for the reward of two pfennig per hundred pieces. At dinner she sat in her father's house "between Herr Mielke, the clerk, and Louis, the apprentice," who thus enjoyed a commensal life with the family.[1]

Only a few years before the turn of the century, almost half the male sales-clerks in Germany received free room and board.[2] This combination of board and pay does not compare with the salary of today's white-collar worker, who performs his appointed tasks and receives fixed wages as compensation. In return for devoting his life to a commercial occupation, the clerk in times past received a subsidy for his living expenses. Where he lived in order to work, the hardships of his apprenticeship being mitigated by the prospect of future independence, the salaried employee of today works in order to live. As is also true of the manual worker, his work is considered not as a part of his life but rather as a sacrifice of his life. And where the white-collar worker, as wage earner, strives toward a shorter workday, the merchant's assistant did not consider such a reduction urgent. He worked twelve hours or more a day, including Sundays, as long as his guild, the commercial profession, or his employer demanded it. Persons with engaging occupations are not usually concerned with limiting the workday.

Clerical Personnel in Small Enterprises

The mass of modern white-collar workers, with its wide array of occupations, did not evolve exclusively from the species of commercial clerk. It would be a mistake to regard the novelist Gustav Freytag's upright clerks as the social ancestors of all the tortured creatures described in Priestley's *Angel Pavement*. Only those white-collar workers who are employed in small commercial establishments, in small and medium-sized cities, and, above all, in retail shops, are genuine descendants of the old-time clerk who lived in class equality with his employer.

In the Weimar Republic these employees worked under conditions and modeled their lives and thought on patterns similar to those of the earlier clerks. Although they did possess greater opportunities for attaining independence (possibly through marriage), their duties were not yet radically specialized, their workday had been shortened very little if at all, and their pay was exceedingly low. They regarded themselves as members of the lower middle class, a term which then lacked its contemporary disparaging sting. They had personal contact with their employers, with whom they dealt directly. The pro-union stance of the modern wage earner had always puzzled them, for experience had not taught them the necessity of collective action, since their workplaces were small and their isolation great. They preferred Christian associations to trade unions, especially in the small towns. In 1932, a study of youth employed in commerce in middle-sized East Prussian towns found a proportionally high percentage to be still connected with the church and devoted to religion. Young Catholic and Protestant men alike favored Christian associations. Young women were also religious, some clinging to the naive piety of children while others undertook their religious duties out of genuine conviction.[3] Family and church ties, as well as social distinction from manual labor, remained an entrenched and unbroken tradition.

If a small-town white-collar worker lost his job, he felt more stigmatized than his unemployed colleague in the big city. This was true even at the time of the Great Depression: "one is immediately ostracized . . . déclassé, without means of support, unemployed—well, that's equal to being a communist."[4] For all these reasons, the position and perspective of the commercial employee in the small enterprise was close to that of the old middle class, with which he shared an aversion to industrialization and its social creatures—the capitalist industrialist and the class-conscious laborer.

This relationship between independent and dependent persons in the *old* middle class was only occasionally apparent in economic and social policies because rural and small-town employees and those in small enterprises were either very poorly organized or, if organized, shared membership with employees of large establishments. It was nonetheless quite significant that in 1932 the middle-class organizations of salaried employees—the Deutschnationaler Handlungsgehilfen-Verband (DHV), the Verband der weiblichen Handels- und Büroangestellten (VwA), the Central German Board of Retail Trade, and the Gewerkschaftsbund der Angestellten (GdA)—published a pamphlet, *Mensch oder Maschine in der Warenverteilung* (Man or Machine in the Distribution of Merchandise), to protest against automatic merchandising after store hours.

Only the socialist Allgemeiner freier Angestelltenbund (Afa-Bund) did not oppose technical progress. Together with the free and Christian trade unions of manual workers, it advocated the use of automats for distribution, because their manufacture necessitated increased employment of labor, and their installation made shorter working hours a possibility for store employees. Likewise, the associations of the Afa-Bund never pleaded for the break-up of large business establishments, as occasionally advocated by the DHV.[5] It is significant that the associations opposing the installation of automats also contained the largest proportion of members from small and medium-sized cities. According to H. Hamm's investigation of 1,000 members of each organization, the following numbers lived in Berlin and other large cities of more than 100,000 inhabitants:[6]

	DHV	GdA	ZdA
All cities over 100,000	412	556	660
Berlin	72	127	176

Inasmuch as the functions of white-collar workers in small establishments had changed very little, they resembled their social predecessors more closely than did any other employee stratum. For this reason, they did not display the characteristic features of modern salaried employees in capitalist society. Nonetheless, to disregard them in speaking of "the" salaried employees would be a mistake. Neither their economic nor sociopolitical development permits their neglect. If big industry would inherit the future, small establishments were the bastions through which the past defended itself in the present.

The sociology of the entire mass of wage earners will have to be reconstructed by taking into account the differences in size of enterprises and the resulting differences in employees' outlooks. Up to now large enterprises have provided the only point of departure. This reconstruction is necessary both for salaried employees generally, who possess substantially different outlooks, and particularly for those in commerce, where the majority of white-collar workers continued to be engaged. Not less than 21.8 percent of the salaried employees in commerce and insurance worked in establishments of five persons or less, 39.2 percent in those of up to ten persons, and more than half (58 percent) in establishments of up to fifty persons. One-third (33.5 percent) of the employees in handicraft and industry were active in enterprises employing up to fifty individuals.[7] This means that, excluding the technical personnel in small and medium-sized establishments, this group included altogether approximately 1.1 million salaried employees (1925), or about one-third of all commercial and office employees, foremen, technicians, and other wage earners considered to be white-collar workers according to prevailing opinion and practice.

Employees in small establishments, whose activities and social position within the enterprise had been generally unchanged despite the passage of time, continued to serve as the primary carriers of middle-class traditions, just as they had in pre-capitalist days. In commerce especially, these employees of the old type, like the small establishments in which they worked, held a relatively fixed position. In 1925, only 11.7 percent of salaried employees in commerce and insurance worked in enterprises of two hundred or more persons. As the business establishment increased in size, the traditional type disappeared and the modern wage-earning, commercial employee of capitalist society came to the fore. The giant enterprise destroyed the position of assistant to the employer. At one end of this development stands the assistant in the small-town general store, at the other the salesmen of standardized articles in chain stores in large cities and most sales personnel in department and one-price stores.[8] Department stores collected 4.3 percent (1928) of total German retail-trade receipts, and the one-price stores accounted for 1.5 percent (1932). Excluding peddlers, consumer cooperatives, company stores, mail order houses, department stores, and one-price establishments, small and medium-sized retail businesses took in 80.6 percent of total receipts in 1928.[9]

As business establishments grew larger, the activities of the individual encountered greater limitations. The tasks divided among employer, assistant, and apprentice in small establishments underwent specialization and, as far as possible, standardization. Minutely differentiated hierarchies developed within the enterprise. More and more people were detached from their former vocational groups and were delivered to a dependency defined in hierarchic gradations.

In addition to the hierarchy within the enterprise, employees were further ranked according to the type of retail store for which they worked. For example, the social prestige of the salesforce depended on volume of sales, sales appeal, and type of customer. Salesclerks in shops selling expensive merchandise enjoyed higher esteem than those selling cheaper goods in ordinary stores. Thus, the personnel in luxury stores constituted the highest group, while purveyors of provisions were the lowest. Selling necessities costing little per unit conferred little prestige, selling expensive articles not bought by the lower strata (for example, leather goods, velvets, silks) increased the salesclerk's social value. This estimation, so strongly emphasized by the personnel themselves, shows that the social standing of the buyer of the merchandise left its mark on the rank of the seller.

White-collar workers have not been part of the capitalist order for as long a period of time as have manual laborers. In capitalist society they are the technical personnel in large enterprises and the commercial employees in those enterprises who perform administrative and organizational functions that formerly—or even in today's smaller establishments—were unnecessary or undeveloped. The work done by these new groups is not informed by tradition. Unlike the clerk in small business whose tasks were handed down from posterity, their work is the requirement of a more concentrated and organized stage of capitalistic economy.

Foremen

Technical personnel, who make up a large part of today's workforce, are a product of the large enterprise and, as such, are a much "younger" phenomenon than either the worker or the original white-collar employee. They are also much "younger" than the foremen, whose history is closely related to that of manual workers. Foremen were needed to assist the business management even when production was still concentrated in small industrial establishments that lacked a special staff of technicians and possessed only a few commercial employees. But the present economic system provides less room for the old-style foreman, who was closely related to the master craftsman, than for the salaried employee of the small establishment, because the development of large enterprises has changed the foreman's functions considerably.

The old-style foreman could be most frequently found in industrial establishments employing many manual workers but few other white-collar workers. He has retained his previous work responsibilities and social position only in those branches of industry that still permit small enterprises, particularly in certain manufacturing industries and in areas where technical progress had made little headway, as, for example, in the building trades. This is also the case in the textile industry, where half of all salaried employees are foremen or hold similar positions.[10] Only in small establishments did the foreman still come into contact with customers and wholesale contractors. Sometimes he was even recorded in the Commercial Registry as a confidential clerk with power of attorney.

With the transition to a methodical and scientific mode of production, the two main functions of the foreman, direction and supervision, were separated. Direction, comprising calculation and preparation of work, was more easily rationalized than supervision. (The latter was, of course, partly eliminated as a result of the mechanization of work processes.) In some establishments, industrial experience, originally personified in the foreman, was systematized and depersonalized. Calculators, timekeepers, engineers, and others were made superior to the foreman, or at least were empowered to supervise the functions still left to him. Having so many more authorities to answer to, many foremen came to feel they would "sooner face God than the manager."[11] Inexperienced newcomers from universities or technical schools, usually much younger than the foreman, also relieved him of his theoretical work. "The office on one side and the workshop on the other—these two words characterize the foremen's struggle to maintain the functions of his job."[12]

The centralization of industry thus increasingly deprived the foreman of his former functions, from purchasing materials and calculating needs to instruction and the distribution of work. Generally he was relegated to a mere overseer and driver.[13] In one respect, therefore, the foreman fell closer to the worker's level, but in another the gap between them widened.[14] By supplementing their income through bonus payments (sometimes of very large proportions), foremen at least retained the possibility of maintaining an economic distance.

Geck has asserted that the worker has become less personally dependent and less subject to the arbitrary power of his superior because of the hierarchical structure of modern business establishments and the resulting changes in the foreman's role.[15] This assertion is certainly true, but its scope should not be overestimated. I know, for example, that in the early 1930s the workers in a large, thoroughly rationalized machine factory on the outskirts of Berlin tried to bribe their foremen with presents, not of money, to be sure, but in kind. (This factory employed many workers from rural districts.) At least in this instance, the rationalization of industry had not diminished personal dependence to the point of eliminating such practices.

The foreman's knowledge that he performed and supervised productive factory work gave him a subjective sense of superiority over the commercial employee. This fact was responsible for occasional political arguments. Shortly after the revolution of 1918, for example, it provided a source of tension between the conservative Deutscher Werkmeisterverband (DWV), with a membership of 80 percent of all organized foremen, and the socialist Zentralverband der Angestellten (ZdA). The then president of the DWV contemptuously called attention to the fact that in western Germany the ZdA was represented not in factories but in retail trade and offices in large cities such as Berlin.[16]

Foremen constituted a group of salaried employees in which every single member had supervisory authority over workers. This authority was protected by law under paragraph 123 of the Trade Code. While, as a rule, insults and acts of violence among workers had no legal consequences, such offenses by workers against their foremen were cause for immediate dismissal. The foremen's position as buffers between management and workers alienated them all the more from workers (although they usually came from this class) as conditions strengthened their opinion that they had outgrown the working class through promotion. The foreman was proud of having attained, by virtue of hard struggle, a social position into which he could never have been born, and he was anxious to retain it.[17] He was not averse to regarding as social distance the functional difference— so essential in the shop—between himself as superior and the workers as subordinates. Of course, exceptions only proved the rule that the foreman was the most disliked man in the shop.

A few decades ago the foreman's sense of superiority, closely attached to his position of trust, was even more pronounced. In 1909 the DWV laid a solid foundation for this attitude by stating that the foreman had a stronger feeling of loyalty to the firm than did the average worker. Thoughts of economic strife, strikes, and similar struggles, it claimed, never occurred to him. On the contrary, he aspired to a lifelong position.[18] As late as the beginning of the 1930s, the foreman's feeling of being more closely connected with the business could not be dismissed as mere ideology. The foreman was less vulnerable to the dangers of dismissal than the worker. More than anyone else, he had to uphold the standards of the factory, and one of his functions, considered especially valuable in younger industrial countries, was to prevent an excessive turnover in personnel.

If he was dismissed, it was difficult for him to obtain new employment because of his age and the difficulty of retraining him. He knew that he would be fortunate, especially during bad periods in the labor market, to obtain a new position, if only as a skilled worker.[19] The high average age, the small percentage of unmarried persons, the great number of large families, and the relatively high percentage of those who turned to agriculture as an avocation were additional factors in the foremen's conservatism. In 1925 31 percent of male salaried employees (38.2 percent of all the gainfully employed) were over forty years of age.[20] While 34.4 percent of technical employees and 30.1 percent of commercial employees were in this age category, 65.7 percent of all male foremen were over forty years of age. Of male commercial employees in trade and communication, 53.3 percent were single; in industry and handicraft, 47.4 percent; of technical employees, 40 percent. By contrast, only 7.8 percent of foremen were unmarried. According to the GdA survey, of 100 married male employees, 29 were childless; of foremen, only 16.[21] Of the foremen and supervisory personnel in industry and handicraft, one-eighth had agricultural side interests, while only one-twentieth of the technicians and one-fiftieth of the commercial employees had them.[22]

All these circumstances promoted apolitical opportunism. As early as 1924 the DWV attributed the decline in its membership not only to the economic crisis, general retrenchment, and demotions of foremen to workers—10 percent of the loss in 1924 was due to this cause—but also to the belief of some foremen "that, in view of the shift in authority, their union activities would constitute a danger to their existence. . . . Some are also of the opinion that the establishment of official salary schedules has made their union unnecessary."[23] Political opportunism, a symptom of the embourgeoisement of the proletariat, was the foremen's salient political attitude.

Technical Personnel

The importance of the technical employee is apparent from the foregoing discussion of the foreman's changing functions. Technicians did not become a prominent part of the workforce until the last quarter of the nineteenth century, when German industry took a decided upward turn.[24] Also, the number of technical students increased rapidly, especially after the Franco-Prussian War. In 1873 alone, for example, five times as many students matriculated at the Berlin Academy of Architecture as at the entire Technical Academy in the previous year.[25]

Engineers were instrumental in undermining the patriarchal position of the foreman. Their academic training was rated more highly than practical experience, thereby lowering the standing of the foreman in the rank order.[26] At the same time increasing specialization in engineering work created a growing need for technical assistants who could perform the simpler functions. This demand was met by a wage-reducing oversupply fed by graduates of technical secondary schools and—even more so—of the private schools that proliferated to excess. As technical functions became differentiated, sharp distinctions developed between higher- and lower-skilled groups. Just as the architect, bound by tradition, had up to that time considered himself superior to the aspiring mechanical engineer, so, toward the end of the century, did the vertical division of work in the factory lead to social differentiation among the growing technical personnel. Draftsmen and factory officials thought themselves better than workers, technicians from professional schools felt superior to draftsmen, and university graduates believed they surpassed professional technicians in social prestige and self-esteem. These social rivalries and antagonisms were reflected in the professional associations and trade unions of the technical employees. Aside from the technicians' clubs, which were composed of independents and employees and had been founded about the middle of the last century for the promotion of professional standards, it was not until 1884 that the first organization to make a feeble attempt at social work for its members was founded—the Deutscher Techniker Verband, or DTV (German Association of Technicians). The immediate cause for its foundation was the desire of underpaid architects, engineers, and technicians to put distance between themselves and the workers. According to the National Sick Benefits Law of 1883, every technical "official" earning less than RM 6.66 a day had to join a sick-benefit fund intended "for journeymen and day laborers." The first issue of the *Deutsche Technikerzeitung* (German Technicians' Journal) contained a draft of bylaws for a separate sick-benefit fund.[27]

In 1904 the Bund der technisch-industriellen Beamten, often known as Butib (Association of Technical-Industrial Employees), was established. Its principles, program, and tactics assumed great importance for the entire group of technical employees. Butib's members were recruited mostly from the large plants of the machine and electrical industries, while the DTV drew its members mainly from government offices and the above-ground building trades. Butib admitted only salaried employees, although assistants and women were included. Since it acted strictly on trade union principles, it soon provoked the wrath and active opposition of the employers, even though, unlike the leftist radical organizations of commercial employees, it never opposed the capitalist social order as such. Butib refused to join the working-class movement as an organization.

The Verband deutscher Diplom-Ingenieure (VdDI; Association of German Academic Engineers) was founded five years after Butib for the purpose of creating a separate organization for university-trained men in keeping with their social rank. Butib regarded this association as "an organization founded and conducted in the interest of the employer."[28] In 1911, when the iron-construction engineers of Berlin went on strike, the VdDI induced its members to "attack the fighting strikers from the rear by acting as scabs."[29]

Butib soon assumed the leadership of the progressive organizations of salaried employees, and in 1911 forced the DTV, with which it merged after World War

I to form Butab (Bund der technischen Angestellten und Beamten), to accept trade union principles.

The rank order of the technical employees did not necessarily correspond to stratification according to income. Before World War I a young academic engineer sometimes received an initial salary of only RM 60 a month. As a rule he was paid less than the foreman. The engineer's income was determined to a large extent by supply and demand, while that of the foreman was established in proportion to the workers' wages.[30] But his "higher" social origin, his certified education, and his existing or possible social contact with higher employees and executives distinguished the engineer from the technicians of lower rank, even if the latter were better-salaried. In addition, the hierarchy was not one of pure achievement. Execution of more responsible functions was tied up with education, and the latter generally with the social position of the employee's parents.

Upon their entry into industry engineers with university degrees were below the par of technical school graduates because they lacked practical experience. The turning point came after about five years. "If the university graduate has been fortunate enough to gain the necessary practical experience within this period of time, the prerequisites for advancement are generally better because of his higher education."[31] To be sure, certain tasks that accompanied the introduction of scientific methods into industry and that were moved from the factory to the technician's office could be solved only by technicians with long practical experience. For example, the time-study clerk's preparation of exact calculations required an intimate knowledge of the manual operations involved in production and of the worker's psyche. Yet, like his other duties, these functions, which only the practically trained employee was qualified to perform, did not bestow higher rank. If the non-academic technician was a construction engineer, he concentrated upon details; if he had to make plans, he designed only small projects; if he ever worked on blueprints, he had to change them according to directions. Even as a plant technician, he could, as a rule, occupy only certain positions, just as in the office. These involved more or less subordinate work and no high degree of responsibility. Distinctions between technical employees and commercial white-collar workers in small establishments were not confined to the different fields in which they performed their functions—technological and production-related work, and commerce and distribution, respectively. In addition, these two types of employees tended to work in enterprises of different sizes. Moreover, the nature of their social contacts and conflicts at the workplace were not the same.

Technical employees were engaged primarily in large industrial establishments. In 1925 57 percent of technical office and supervisory personnel were employed in places with a staff of more than 200 persons, while 30.2 percent were in places with more than 1,000 persons. On the other hand, the number of commercial employees in industry and handicraft in enterprises employing 200 persons was only 40.8 percent, with 17.5 percent in places employing over 1,000. Statistics make it clear that the number of technical rather than commercial white-collar workers was the real index of capitalist transformation of the workforce. Table 1.1 illustrates this fact and destroys the notion that the commercial employee played a more important part in giant enterprises than the technician.

Accordingly, as of 1925 the majority of commercial employees were not in the industrial strongholds of the capitalist economy but in commerce and in middle-sized industrial establishments. As establishments grew in size, the proportion of technical employees within the entire workforce increased. The proportion of commercial staff increased only up to the medium-sized enterprise employing eleven to fifty persons; as the size of establishment expanded further the proportion dropped. This trend may reflect the fact that the mechanization of production had made its greatest progress in giant enterprises. Increased production capacity required additional technical experts and assistants for calculation, timekeeping, planning, submitting estimates, and so forth. In commercial departments, however, growth produced opportunities for rationalizing the larger administrative apparatus in order to cut down on personnel.

The different social contacts and conflicts of technical and commercial employees in the workplace derive from the very origin of the technical employee group. The permanent social and economic dependence of retail white-collar workers was a consequence of the increasing importance of large enterprises, in which the social characteristics of the old commercial clerk could no longer be found, whereas the dependence of technical employees arose *within* the industrial establishments. From the very beginning they had almost no prospect of achieving economic independence within their profession, and ascent within the hierarchy was limited because high positions were reserved for persons with a better ed-

Table 1.1: Distribution of Occupational Groups according to Size of Enterprise, 1925

Enterprises of	1–5	5–10	11–50	51–200	200–1,000	1,000+
	Per thousand of total employed (industry and crafts)					
Technicians and Foremen	6	16	29	39	46	59
Commercial Employees	13	50	80	76	67	58

SOURCE: G. Fürst, "Die Angestellten in Klein-, Mittel- und Grossbetrieben," p. 49.

ucation or a more esteemed social origin. At the outset the dependence of technical employees was gradated according to their position in the rank order within the firm, an unavoidable circumstance especially among the assistants, who constituted the majority. That this feeling of dependence was tangible and widespread made it all the more effective a spur to free trade union orientation among intermediate- and low-rank technicians.

Because of his preparatory training the technician who lacked a university education had a better understanding of workers than did the commercial employee or the academically trained engineer. The student of a technical trade school had to have several years of practical experience behind him. In the machine industry, for example, engineer apprentices were not given preference over other apprentices in the factory. The student at a technical college, however, got his practical training during his vacations, and his closer contact with workers was seldom more than an interesting and strange adventure. It was thus the non-academic technician who, through his shop experience, acquired both an insight into collective action and an understanding of workers. Technical college graduates were very seldom unionized. When they did organize, they preferred associations with a majority of university men—either scientific societies or those where a middle-class atmosphere emphasized the social superiority of its members over non-academic technicians.

When economic misfortunes moved the higher technician closer to the worker and to his dependence on the business cycle, he held "the system" responsible for his humiliating loss of social prestige. His radicalization was directed against democracy, trade unions, and the spirit of Weimar. Thus Butab, the most prominent organization of technical employees, with a majority of trade school graduates among its members, pursued a vigorous, socialistically oriented trade union policy, while the younger generation of graduate engineers, fresh from the technical colleges, became National Socialists more readily than other university men. The majority of German students elected National Socialists to their academic representational bodies several years before the NSDAP's electoral triumph in 1930, but students at technical colleges, in double quickstep, surpassed the enthusiasm of university students on their common march into the Third Reich.[32]

Commercial Employees in the Larger Establishments

Dependence based on position in the rank order was also characteristic of commercial employees in larger establishments. But unlike the technicians they had no contact with blue-collar workers, which contributed to their clinging to middle-class orientations. The prevalence of such orientations is reflected in the relative strength of the non-socialist union organizations among them (see chapter 13). The middle-class tendencies of commercial employees in the larger enterprises are also connected with two other facts of office life, namely, that the work experience lacks a mass character and that the individual is assigned a place in a hierarchy.

The majority of commercial employees worked in medium-sized establishments, where a proletarian attitude generally seemed more out of place than in giant enterprises. Only in giant establishments could the feeling of belonging to the proletariat directly shape the employee's behavior and thought, for here proletarianism not only manifested itself in the employee's dependence on the business cycle and in his obligation to accept minutely divided work—it also was directly and concretely comprehensible within the enterprise. This was possible only where the division of labor had made great progress and the enterprise had expanded considerably. Characteristically, however, the possibility of proletarianization existed primarily for the lowest category of white-collar workers in large establishments—that is, for a very small minority of commercial employees—because only in large establishments did many specialized workers of equal rank work together.

In medium-sized establishments, in contrast, specialization had not advanced to a point where one employee performed a single function continually. Rather, many subordinate employees worked individually on complex tasks. "Only in stenographers and saleswomen are the 'pure' worker types to be found."[33] The characteristic of medium-sized business was not a mass of wage earners of equal rank but a hierarchical gradation of employees. The development of hierarchy was first and foremost due to the division of labor, which was in turn a response to the expansion of business, the higher degree of organization, and the resulting strict control, planning, and supervision of activities within the enterprise. Tasks formerly performed by one person were in many instances divided and assigned to various employees or special departments, which cooperated with each other to form a hierarchical structure of their own.

Nevertheless, not all the work performed by commercial employees, especially those in large enterprises, can, without reservation, be explained by a division of tasks. Not all modern commercial employees are specialized workers whose duties were formerly performed by one person. Rather, a part of their functions must be regarded as having sprung automatically from the need for special administration, which was not required in smaller establishments. From the point of view of the sociology of business, management, and especially personnel management, can be explained by the need to reintegrate the minutely differentiated giant enterprise. This interpretation corresponds to the scientific conception of management as a "circle of all those business functions whose objectives do not come within the sphere of the true aims of the business, but whose field is the enterprise as a whole or parts of it as groups of business factors."[34]

Employees with administrative functions were also placed in a hierarchical order. It is noteworthy that the rank of an employee on the business ladder was of greater importance to his prestige and behavior than whether he was active in distribution, management, or planning. The assistant in the statistical office was of lower rank than the head of the correspondence department, even though he was part of the management by which the owner conducted the business.

The Lowest Commercial Employees

In chapter 8, which deals with the masked class membership of white-collar workers, the significance of hierarchical order in the office will be discussed in more detail. At this point some of the more important types of commercial employees who found themselves in a particularly dependent and precarious position are surveyed. Most of them were late social products of economic development: saleswomen in one-price stores, lower office personnel in giant enterprises, typists, and machine operators. These creatures of modernity shared certain negative characteristics. Unlike employees in a small firm, they had no personal contact with the principals and could not be regarded as members of the old middle class. Nor did they share in the prestige of the entrepreneur, as was sometimes true of employees in medium-sized establishments. Instead, they were insecure and resembled true proletarians.

Saleswomen in One-Price Stores

The discrepancy between salespeople and their workplaces increased as workplaces became larger and more impressive in appearance. At the same time management became more and more concerned about bridging this wide gap. One large retail establishment cautioned its sales personnel against growing too friendly with each other and using "du" (the familiar form of "you"), "especially in the presence of customers." This regulation made the employees themselves responsible for an intimacy that actually originated in their social background and conditions of work. The reason management gave for the regulation—"to be too intimate with strangers lowers your prestige"[35]—obscured the purpose of the order. Management was unaware that *it* had revealed the social conditions behind its exhortation and endangered the success of its admonitions by itself using the familiar "du" when addressing employees in executive orders. That this implied a value judgment on management's part is shown by the more elegant forms used when it wished to impart notices to customers. What store would dare hang out signs reading "Du darfst umtauschen" ("you may exchange")? A neutral form was chosen: "Exchanges Are Excluded," or it was politely said, "Please Watch Your Coat and Hat." Another list of instructions for salespeople of a retail association was more to the point: "The use of 'du' among personnel in the presence of customers makes a most unfavorable impression." Personal contact with salespeople was unavoidable to the consumer of almost all commodities. Before the rise of the supermarket it was almost impossible to do away with the clerk behind the counter. This was a decisive factor in preventing, although incompletely, the automation of the selling process and pointed it to different, narrower paths of rationalization than those followed by production. But the activities of the salesforce were not completely closed to modern efficiency methods.[36]

Standardization of merchandise and prices systematized sales so that eventually only a very limited acquaintance with the merchandise was required, and the work could be performed in a routine manner. The type of saleswoman created as a result was generally found in large cities, and she differed from employees in small retail establishments whose functions were handed down by tradition. In a sociological survey saleswomen must be classified with those employees who are products of late capitalism.

The saleswoman with the most proletarian characteristics was found in one-price stores. Only for the customer's sake did her functions remain less than automatic. She was distinguished from an automaton only through the scrap of personality that satisfied the sovereign demand of the customer on whom she waited. On the job she was on the borderline between human being and disembodied, minimally functioning brain: a vocabulary of thirty words and mastery of the multiplication table sufficed for the execution of her duties; she was not allowed to change anything larger than a twenty-mark bill. The regulations of a chain of one-price stores stated in 1931 that "all employees and all persons entering the establishment for the purpose of bringing them food must submit to a search by duly authorized persons upon entering and leaving the store. . . . Saleswomen are not allowed to have any money on their person during working hours." And the special instructions for saleswomen of the same firm contained the following directions: "Customers seeking information about the store or its stock are to be referred to the manager or his assistant. . . . Saleswomen are not allowed to leave their counters without permission of the floorwalker. . . . All employees are supposed to conduct themselves as educated ladies and gentlemen at all times."

The lowest-rank sales personnel in large retail stores resembled manual workers in that they formed the base of the establishment's hierarchy. Also, in contrast to commercial employees of equal rank in industry, they had no other workers beneath them. They differed considerably from blue-collar workers, however, because they were the business's direct representatives to the outside world; in its name sales personnel talked to that part of the world made up of customers. To be sure, in all large enterprises an illusion of belonging to the firm had replaced the real tie that existed between employer and employee in times past. This illusion, however, often affected the attitude of employees with the force of reality.

The semblance of responsibility created by independent contact with the customer, and the apparent freedom aroused by a comparison of occupational activity with the drudgery of homelife, made the work more tolerable for the saleswoman. Furthermore, the laws of social valuation were tempered for sales personnel because the customer, as such, was classless. To the extent that the customer's higher social rank was noticed by the saleswoman, it conjured up the image of a social order in which all work, even that lacking any distinction, was more bearable. The taint of social inferiority associated with the performance of very simple tasks was weaker because of contact with persons of a higher class.

Lower Personnel in Giant Establishments

Although sales activity has not been as fully rationalized as production, the large office offers a much wider field for automated efficiency. The introduction of office machines, which made their appearance on a large scale after 1925, the use of bookkeeping machines, combined adding machines and typewriters, franking and letter-opening and -closing machines, the installation of pneumatic tubes to lessen legwork, and automatic-delivery and similar devices are not the only factors to be considered. Not the least important consideration is the general standardization of employees' activities, which was based upon specialization and prepared or supplemented true standardization and automation. Systematic arrangement was its motto, statistics was its science, and increased business its goal. It resulted in loss of individuality for workers and an impoverishment of human relations. Personal contact with people outside the enterprise, demanded by the nature of salesclerks' work, was nonexistent for other employees. Even contact among employees was reduced to a minimum. One report stated:

> The work in large offices is performed almost without a sound, although there are more than 1,000 people present not separated from each other by any kind of partition. The most important aid to this silence is the automatic telephone on each desk. . . . There is no necessity for running from desk to desk or . . . for shouting over several tables in intra-office communication. The telephone is even used for conversations between adjoining desks.[37]

Even if this description were an overstatement, there is no doubt that the individuality of employees working in such places was markedly reduced. Work was not performed individually but collectively. Employees' activity appeared varied only in the light of cooperation. Individuals performed one task of narrow scope in a perpetual chain of boring repetitions. This phenomenon, the product of organized distrust of everything incalculable—such as chance, personality, and tradition—was of course possible only where administrative or distributive activity was very extensive and where many stereotypes and specialized functions were performed regularly. This was especially so in statistical bureaus, large banks, and offices of giant enterprises, and the machine operator was found only in these places.

A comparison of bank and insurance employees is enlightening. Before World War I the former were regarded as the aristocracy of salaried employees, while the low-salaried insurance employees were the pariahs—if one disregards saleswomen. As a result, insurance employees were strongly inclined toward unionism. The so-called Münchener Verband (Verband der deutschen Versicherungsbeamten, Association of German Insurance Employees) was one of the founders of the ZdA. In April 1920 it seceded from that organization on account of lax representation of its interests, and the liberal-national Allgemeiner Verband der Versicherungsangestellten (General Association of Insurance Employees) came into being. In the case of bank employees, on the other hand, the inclination to regard themselves as a kind of civil service was especially pronounced. The radical Allgemeiner Verband der Bankangestellten (General Association of Bank Employees) never achieved much success in the field of organization and could never break the domination of the Deutscher Bankbeamtenverein (DBV). After World War I the status of bank and insurance employees was almost reversed. Bank employees were especially hard hit by office rationalization and mergers. When the Deutsche Bank and the Diskontogesellschaft merged in 1929, one executive declared that, if no dismissals could be effected, the merger would be to no purpose. Insurance employees fared better than all other employee groups. Aside from cuts in salaries occasioned by the emergency decree of December

1931, their wage scale was not reduced until the peak of the Depression. This may be attributed partly to the relative solvency of the insurance business, and partly to employers' efforts not to endanger the prestige of their firms in the eyes of policyholders. Despite these changes the old organizational structure attuned to former conditions was kept intact by both groups of employees. The social functions of bank officials were still better attended than their union business meetings, while insurance employees retained their union traditions. At elections for employees' representatives on the shop councils of large banking institutions, however, it was noted that the leftist radical Allgemeiner Verband at times achieved much better results in proportion to its membership quota than did the DBV.

Typists

Stenographers are found in businesses of all sizes. Women were used extensively to fill subordinate office positions for a long time; their influx into offices did not begin only with World War I. Indeed, the rationalization of script (stenography), the mechanization of writing (the typewriter), and the advent of the telephone released this stream of workers long before the war. The increase of female help contributed extensively to the growth of the employee class. Their positions were based upon knowledge and skills which, according to the Christian-national VwA (Verband der weiblichen Handels- und Büroangestellten, Association of Female Business and Office Employees, connected with the DHV), male apprentices and clerks in their conceit refused to acquire.[38]

In addition to the possibilities of easy replacement and the possibility of working in different lines of business, typists, and especially stenographers, have steady contact with employees of higher rank. Stenographers are the hands of their superiors. Both the nature of their duties and association with persons of distinction within the establishment shaped their behavior and consciousness. These persons of higher prestige were generally men. The difference in sex gave the rational business atmosphere a touch of life and relieved tension with the superior. If this tension existed because of the nature of the organization, it was often mitigated in an erotic manner. The work of the stenographer was in itself dull, mechanical, and very strenuous. According to Fuykschot, this work can be paid by the job, because "it demands attention but absolutely no thought."[39] Teachers of typewriting claimed that stenographers could not pursue their vocation for more than ten years.[40] According to an investigation by the Afa-Bund "disorders, caused by overexcitement of the nervous system, were features of typing work." In one-half of all cases polled, it found that impairment of health was attributable to the occupation.[41] According to a questionnaire distributed by the ZdA in 1930, one-half of 5,630 female employees worked more than the normal workweek of forty-eight hours. Of those who worked overtime, 42 percent were less than twenty years of age.[42] In the light of these facts about the occupational life of stenographers, one may judge the worth of the ideology, widely disseminated among stenographers in establishments of all sizes and propagated by the National Central Office for Employment Exchange and Unemployment Insurance, that the stenographer is the "merchant's assistant." She finds it "so very interesting," it was claimed, "to work with her superior," and "the time flies so fast that it is almost annoying when the work day is over, since one would love to do much more."[43]

Machine Operators

The typist has a certain unproletarian character because of her personal connection with her superior and because her occupation is often only a temporary arrangement (before marriage). In the case of the true subordinate employee who operated an office machine, however, the difference between worker and salaried employee actually disappeared. He resembled the unskilled or semiskilled worker in the factory.

The conception of "unskilled employee" is, of course, broader than that of the machine-operating employee. The following account, written by an employer about the structure of the employee personnel in the Berlin metal industry, is enlightening:

Side by side with the trained "businessmen" is the vast army of the untrained, also calling themselves "businessmen," but really never performing commercial tasks. Some of the latter have acquired, through close application and unusual intelligence, a fine knowledge of commercial practices. These have an opportunity of advancement in the business occupation. The duties of many of these unskilled forces, however, are confined to purely administrative departments of the business. This includes the great number of factory clerks, stenographers, filing clerks, employees in the payroll and personnel departments, clerks in the sick-benefit fund, statisticians, registrars and other administrative clerks. The work of these employees in present-day giant enterprises is almost manual.[44]

In establishments where a great number of customers or other persons had to be reached regularly (consumer cooperatives, insurance offices, sick benefit funds, finance and post offices, municipal bureaus, magazine publishers), the old, relatively expensive, and slow method of reproduction by typewriter could be replaced by the new Adrema addressograph, which because it worked fast and accurately, quickly found wide favor. In Cologne, for example, 1,000 of these machines were in use at the beginning of 1930. An operator was trained in two weeks, usually by the manufacturer, just as many modern office machines are supplied together with the personnel to man them. Operation was as simple as it was monotonous. It was less exhausting than work on the typewriter, did not demand any general training, and could be paid on a piecework basis. This last feature led to the conjecture that this work would, in the course of time, come down to the level of wage labor.[45]

This example demonstrates what experience corroborates—mechanization and automation of office work led to a direct change in personnel status wherever the machine work was not treated as a side issue, as it was in many medium-sized businesses, but was performed exclusively by specially designated persons. Experienced white-collar workers were crowded out by trained operators, mostly young girls. But not all qualified employees became dispensable as a result of office mechanization. As a matter of fact, with the creation of new spheres of activity their number diminished, but new, specially trained or unskilled help was required. The composition of the personnel needed to operate the widely used tabulating machine furnishes an instructive example. A holepuncher, a checker, a sorter, and a tabulator were required. A knowledge of bookkeeping and similar special work was essential to the tabulator, but he alone performed work done by several skilled employees prior to the installation of the machine. His new female colleagues, however, were semiskilled help. The holepuncher was often "requisitioned from the employment agency for unskilled young people with the stipulation: previous experience not essential; must be able to read six-digit numbers."[46]

With the advent of the machine-operating employee, the associations of salaried employees were confronted with entirely new social and political problems. Not long before (1930) the DHV had proclaimed that the bookkeeping machine operator was the master and not, like the laborer, the servant of his machine. Now this organization emphasized that, through rationalization, new dangers of proletarianization had arisen and that these "affect the salaried employees to an especially large degree."[47] All associations opposed the effects but not the process of this rationalization.

Government Employees

In the preceding discussions, white-collar workers in government offices have not been mentioned, although, numerically, they constituted an important and, sociologically speaking, interesting group of the salaried employees. They are, because of their proximity to a true bureaucracy, deserving of a separate investigation. The following remarks may suffice here.

Government employees are confronted with situations of social conflict and contact unknown to any other group of white-collar workers. Their typical opponents are, first, civil servants, who generally have executive power over employees holding subordinate positions within the hierarchy. The permeation of public officialdom with these employees—more prominent in small *Länder* (states) than in large ones—produced an antithesis of interests among persons in government service. The civil servants and their associations spoke about a "silent destruction of the professional civil service" and regarded this class of employees as interlopers who threatened their "vested rights." They pointed out that contributions to the insurance premiums for such employees were burdening municipalities and *Länder*. Not to be outdone, government employees called attention to the increase in public expenditures caused by the pension system. The spokesmen of the government employees were the enemies of bureaucracy. They contended that there was a basic equality of technical functions between civil service and private enterprise. They pitted the employee as the prop of a modern, rationalizing spirit against the public official, the representative of bureaucratic pedantry. They even demanded, with a hint at the systemization of big industry, the sacrifice of the vested rights of the officials. This would destroy the secure public official's sense of sinecurism, which their enemies alleged was so injurious to efficiency.[48]

Contrary to the widespread opinion that white-collar workers in government were generally appointed temporarily, it must be emphasized that their status was permanent. According to a survey of the GdA in 1929, 13 percent of the male and 15 percent of the female employees in civil service had been employed up to two years, 22 percent and 16 percent respectively up to four years, and the rest longer. Not less than 41 percent and 36 percent, respectively, had served more than eight years.[49] Because of this permanence, their position was more advantageous than that of their colleagues in private industry. In this respect, the situation of public officials was reflected in that of government employees. (The latter did not, however, enjoy the privileges of the former.) On the whole, government employees were poorly organized. Their relationship to public officials followed from the fact that a comparatively large number of these employees belonged to organizations of public officials. Here we see a return to the old "harmony associations" of employers and employees of prewar days. The small dues of these organizations, as compared with the unions of salaried employees, were an added membership inducement. In municipal offices, officials exercised a certain pressure upon employees to join their organizations. Conversely, membership in unions of salaried employees was usually interpreted as a sign of antagonism toward the officials.

The second typical and special adversary of the government white-collar worker was the employee entitled to the privileges of a veteran of twelve years of army service. The twelve-year veteran was especially favored for placement. According to the 1931 report of the Reichsverband der Zivildienstberechtigten, its members (130,000 in number) were in the following positions; 66 percent career civil servants; 12 percent retired or retired subject to recall; 3 percent on probation; 10 percent in public service; 1 percent living on pensions. Only 3 percent were in private business, and 5 percent were civil service applicants.[50] In order to comprehend fully the special rights of the veterans who competed with other white-collar workers for employment, one has only to compare these figures with the vast number of unemployed white-collar workers. Moreover, the veteran employee guaranteed the militarization of the lower bureaucracy.

II Social Origin of Salaried Employees

The number of salaried employees grew considerably during the first decades of this century, but this stratum's natural capacity for regeneration was smaller than that of all other social strata.[1] Hardly one-fifth of those who occupied white-collar positions in 1930 had fathers with similar occupations. The remainder, a very large majority, was recruited from other strata, principally the middle class. In 1929 the most comprehensive statistical survey of the social origin of salaried employees discovered that,[2] including those employees who inherited their occupation, 71.7 percent originated in the middle class and only 3.3 percent in a higher stratum; manual labor contributed 25 percent.[3] White-collar workers were of distinctly urban origin; only 4 percent were of rural parentage. The number of blue-collar workers coming from the country was probably much larger, although the agricultural districts were no longer the principal recruiting ground for the labor proletariat that they had been about the middle of the last century, nor were they as important as they had been shortly before World War I.

At the beginning of the Industrial Revolution agriculture and artisanry were the most common sources of origin of the wage-earning class, but they were never significant sources of origin in the history of salaried employees. While the labor proletariat largely descended from farmers and artisans, the mass of salaried employees was drawn from the ranks of independent tradesmen, merchants, and public officials. This "descent," however, lost its significance as proletarianization progressed and workers' children "ascended" en masse into white-collar professions. The similarity of many white-collar workers' functions to those of manual labor was manifest in this process, as was a corresponding lowering of the former's average rank. The new middle-class generation no longer held the occupation of salaried employee in such high esteem as to check the advance of proletarian youths; instead, they left to the latter the poorest positions and attached increased value to social distance. As mechanized activity increased, a greater number of white-collar workers sprang from the ranks of manual labor. Considered from this point of view, as the chances for workers' children to ascend into the ranks of salaried employees increased, the more this movement from one stratum into another lost the character of ascent. The offspring of laborers found ascent into a higher stratum easier because in this phase of economic development the goal—white-collar employment—was less highly valued.

Even before World War I the number of white-collar workers with a working-class background was considerable, varying between 8 percent and 19 percent in the case of male technicians and commercial clerks according to more comprehensive studies (see table 2.1). More workers' children entered the ranks of commercial than of technical employees. The percentage of those whose parents were public officials, salaried employees, or in the free professions, that is, members of strata with higher levels of educational attainment, was higher among technicians than commercial employees. Jaeckel's investigations found that 42 percent of all technicians came from these strata,[4] while Günther's studies found only 29.5 percent, and a DHV survey disclosed that only 31 percent of its members were from these backgrounds.

Even before World War I the proportion of white-collar workers of working-class origin was higher among women than among men. Table 2.2 shows that female technical personnel held the highest social position and that the female office worker was ranked higher than the saleswoman. Even in prewar days the working class to an increasing extent contributed women to the ranks of female salaried employees (see table 2.1, lines 4–10 and 13). This tendency continued after World War I and broadened to apply to all white-collar workers, as shown in table 2.2. Among the apprentices of the GdA, working-class origin was much more frequent than among the clerks. Whereas one-fourth of the clerks originated in the working class, the average for apprentices, who chose their vocation when it was already in a later, more advanced stage of proletarianization, was two-fifths. (In the industrial centers of Saxony the proportion increased to 50.3 percent; in the Rhine district it shrank to 28 percent.) And since there are no untrained salaried employees of the same age as apprentices, the distance between the generations becomes even greater. If we compare the distribution of commercial employees of the same social origin over the lowest and highest age groups, it becomes evident that, within a period of twenty-five years, the rank order of the originating strata had been exactly reversed (see table 2.3).

Among the highest and middle age groups, therefore, the three largest sources of origin were the employers' strata (tradesmen, farmers, and independents), while the younger generation derived from the wage-earning classes. In the older gen-

Table 2.1: Salaried Employees of Working-Class Origin (according to prewar surveys)

Number Polled	Year	Job Classification	% of Working-Class Origin
32,741	1908	Male Commercial Assistants in DHV[1]	18.96
53	1914	Trained Bank Clerks[2]	4.2
21	1914	Untrained Bank Employees[3]	11.7
494	1897	Saleswomen[3]	13.1
137	1897	Female Forwarding and Stock Clerks[4]	13.6
109	1897	Female Technical Personnel[4]	9.1
	1902–03	Saleswomen in Berlin[5]	33.6
549	1906	Saleswomen in Karlsruhe[6]	44.7
364	1909–11	Older Saleswomen in Munich[7]	40.3[a]
717	1909–11	Younger Saleswomen in Munich[8]	66.9[b]
697	1898	Female Office Employees[9]	4.4
1,512	1902–03	Female Office Employees[5]	10.1
400	1907	Female Office Employees in Leipzig[10]	27.0[c]
998	1913	Students of the Commercial School for Girls of the Merchants' Association of Berlin[11]	11.7[d]
3,265	1907	Technical Employees in Greater Berlin[12]	7.96
2,403	1907	of these: Secondary School Graduates[12]	10.36
862	1907	Technical School Graduates[12]	1.28
11,145	1910	Technical Employees in the DTV with a completed Secondary School Education[13]	15.5

SOURCES:
[1] DHV, ed., *Die wirtschaftliche Lage der deutschen Handlungsgehilfen*, p. 6 and table 4.
[2] O. Stillich, "Die Herkunft der Bankbeamten," p. 401.
[3] J. Silbermann, "Zur Entlohnung der Frauenarbeit," p. 1424.
[4] Ibid., p. 1429.
[5] J. Silbermann, "Die soziale Herkunft der Berliner Handlungsgehilfinnen," p. 1305.
[6] M. Baum, *Drei Klassen von Lohnarbeiterinnen in Industrie und Handel der Stadt Karlsruhe.*
[7] K. Mende, "Münchener Jugendliche Ladnerinnen zu Hause und im Beruf," diss., p. 14.
[8] Ibid., pp. 12–14.
[9] J. Silbermann, "Zur Entlohnung," p. 1413.
[10] I. Kisker, *Die Frauenarbeit in den Kontoren einer Großstadt*, p. 56.
[11] "Die Schülerinnen," etc., in: *Archiv für Frauenarbeit*, vol. 1, p. 76.
[12] R. Jaeckel, *Statistik über die Lage der technischen Privatbeamten in Grossberlin*, pp. 26ff.
[13] A. Günther, *Die deutschen Techniker*, p. 55.

[a] Of these, 36.5% from a "higher" stratum of labor, including letter carriers, subordinate civil servants, coachmen, domestic janitors, and conductors, and 3.8% from a "lower" stratum, including peddlers.
[b] Of these, 52.7% from the "higher" and 14.2% from the "lower" labor stratum.
[c] Including foremen: only 1% descended from unskilled workers.
[d] Foremen and skilled workers.

Table 2.2: Salaried Employees of Working-Class Origin (according to postwar surveys)

Number Polled	Year	Job Classification	% of Working-Class Origin
99,695	1929	GdA Employees as a Whole[1]	25.0
76,381	1929	Male GdA Employees[1]	23.9
23,314	1929	Female Employees[1]	28.4
	1929	Male Commercial GdA Employees[2]	24.1
	1929	Female Commercial GdA Employees[2]	28.6
904	1925	Honorary Functionaries in the ZdA[3]	50.0
139	1925	Active Functionaries in the Zda[3]	37.0
500	1931	Provision Saleswomen in Cologne[4]	62.5
318	1932	Saleswomen in Cologne[5]	51.5
1,555	1927	Male Apprentices in DHV, Swabia District[6]	18.8
	1929	Male Apprentices in GdA, Würtemberg[7]	35.6
5,164	1929	Male Apprentices in GdA, Average for Reich[8]	33.6
2,560	1929	Female Apprentices in GdA, Average for Reich[8]	42.9
7,724		Total Apprentices in GdA, Average for Reich[8]	36.7
	1929	Male Technical Employees in GdA[9]	23.9
	1929	Male Foremen in GdA[9]	33.8
	1929	Male Pharmacists in GdA[9]	7.7
1,492	1929	Male Agents in GdA[10]	1.0

SOURCES:

[1]GdA, ed., *Die wirtschaftliche und soziale Lage der Angestellten*, p. 43.
[2]Ibid, p. 45.
[3]K. Stehr, "Der Zentralverband der Angestellten."
[4]A. Wissdorff, "Die Verkäuferin im Lebensmittelhandel," p. 4. Of these 62.5%, 47.5% were skilled and 15.0% unskilled workers.
[5]Census among girl students of the sales classes in the Vocational School of the City of Cologne by H. Schröer, *Die betriebliche Ausbildung des Verkaufspersonals in Einzelhandel*, p. 61. Of these 51.5%, 8.8% were unskilled, 42.7% skilled laborers and artisans, subordinate civil servants, and lower-grade commercial employees in warehouses and offices.
[6]F. Behringer, *Herkunft, Vorbildung und Berufsausbildung der Kaufmannslehrlinge*, p. 19.
[7]GdA, ed., *Die kommende Angestelltengeneration* (Berlin, 1933), p. 23.
[8]Ibid., p. 22.
[9]Ibid., p. 45.
[10]Ibid., p. 46.

eration fathers were found chiefly among independents; in the younger, among workers.

Table 2.2 also reveals that working-class origin was still quite rare among those white-collar occupations whose content least approached that of workers. Only 8 percent of the agents and representatives organized in the GdA who were still relatively close to the old-style independent merchant, and only 1 percent of the pharmacists who, as university graduates, had to expend larger sums for

Table 2.3: Social Origin by Age Groups, 1929 (in %)

Social Origin	Female Commercial Employees (by age)			
	To 25	25–49	50+	
Workers	66.7	32.7	0.6	100
Salaried Employees	60.8	38.4	0.8	100
Civil Servants	58.6	39.9	1.5	100
Tradesmen	48.2	49.0	2.8	100
Farmers	31.0	65.3	3.7	100
Independents	29.2	65.2	5.7	100
Social Origin	Male Commercial Employees (by age)			
	To 25	25–49	50+	
Workers	34.7	50.9	6.3	100
Salaried Employees	31.7	60.9	7.4	100
Civil Servants	29.1	60.4	10.5	100
Tradesmen	22.3	63.4	14.3	100
Farmers	16.3	67.8	15.9	100
Independents	17.0	63.2	19.8	100

SOURCE: GdA, ed., *Die wirtschaftliche und soziale Lage der Angestellten*, p. 60.

their education, were of proletarian origin. In prewar days proletarian origin among bank employees was also comparatively rare, because banks usually demanded a secondary school diploma. Banks also introduced the typewriter much later than did industry, from which, as enterprises with an older tradition, they sharply differentiated themselves. Bank employees, therefore, constituted the elite of white-collar workers before World War I. The war, and above all the inflation of the postwar period, brought with them increased efficiency and profits through mechanization and caused a radical change. As unskilled white-collar workers entered the unusually strongly mechanized bank business, the average social origin of its employees was destined to be transformed.

Table 2.2 also provides a certain insight into the social composition of employee associations. Even before World War I 19 percent of DHV members had proletarian antecedents. The DHV's regional census of the social origin of apprentices in the Swabia district turned up the same percentage. Inasmuch as the proportion of salaried employees of proletarian origin had increased in general, this probably signified that some of these employees turned away from the DHV. In any case, a greater percentage of their number joined (until 1933) more leftist organizations. Among the apprentices of the GdA in Wurtemberg, regionally comparable with the DHV district of Swabia, the proportion was nearly twice as high. Unfortunately, sufficient figures on the social origin of ZdA members are not available, but they were unquestionably more heavily derived from the working class than were the members of the GdA.[5]

Valuable inferences concerning the origin of the ZdA membership are suggested by Stehr's study of this union's officers. No less than half the honorary functionaries were of working-class origin, although proletarian origin was much rarer among the active functionaries.[6] Assuming the composition of the entire membership corresponded to that of the organizational elite, then the ZdA, with about 50 percent, had the highest proportion of members of proletarian origin, while the DHV had the lowest with about 20 percent, and the GdA held the middle ground with 25 percent.[7] Generally, these levels of proletarian-derived membership corresponded to the political and ideological attitudes of the three organizations up to the end of the Weimar Republic in 1933.

The social origin of salaried employees varied with the size of the locality. The smaller the city, the more members of this group were recruited from agrarian strata, but the number of male salaried employees whose fathers were agricultural workers was no more than 9.7 percent (GdA) even in small cities of less than 5,000 inhabitants. An increase in the size of the city, however, meant a proportional gain for independents, for those in trade and commerce, and for the employees themselves. (In the case of civil servants, the movement was not so clearly defined.) Consequently, most white-collar workers who followed in their fathers' footsteps were to be found in the large cities. Correspondingly, the opportunities for acquiring independence were most slender there.

This general pattern notwithstanding, it is unclear why the proportion of white-collar workers of working-class origin varied in cities of different sizes. The assumption that their share of salaried positions grew with size of locality was true only in the case of female employees: relatively more daughters of workers became salaried employees in large cities than in the small towns,[8] whereas comparatively fewer male white-collar workers originated in the proletariat in large cities than in small towns. This phenonenon might be attributable to a vocational outlook that raised fewer illusions in young men and caused them to prefer learning a trade over commercial apprenticeship. The pattern might also have something to do with the nature of available positions. Young women had more opportunities than workers' sons to obtain jobs requiring no special training—for example, in shops, department stores, and urban offices. Table 2.4 shows that the desire of young women to obtain white-collar positions increased absolutely and relatively between 1925 and 1931; the figures on their realization of that desire during the same years move in the opposite direction.

In the Weimar Republic the working class was the primary stratum from which salaried employees were recruited. This ascent took place predominantly

Table 2.4: Occupational Wishes of Young Women and Positions Obtained, 1925–31

	1925–26	1926–27	1927–28	1928–29	1929–30	1930–31
Number of young women seeking employment advice (in thousands)	152	173	176	167	172	178
Of these: Applicants for white-collar positions (in %)	27	29	33	37	37	37
Of these: Desired employment obtained (in %)	36	42	46	44	36	30

SOURCE: *Rundschau der Frau: Materialen für weibliche Funktionäre des ZdA*, no. 3, May 1932, vol. 3.

from the ranks of skilled workers; children of untrained workers had comparatively few chances to rise to white-collar positions.[9] As everywhere else in society, this ascent was normally into the immediately adjacent stratum; to skip over a stratum was very rare. The children of unskilled workers found it difficult to obtain white-collar positions because they could not meet the financial requisites (expenses for commercial school, clothing, and so forth)—requisites that were present even at the beginning of one's social ascent.

A review of the conditions governing social origin, therefore, results in the following comprehensive schematic picture; proletarian origin is comparatively rarer or more frequent:

Rarer

| Prior to World War I | among men | among older people (clerks) | among pharmacists, agents (technical personnel) | in DHV | among women in small and medium-sized towns | among men in large cities |

More frequent

| After World War I | among women | among youths (apprentices) | among foremen, office employees, salesclerks, commercial employees | in GdA ZdA | among women in large cities | among men in small and medium-sized towns |

Keen competition during periods of large-scale unemployment devalued the origin and education of members of higher strata and made it easier for employers to hire cheaply those persons with the most refined backgrounds possible. The positions available in offices and stores to the children of workers were not highly esteemed. The security offered by these positions was less than that of the average white-collar worker's. The privileges that were simultaneously attacked—if enjoyed by others—and desired by the working class (in some cases, weekly wage rates and, correspondingly, notices of dismissal a week in advance) were most seriously threatened in such positions, and the income they provided was often less than that received by factory girls. These conditions considerably impeded the efforts of white-collar workers to execute the "cultural mission" which, according to the middle-class theory they "had to perform as the connecting link between the labor proletariat and the industrial leadership."[10]

III Promotion

Formerly, the typical opportunity for employees to advance was by achieving independence. But as the main weight of employment shifted from commerce to industry, and as giant enterprises gained in importance, this opportunity was displaced by the possibility of promotion within the business hierarchy. To be sure, in the Weimar Republic the old road of ascent was not entirely blocked, especially in small-town retail establishments; sometimes it was opened by marriage. The problem for employees, however, was no longer the extent to which they could become employers within the old middle class, but how they could rise above a subordinate rank to reach higher positions within the new middle class. Not removal from the wage-earning class, but promotion to a higher rank within that class was uncertain.

This change reflected the transformation of liberal capitalism into monopoly capitalism and, in the upper reaches of society, the displacement of the businessman by the organizer and of the employer by the executive.[1] Just how far conditions had outdistanced the former possibilities of social advancement, and how the employee had forgotten to reckon with them, may be gleaned from the fact that a change in employment from a small or medium-sized business to a giant enterprise was often considered an "ascent." Indeed it was an ascent, but only insofar as working conditions in such enterprises were better and the salary higher.

More importantly, during the economic crisis possibilities for achieving independence completely lost their positive significance, for a new mass of "independents" emerged, often as a result of *descent*. This mass of independents was composed of déclassés—of dismissed people who, with their last savings, had opened a baker shop, of children,[2] and of a legion of absolutely indigent sales "agents" on commission who led a miserable existence begging from door to door. This type of agent, a salaried employee whose rank and standard of living fell even below that of the proletariat, was an independent, but his independence consisted in the necessity of bearing his misery alone, without the social protection enjoyed by wage earners. More and more people from the multitude of discharged white-collar workers and civil servants were continuously condemned to this parasitical independence.

The labor market of commissioned agents differed from that of all other employees' groups. An official report stated: "The demand for commissioned agents was strong again, just as in previous months. Almost exclusively, however, canvassers and representatives on commission were required. Employers often tried to obtain suitable persons on relief from the official employment agencies, with the relief payments continued. . . . Upon investigation of the various offers, it was discovered that in many cases would-be employers were themselves relief recipients."[3]

Dating from the time of the postwar inflation, employers tried increasingly to convert the status of the salaried representative into that of an independent agent[4] (in the sense of article 84 of the Commercial Code) who, like a full-fledged merchant, bears the risk of the business and is paid only a commission. This development was paradoxical: the more the agent lost all opportunity of becoming independent, the more the employer sought to subsume the employee under a law which presupposed independence. But the transformation of a traveling salesman into a commissioned agent was not *necessarily* harmful to the salesman, since commissions were usually higher than a fixed salary. Such changes had been less frequent in the late 1920s than in the early 1930s, when they usually constituted a disadvantage. They were also less frequent in medium-sized localities and establishments, where close contact between employer and representative still survived, than they were in large cities and giant enterprises. This was another paradox, for the tendency toward buraucratization at the expense of personal liberty emanated most strongly from big business. Here, also, economic considerations triumphed: wherever the personal independence of the economically dependent was cheaper, the breadgiver granted it, if only in a pitiful form.

Writers who expounded the middle-class theory made no mention of such phenomena, nor did they systematically examine the disintegration of bourgeois society caused by millions of unemployed. On the contrary, these writers pictured career opportunities for a "normal" body of salaried employees in a "normal" society. The countertendencies and obstacles which the theoreticians overlooked lay not only in the risk of unemployment, but also in the disproportionate increase in unqualified help, in the bureaucratization of giant enterprises, and in the monopolization of remaining promotion opportunities by employees of higher rank. By ignoring all these phenomena, the middle-class theory offered not so much an understanding of reality as it did proof of the longevity of those obsolete notions in which liberal and bureaucratic ideals were fused. The ideology of promotion and social ascent was not abandoned during the period of rationalization and the great economic crisis. In 1921, for example, the DHV discussed "the treatment of subordinates" on the assumption "that the clerks of today include the employers, managers and executives of tomorrow."[5] But while this statement conceivably retained some accuracy, the manner in which the GdA enrolled trainees in its "model firms program" was highly questionable. A recruiting pamphlet read: "Apprentice by day—manager of a worldwide business by night. . . . The ladder of success has many rungs, and all must be climbed and mastered. Determination is the only requirement." A functionary of the VwA wrote in 1932 that "the possibility of a step-by-step ascent to better and better paid work is typical of employee activity. . . . This opportunity basically distinguishes the salaried employee from the worker. . . . Gradual ascent is the rule, and every employee hopes for it in normal times."[6]

The officers of middle-class unions were inclined to regard even positions calling for simple standardized work as starting points to higher posts,[7] and contented themselves with demands "that machine work must constitute only a stepping stone to better positions in commercial life."[8]

More objective than these German spokesmen was H. Fuykschot, a Dutch citizen. In 1929 Fuykschot presented a report on "Repercussions in the Use of Office Machines" to the fourth international congress of the International Federation of Christian White Collar Workers' Unions. According to that report,

> It would obviously be commendable if young employees were to perform purely standardized work for a short time and then gradually be drafted for more responsible tasks. The difficulty lies in the fact that, for the majority of such employees, no opportunity for advancement exists, so that these young persons will be assigned to this type of work for many years, perhaps for their whole life. The development is the same as that of the skilled artisan, who once was the complete master of his craft but has been reduced to an industrial worker condemned to piecework.[9]

Fuykschot's opinion, based upon unusually extensive international data, completely contradicted the notions of German writers in the same union camp.

In the German middle-class theory the obstacles that irreparably diminished the individual's chances for advancement were hardly considered. Nevertheless, large numbers of employees were eliminated from the process of production during the Depression, especially as a result of replacement by younger persons. In addition, general phenomena lying beyond the crisis in the business cycle, such as the collectivization of the middle class and the bureaucratization of giant enterprises, should have prohibited talk of a "normal" ascent by the white-collar workers.

Lower, easily replaceable employees had increased in greater numbers than those in the upper strata. But the larger the number of lottery tickets in proportion to the number of available prizes, the smaller are the individual player's chances of winning. Not enough higher positions were available even for the ablest people, provided they even had occasion to prove their ability. And how often they could not even show they deserved promotion! While they waited for a chance, they grew older and thus drew nearer to dismissal.

A July 1926 law concerning protection from dismissal stipulated that employees above the age of thirty who had been employed for at least five years be given a dismissal notice three months prior to termination. This notification period increased for employees of longer tenure, reaching six months after twelve years of service. The 1926 law was especially unfavorable for older employees in small and medium-sized enterprises. For economic reasons such older employees who felt entitled to promotion were frequently replaced by cheaper and younger persons not protected by the law. In giant enterprises high managerial positions were increasingly filled from the outside. The desire of those who deserved well from their enterprise was often disregarded.[10] For those in intermediate positions, too, promotion often depended on unforeseeable conditions.

In many large establishments, the various departments were so distinctly insulated from one another that the employees of one department were sometimes, despite prolonged employment by the same firm, barely aware that other departments existed and, in any case, had scarce personal contact with any colleagues in them. This separation was sometimes maintained even in the lunch room and the various factory sport clubs, where the employees of a department sat only at their own table or pursued their own sport activities. The departments promoted a particular brand of egotism, jealously guarded by their heads. They vied with one another to keep down their overhead as much as possible, outbid one another, and strove to prevent any infringement upon their official jurisdiction. This intra-organizational rivalry, occasioned by that "organized economic irrationalism" which H. Bente made the subject of an interesting investigation,[11] left its mark upon the occupational career of the individual employee. If he was capable, his superior tried to retain him, regardless of whether he would be more valuable in some other position with better opportunities for advancement. If he was inefficient but had connections, not necessarily with the heads of the firm but with some other influential employee whose wishes had to be considered for some reason by a more authoritative executive, an attempt was made to hold him despite his poor showing or to pass him off as competent to another department rather than to urge his discharge. Anyone familiar with conditions in large enterprises knows how often the process of selection is guided by such reasoning and by laws other than those considered natural by liberal sociology.[12]

Despite the discrepancy between reality and the middle-class theory, it is not without reason that the ideology of promotion was so tenaciously defended. Employees with a middle-class background, who, as shown in the preceding chapter, were organized predominantly in associations that advocated a middle-class ideology, enjoyed somewhat better chances for advancement than white-collar workers of working-class origin.

According to a GdA survey, 15.1 percent of male commercial employees in responsible positions came from the class of independents; 12.9 percent and 12.4 percent had agrarian and craft or trade origins, respectively; 10.2 percent had public officials as fathers; 9.6 percent were the children of salaried employees; and only 7.3 percent of workers. Proletarian origin was generally synonymous with inferior education. The GdA survey established that, of the male employees from working-class families, 79.8 percent had only an elementary school education; the corresponding proportion among sons of public officials was 44.3 percent, and among sons of independents, only 15.4 percent. In a society in which the monopoly of education by the middle class was unbroken—the abolition of the formal privileges of education notwithstanding—class origin became an additional factor of insecurity for the employee of proletarian parentage. It was therefore much easier for sons of the bourgeoisie to deny the social and economic dependence of salaried employees or to dispute its consequences. They could advance more easily and were somewhat less exposed to the consequences of economic dependence. By comparing employees between the ages of thirty and forty-nine who had advanced to a position of independence and responsibility (levels 4–5) and who possessed the same occupational preparatory training, table 3.1 shows that the type of school attended retained its importance decades after graduation. The same occupational instruction at a training school or an equal period of apprenticeship and seniority in the business did not offset the deficiencies of elementary school graduates.

Most noteworthy and almost puzzling is that graduates of secondary schools among thirty- to forty-nine-year-old employees were on an almost equal footing with the graduates of elementary schools. Only graduation from higher schools

Table 3.1: Position, Education, and Training of White-Collar GdA Members 30–49 Years of
Age[a] (in %)

Level of Activities	Elementary School		Secondary School		Higher Schools	
	A[b]	B[c]	A	B	A	B
Lower (1–3)	80.3	63.1	81.3	60.1	55.5	48.4
Upper (4–5)	19.7	36.9	18.7	39.9	44.5	51.6
	100.0	100.0	100.0	100.0	100.0	100.0

SOURCE: GdA, ed., *Die wirtschaftliche und soziale Lage der Angestellten*, p. 73.

[a]Total sample: 24,564.
[b]A = training school only.
[c]B = training school and three years' apprenticeship.

made a marked difference. To be sure, the GdA survey established that occupational training was more important for the career of primary and secondary school graduates than their type of school education. But, inasmuch as the proportion of employees with higher education was larger among persons of middle-class origin, they fared noticeably better than persons with working-class origins in reaching more responsible positions.

Advancement opportunities varied for employees of different occupational groups. Foremen had none, and those for office girls and government employees were very slim. The chances were better for saleswomen, of whom a small percentage could become supervisors, section managers, instructors, and so forth,[13] than they were for female office workers, while the reverse prevailed among male employees of these two groups. The female stenographer of middle-class origin had some chance of becoming a private secretary.

The higher proportion of skilled persons among technical employees seems to indicate that promotion was less difficult for them than for commercial assistants. This trend is contradicted, however, by the particularly large number of unemployed technicians and by the fact that university graduates interfered with their promotion. In addition, as a result of increased scientific management on one side and an oversupply of technicians on the other, academic technicians had to compete with non-academicians even for intermediate positions. Because intermediate chemical technicians in the sugar, dye, soap, oil, and other industries could not dislodge the university men, their promotion opportunities were conspicuously poor.[14] In the larger machine and electrotechnical firms, the secondary school technician could not count upon promotion. In the few exceptional cases "where the construction and operating engineers with academic and secondary school education have the same basic opportunities for advancement, the rate is usually different. A change from factory to factory is much easier for the university graduate, because of his connections and his social bearing. . . . The secondary school technician, on the other hand, has to take the low path."[15] The secondary school technician's chances for promotion were somewhat more favorable in field service and in smaller enterprises.

For female salaried employees promotion was less possible than for the men. Their most likely chance of ascent lay in marriage into a higher social stratum. Statistics on this subject are inadequate. However, a census in Bavaria in 1927 established that 60.5 percent of men who married female civil servants and employees were independents, upper or intermediate public officials, and salaried employees. Only 38.3 percent of the husbands were manual workers, servants, domestics, or hired laborers of various kinds. Twenty-five percent of male employees in industry and 30 percent in commerce and transportation married female blue-collar workers.[16] These figures indicate that the insecurity of female help was greater than that of men.

IV Social Stratification

Both GdA and DHV used their extensive surveys to try and determine the social stratification of salaried employees. Both distinguished five levels of activities as follows:[1]

DHV	GdA
1. purely standardized	standardized work
2. simple	semiskilled work
3. semiskilled	partly independent work
4. independent	independent work
5. difficult, responsible	executive work

The DHV categories applied to male commercial clerks, those of the GdA to commercial and office personnel of both sexes. The GdA also surveyed and categorized other types of salaried employees. Its designations for technicians, for instance, differ from those for commercial personnel only in the third and fourth categories, which were changed to "independent" and "independent-responsible," respectively. Consequently, according to the GdA, technicians in categories 3 and 4 performed more highly skilled work than commercial employees at the same levels. Foremen were also divided into five groups: overseers, assistant foremen, foremen, expert foremen, and chief foremen. Workers employed by law offices and notaries were arranged into four categories with office manager belonging to the highest (level 4). The distribution of all persons polled among these groups presented the following picture (table 4.1). The DHV concluded from its findings that standardized work "did not play any part" in the activities of commercial clerks. They were instead located predominantly in the skilled work levels 3 and 4, which included no less than two-thirds of all commercial employees surveyed by the DHV. The GdA also registered 55.9 percent in these upper brackets. Thus, about 10 percent of all commercial employees performed

48

Table 4.1: Male and Female Salaried Employees according to Levels of Activity

	1	2	3	4	5	
According to DHV						
1. Commercial Employees (M)	0.27	25.06	41.19	24.58	8.90	100
According to GdA						
2. Commercial Employees (M)	2.4	30.9	38.3	17.6	10.5	
3. Government Employees (M)	1.2	28.3	67.1	2.3	1.1	
4. Employees in Law Offices (M)	12.6	37.8	7.5	42.1	—	
5. Commercial Employees (F)	6.3	66.2	23.9	2.4	1.2	
6. Government Employees (F)	6.7	57.2	35.2	0.9	—	
7. Employees in Law Offices (F)	5.7	77.2	11.9	5.2	—	
8. Technicians (M)	2.8	27.1	37.1	20.4	12.6	
9. Foremen	8.0	12.5	17.2	59.7	2.6	

SOURCES: DHV, ed., *Die Gehaltslage der Kaufmannsgehilfen*, p. 52; GdA, ed., *Die wirtschaftliche und soziale Lage der Angestellten*, p. 18.

highly skilled work, 50 to 70 percent congregated in the middle levels, and only 20 to 30 percent performed simple and formalized work. Purely standardized functions were exceptional.

Since the ideology of both associations would have been discredited had the lower groups been more strongly represented, the criteria on which these classifications were based should be scrutinized with caution. For example, the associations' desire to obtain collective salary agreements may have interfered with an impartial classification: the statistical grouping of some skilled employees into lower categories might have weakened their arguments for reclassifying those employees into a higher salary group. In any event, as sample tests demonstrated, the classification was not made by applying sociological criteria. Since classification in ambiguous cases was undoubtedly based less on work functions than on compensation and age,[2] many employees performing standardized work appeared in levels 2 and 3 when, from a sociological point of view, they belonged to a lower category.[3]

The GdA survey is also inconclusive with respect to the entire stratum of salaried employees. For instance, if the age divisions presented in its survey findings accurately portrayed its entire membership, then the GdA was somewhat "overage." The GdA found 29.2 percent of male commercial employees to be over forty years of age, as compared with only 14.9 percent in the DHV. It is precisely for this reason that level V, containing the most highly skilled employees, was more strongly represented in the GdA's survey findings than in those of the DHV. Theodor Geiger, who attempted to determine the social stratification of salaried employees from the statistics of the GdA, overlooked these points. The "elite character" of this organization dissolves entirely into an "age character," as table 4.2 shows.

The figures in table 4.1 are no more than guideposts. Thus, in reality the lower groups were more strongly represented than the upper groups; the social pyramid has a wider base than the table would have us believe. The proportions of 4.2:4.2:1.6 for the lower, middle, and upper strata, which M. Rössiger cites on the basis of GdA statistics,[4] would have to be changed in favor of the lower groups in order to provide a more accurate picture.

Even only as guideposts, however, the figures in table 4.1 reveal a number of fundamental differences between the various occupational groups. Government employees, for instance, are shown to work within an especially unfavorable social structure. They were almost entirely unrepresented on the two uppermost levels, where positions were filled instead by public officials. Inasmuch as public officials obstructed the advancement of government employees, the relations between the two groups were characterized by a distinct social contrast, as even a statistical summary can attest. The typical superior of the government employees was the civil service official. Of the 186,000 government employees in permanent administrative posts of the *Reich, Länder*, municipalities, and counties (including the Hansa cities), 83.2 percent fell into the "lower" or "lower-intermediate" brackets (31 March 1930). The corresponding figure for civil service employees

Table 4.2: Age Group Distribution of Members of Various White-Collar Unions (in %)

	Age	
	To 30	Over 40
Male Commercial Employees		
In 1925 National Census[1]	56.3	23.1
In the GdA[2]	42.3	29.2
Female Commercial Employees		
In 1925 National Census[1]	80.1	7.0
In the GdA[2]	63.2	8.7
In the ZdA[3]	84.0	5.0
Male Technical Employees		
In 1925 National Census[1]	38.9	34.4
In the GdA[2]	31.3	39.5

SOURCES:
[1]G. Fürst, "Die Altersgliederung der Angestellten," p. 65.
[2]GdA, ed., *Die wirtschaftliche und soziale Lage der Angestellten*, p. 64.
[3]S. Suhr, *Die weiblichen Angestellten*, p. 8.

was only 46.5 percent.[5] Law office and notary employees had relatively more members in the lower levels than commercial employees. The most skilled occupational group, technical employees, also obtained the highest proportion of executive work. According to Theodor Geiger's estimate, 22 percent of all male technicians achieved executive positions, as compared to only 3 percent among sales and office employees.[6] The average performance of technicians required greater skills than that of commercial clerks; almost half of the technical personnel were architects, engineers, or chemists.

Table 4.1 also yields important information with respect to the sexual stratification of salaried employees. While the conception of a pyramid more or less accurately depicts the social structure of the entire body of salaried employees, it fails to describe the arrangement of either men or women considered separately. Women were represented much more strongly in the lower categories than men, who by contrast, were located more in the intermediate and upper brackets than in the lower. Clearly then, a substantial difference existed between male and female job classifications. Since we are concerned here only with the relationship between the figures, the following table by M. Rössiger is presented without corrections:

Employees	Total	Male	Female
Upper Stratum	15.76	20.29	2.51
Middle Stratum	41.90	47.53	25.44
Lower Stratum	42.34	32.18	72.04

Thus, of every ten men, seven belonged to the upper and middle strata and only three to the lower level; but of every ten women, seven belonged to the lower stratum and only three to the upper and middle ranks. Among females generally, 64 percent of the government employees, 83 percent of the law clerks, and 73 percent of the commercial employees occupy the lowest rungs, levels I and II.

Considering that the least-skilled female employees were especially difficult to organize and that women were more strongly represented in the ZdA than in the GdA and the Gesamtverband der Angestelltengewerkschaften (Gedag, Federation of Employees' Unions), it appears that about 80 to 85 percent of all female employees performed entirely subordinate functions. Only one-fifth of all female salaried employees attained positions in the middle and higher categories, and virtually none attained level 5, where positions were filled almost exclusively by men. In other words, the barrier at which aspirants to higher positions generally came to grief was lower for women than for men, namely, on the border between the lower and intermediate groups. It is true that, due to marriage, women generally left their occupations earlier than men, but even so, the social stratification of the workplace was at the same time a stratification according to sex. Men generally possessed authority while women were typically subordinates. This circumstance offered "objective support" for the demands for special prestige pressed by commercial clerks, demands that reflected the traditional anti-feminist ideology of men. Proletarianization affected the whole class of salaried employees, of course, but especially as it advanced, so also did the desire of male employees to translate their positions and sex into a right to exercise some authority within the enterprise.

It was not by chance that the DHV drew the most extreme conclusions from this social stratification according to sex. The DHV was an association composed exclusively of men, and, besides, at the time the surveys were taken it had relatively fewer male members originating in the working class than did either the GdA or the ZdA. Its experiences during the period of rationalization following 1925 led the DHV to the opinion "that the new work methods . . . do not result in a new proletarianization of commercial clerks. The number of male commercial clerks will, of course, grow less rapidly in the future than that of female clerks. But they will retain their 'delegated' employer function, because they will take over the new functions of organization, statistics, and management arising from the operation of rationalization."[7] As a matter of fact, the influx of female employees in the years after 1925 (when the total strength of salaried employees was 3.5 million) may have been relatively greater than that of their male colleagues. S. Suhr estimated the increase of female employees during the period between 1925 and 1930 to be 200,000 (from 1.2 to 1.4 million) persons. Since the number of salaried employees working in 1930 was approximately 3.9 million, the males had also increased by only 200,000 at the most, and thus at a slower pace than the female.[8] Thus, the ratio between male and female employees had shifted quantitatively in favor of women and qualitatively in favor of men. Moreover, subordinate positions in 1931 were being filled with young and cheap females even more rapidly than they had in 1925 (some of them with temporary workers, as a result of the economic crisis). The occupational inequality between the sexes had widened.

Even as early as at the turn of the century, the DHV maintained that women were thoroughly fitted to perform inferior functions, for example, to do "mechanical typing . . ., just as, for example, in the printing trade male help cannot be employed for any length of time for folding and similar processes." The argument by which this association substantiated its position, even as it battled the occupational claims of women, is not without merit: "Such tasks [mechanical ones] can only be performed by persons who do not consider their work an occupation and therefore carry it out only with indifference and to a certain extent with repugnance."[9]

Later, in the Weimar Republic, the organization ceased to fight against female competition. Many of the inferior functions which it had previously wanted reserved for women, due to their willingness to accept low wages, had been taken over by men. As members of the DHV they considered their work to be an occupation. They were not to perform it with indifference or reluctance but, conscious of their prestige, they were to regard it as a delegated employer function. Thus, for example, according to the DHV, male employees who typed more than 150 syllables per minute did not perform a simple, mechanical task but the "skilled commercial work" of level 3. Ideologies will change!

The social differences between male and female white-collar workers were clearly reflected in the average salaries of their various age groups (see table 4.3).

Table 4.3: Average Monthly Salary of White-Collar Workers by Age Groups and Sex

Age	Male		Female	
	% of Polled Employees	Average Salary in RM	% of Polled Employees	Average Salary in RM
to 18	2.5	97	9.0	81
19	3.7	113	7.9	100
20	4.4	129	9.1	115
21	4.0	145	8.6	126
22	3.4	162	7.4	137
23	3.2	177	6.4	146
24	2.9	191	5.3	156
25	2.9	206	4.9	163
26–28	9.0	239	11.3	179
29–30	6.5	272	5.8	195
31–32	5.9	290	4.4	203
33–35	8.8	308	5.4	208
36–40	12.7	330	6.4	221
41–45	9.5	346	4.1	233
46–50	7.8	351	2.1	239
51–55	5.8	338	1.2	254
56–60	3.8	330	0.5	237
61–65	2.2	317	0.2	214
65+	1.0	299		205
	100		100	

SOURCE: *Statistisches Jahrbuch für das Deutsche Reich*, 1932, p. 287.

According to the GdA survey, women almost never reached the higher salaries above RM 250 per month. However, men twenty-nine years of age or older earned more than the maximum salary for women of any age. Salaries increased up to RM 351 for the male age group of forty-six to fifty years, and gradually decreased at higher ages down to RM 300. The salary inequality between the sexes existed in all age groups, including the lowest. The economic significance of these sex-based salary differences appears even more starkly considering the fact that, in the lower age groups, female workers were relatively numerous and men relatively scarce, whereas the proportions were reversed in the higher age groups.

The figures on beginning and top salaries in collective bargaining agreements also show the economic disadvantages that female white-collar workers had to accept. This was true for all occupations, including those which paid the lowest salaries, such as positions in retail and wholesale trade. In general, the beginning salaries for females in the lowest bracket of the collective agreements were about 10 percent lower than the salaries for male workers, that is, about RM 9 to RM 13 per month. For the higher brackets, which in any event were infrequently attained by women, this percentage was often much higher, increasing, for example, to almost 20 percent in retail trade.[10]

V Relations with Blue-Collar Workers and Entrepreneurs

The status of salaried employees in the Weimar Republic cannot be satisfactorily explained with reference to their economic position in the labor market or to their widely different functions within the enterprise. Neither can their status be reduced to the legal privileges which elevated the white-collar workers above manual laborers in Germany. To the contrary, these legal privileges must themselves be understood as products of claims to and grants of social prestige. In examining the social prestige of white-collar workers, we shall consider their relations first with manual laborers, then with the entrepreneurs.

White- and Blue-Collar Workers

White-Collar Workers of Blue-Collar Origin

Salaried employees with social origins in the class of manual laborers regarded their positions as an ascent. This was true not only of those who had moved up in the hierarchy of the enterprise, like foremen and many technicians with secondary schooling, but also of many low-level commercial employees who occupied their positions as a consequence of generational ascent.

Conversely, among manual laborers, the female office worker was more highly esteemed than the female factory worker. Apprentices in the office were considered to be more "refined" than apprentices in the factory even though they came from the same social milieu.[1] The career wishes of manual workers reflected these social evaluations. As a rule, their career wishes were not utopian hopes for economic independence, but pragmatic and modest aspirations for what was socially near. Thus, for example, when the Section for Women's Work of the Vienna Chamber of Labor asked female industrial laborers whether they wished to have another job, the 40 percent who answered yes expressed a desire primarily for low-level commercial jobs, for example, office work or employment as a saleswoman. Leaving aside the female factory workers doing heavy labor who desired "any other job," the inquiry found "that the unskilled worker aspired to skilled work, the skilled laborer to a job as salaried employee, the highly trained laborer to a social occupation." The hierarchy of these wishes clearly expressed the social ranks recognized by blue-collar workers.[2]

Commensalism and Intermarriage

Manual workers desired both commensalism and intermarriage with commercial employees, or at least refused them only as an act of defiance. By contrast, salaried employees who did not come from the blue-collar class rejected both commensalism and intermarriage according to an unwritten code of honor or for fear of losing social prestige.

Life Style

White-collar workers still cultivated the remnants of a "specific style of life," in which the social "honor" of a stratum is typically expressed.[3] These remnants included the special, economically unjustifiable value that the salaried employees placed upon their housing and cultural needs, as well as their corresponding restriction of expenditures for food.

In 1927–28, the average household of manual workers spent 45.3 percent of its total expenditures on food and 16.5 percent on housing (rent, furnishing, repair, light, and heat). In the average household of salaried employees, the corresponding percentages were 34.5 and 20.5.[4] For selected low- and high-income groups of blue- and white-collar workers, similar differences in expenditures could be observed (see table 5.1). The surveys conducted by the Afa-Bund on life style of salaried employees are especially illuminating, because they distinguish between commercial employees, technical employees, and foremen, whereas the DHV survey is limited to commercial employees. The Afa-Bund's figures show that life style of foremen resembled that of blue-collar workers more

Table 5.1: Percentage of Expenditures for Food and Housing among High- and Low-income Households of Blue- and White-Collar Workers

Income Group in RM	Blue-Collar		White-Collar	
	2,500–3,000	4,300+	To 3,000	5,100+
Heads per Household	3.9	4.9	3.1	4.0
Food	47.3	41.5	41.6	30.5
Housing	17.8	16.9	22.2	20.9

SOURCE: *Statistisches Jahrbuch für das Deutsche Reich*, 1932, pp. 321–22.

than that of technicians or of commercial employees of the same income group (see table 5.2). To some extent, the higher expenditures for food among foremen can probably be attributed to their somewhat higher number of heads-of-household, but even so, the expenditures for housing among foremen were somewhat lower than those of technicians and commercial employees. Similarly, foremen spent considerably less for the satisfaction of "cultural needs" than did the other two groups of white-collar workers. In this regard as well, foremen resembled manual workers more than other salaried employees.[5]

In many cases, the elevated life style of salaried employees (for which they had paid by marrying later and controlling births more strictly than did blue-collar workers) was made more difficult or impossible by dismissals and salary reductions during the last years of the Weimar Republic.[6] The difficulty of maintaining the accustomed life style under economic pressure was due, of course, to the fact that the need for food is less elastic than the desire for other satisfactions. Thus, dismissals and salary reductions had a disqualifying effect, that is, they effectively "curtailed the honor" of salaried employees, but did not silence their claim to a "status-appropriate" life style.

Table 5.2: Expenditures in Households of White-Collar Workers according to Occupational Groups

Occupational Group	Commercial Employees	Technicians	Foremen
Heads per Household	3.1	3.3	3.6
Income	RM 394.71	RM 424.60	RM 391.53
	Expenditures in %		
Food	32.8	30.2	36.5
Housing	21.5	21.8	19.5
Clothing	10.9	10.2	10.7
Cultural Needs	19.5	20.3	16.9
Forced Expenditures	10.3	10.0	10.5
Savings	2.5	3.9	2.1
Debts Payments	2.5	3.6	2.1
	100	100	100

SOURCE: Table 20 in E. Sträter, "Die soziale Stellung der Angestellten," p. 69. Sträter's figures are from the survey of the Afa-Bund, *Was verbrauchen die Angestellten?* p. 55. For members of the DHV see DHV, ed., *Der Haushalt der Kaufmannsgehilfen.*

Monopoly of Career Opportunities

The social rank of the salaried employees is also visible in the monopoly that members of the higher strata held over some employment and career opportunities. This monopoly, which was no less effective for its lack of legal standing, was discussed in chapters 2 and 3.

Legal Privileges of Salaried Employees

Inasmuch as the legal order can guarantee honor as well as power—as Max Weber demonstrated—the special, legal privileges enjoyed by salaried employees were signs of special esteem. Included among their legal privileges were monthly salary payments, continued salary payments in case of illness, longer time periods for termination of employment than was required for blue-collar workers, special protection against the termination of older white-collar workers, preferred treatment of salary claims (but not of wage claims) in the event of bankruptcy, separate social insurance, special representation in the factory council, and so forth.

These privileges were legalized partly because salaried employees were fewer in number than blue-collar laborers. They were partly also a legacy of the precapitalist past, and especially of occupational esteem enjoyed by clerks, which had enabled them to enlist the aid of the state in combatting the beginning dissolution of their estate and the beginning proletarianization of its members. For example, monthly salary payments, privileges in the event of bankruptcy, and continued payment of salary in case of illness corresponded with earlier, special claims to social esteem by persons who rendered services akin to the duties of civil servants. This fact prohibited the payment of wage-like compensation for the work of clerks and, ideally, required the granting of "provisions" appropriate to members of an estate.[7]

To the degree that the socioeconomic position of salaried employees increasingly deteriorated—attributable to the transformation of the stratum into a mass, destruction of the occupational career, partial mechanization of white-collar functions, and inclusion of salaried workers into the phases of the business cycle—their privileges also changed from symbols to safeguards of their social esteem. They were defended not only because their suspension would have intensified the economic insecurity of salaried employees, but also because the loss of prestige would have been inestimable. The DHV recognized this quite clearly when, during the great crisis, the privilege of a fixed monthly salary was abolished. The salary reductions based on shortened working hours transformed the "service relationship" of white-collar workers into that of laborers. The entrepreneurs were interested in "being able to determine the number of working hours according to the prevailing demand and to calculate the wage of the salaried employees from case to case according to that demand. If such a determination of salaries were followed exactly the recipient of a fixed monthly salary would be turned into a wage earner with the attendant uncertainty of his income. This would mean the collapse of the main pillar which has hitherto borne our estate as an estate."[8]

Workers' Attitudes toward Salaried Employees

Finally, the social prestige of salaried employees was evident in challenges to the legitimacy of their rank by the less favorably placed workers. Just as "the more favorably placed person feels the increasing need to be able to regard the contrast which favors him as 'legitimate,' i.e., to regard his own situation as merited and that of the other as somehow incurred by his own 'fault,' "[9] so the less favorably placed person strives to deny his own "fault" and the other's "merit." Asked about their perceptions of salaried employees, manual laborers often replied that white-collar work was largely superfluous and therefore increased the costs of production, but that it was necessary to the interests of entrepreneurs because it had the effect of reducing wages. Apart from salespersons, the worker was acquainted only with foremen, technical personnel in the factory, and such salaried employees as he met in public offices, trade unions, and political parties. He often viewed the salaried employees as alien, distant, or even hateful because of their bureaucratic or military bearing, and at the same time envied their greater economic security. Foremen and technical personnel, on the other hand, were part of the worker's immediate experience, appearing to him as the very instruments of exploitation.[10]

"The worker merely follows his instinct when he senses that the salaried employee is an adversary who, in certain circumstances, can contribute to the further deterioration of the worker's economic situation, which is regrettable already."[11] This was the verdict of the chairman of the factory council in a large enterprise. Another worker wrote, "All these supervisors and overseers, these ministers of control and dismissal would be superfluous, and the money spent on them used for wage increases, if one adopted a fundamentally different attitude toward the treatment of the worker and his work."[12] Still another worker asked, "Why are there white- and blue-collar workers? Yes, why? Why is the manual worker paid by the hour, the day, the week, but the salaried worker by the month? At the time of the inflation the workers were envied because of their short payment periods! Why is it that the manual worker gets paid only for the work he actually does, while the salaried employee is paid also for work he blamelessly misses? Why are the vacations of the salaried employee much longer than those of the worker? Why is the salaried employee, but not the worker, protected against losses resulting from shorter working time?[13] Why is the salaried employee addressed as *Herr* Mueller, the worker as Mueller? Why is it that salaried employees must be given long notices, but the workers can be dismissed on short notice?"[14]

A particularly sharp and partly unjust verdict on salaried employees was delivered by the representative organ of the Christian Trade Unions of workers:

> The salaried employees are located on the free labor market at protected places. The worker must "bleed," because the salaries of the white-collar workers must not be reduced and because superfluous white-collar workers are widely protected against dismissal. . . . The more the salaried employees protect themselves against dismissal, reduction of salary, etc., the more it is the workers who are burdened with economic risks generally and with the specific risks run by the enterprise. And the whole world seems to find that arrangement in order. . . . The salaried employees are granted special privileges, the workers have the pleasure of contributing to the costs of such measures. It does not occur to anyone that it might ever be possible to attain the same privileges for the workers.[15]

Especially illuminating in this article was the indignant allegation that the press protested more strongly against the dismissal of salaried employees than of blue-collar workers. The extent to which public opinion expressed sympathy with the fate of individual social strata is here made into a measure of public esteem.

Also characteristic of working-class attitudes are the proposals which a manual worker made for improving relations between blue- and white-collar workers:

1. All salaried employees, whether commercial or technical, should start at the bottom. Blue-collar workers ought to feel that white-collar workers had obtained their positions through neither favors nor studies.
2. Blue-collar workers should have opportunities for advancement in the factory.
3. With respect to social insurance, both kinds of workers should be equal.
4. Workers' protection against dismissal should resemble that of salaried employees.
5. The unions of white- and blue-collar workers should cooperate closely in the various industries.
6. The laws establishing group councils should be abolished.[16]

In all these judgments of salaried employees, blue-collar workers overlooked the fact that the majority of white-collar employees suffered the fate common to all workers: they lived in economic insecurity. But just as the anti-feudal bourgeosie, in its struggle for social advancement, had painted a picture not of the nobility's impoverished members but of its ruling representatives and strongly provocative life styles of libertines, so the worker focused on those white-collar characteristics that he lacked. This perception was eminently sociological in character, for indeed, every kind of social prestige is founded on differences rather than equalities.

Effects of the Economic Crisis

Despite the proletarianization of the salaried employees and their acute impoverishment in the economic crisis, enough privileges remained to support their accustomed esteem. Moreover, during the crisis conflicts within the enterprises grew sharper, because the bitter struggle for the workplace unfavorably affected the moral climate and increased the friction between those white- and blue-collar workers who came into contact there.

All things considered, the crisis hit laborers harder than salaried employees. Although the reserve army of unemployed white-collar workers was very large, figures of the used capacity of white-collar workplaces showed the unemployment of salaried employees to be relatively smaller than that of blue-collar workers. That is to say, the average salaried employee had a better chance of clinging to his job than the average manual worker. While many of the legal privileges mentioned above were seriously threatened, not all were abolished. Most of the cited attacks by manual workers on the status and prestige of salaried employees had not missed the point.

At the same time, the working conditions of the salaried employees had been equalized with those of the laborers to an extent that varied with rank in the social hierarchy. For example, neither the substitute saleswoman in a large-scale retail enterprise nor the employee working at a machine in a huge office could be distinguished from unskilled workers in many respects, including their weekly pay periods. By contrast, the relatively higher strata of the salaried employees continued to enjoy many of the old privileges. The esteem of the more highly placed employees did not extend to the marginal stratum, whose position melted into that of the unskilled workers. For example, marriage between a substitute bookkeeper and a salesgirl in a department store was generally regarded as a mismarriage. The worker judged "the" salaried employees not by those persons who completely shared his fate, but by those who enjoyed a little more social prestige than himself.

Differences in Unemployment Rates

We still need to consider more fully the unemployment of white-collar workers in relation to that of manual laborers. Table 5.3 shows the number of "recipients of support" among white-collar workers to be lower than 100,000 in the two years 1927 and 1928. Thereafter, unemployment increased continuously, reaching almost 550,000 by January 1933, when Hitler assumed power. Comparing these figures with those for blue- and white-collar workers combined (column 2), and taking into account the proportion of unemployed white-collar workers

Table 5.3: Unemployment of Salaried Employees, 1927–33[a] (in thousands)

1	Blue- and White-Collar Workers 2	White-Collar Workers 3	Column 3 as % of Column 2 4
March 1927	1331	119	9.0
June	736	91	12.4
Sept.	477	79	16.8
Dec.	2391	86	3.6
March 1928	1195	94	7.8
June	717	87	12.1
Sept.	664	80	12.0
Dec.	1830	93	5.1
March 1929	2091	113	5.4
June	930	115	12.4
Sept.	910	107	11.8
Dec.	1985	118	5.9
March 1930	3041	204	6.7
June	2641	224	8.5
Sept.	3004	261	8.7
Dec.	4384	296	6.8
March 1931	4744	339	7.2
June	3954	357	9.0
Sept.	4355	384	8.8
Dec.	5668	430	7.6
March 1932	6034	495	8.3
June	5476	520	9.5
Sept.	5103	511	10.0
Dec.	5773	522	9.0
Jan. 1933	6014	578	9.6

SOURCE: L. Preller, Sozialpolitik in der Weimarer Republik, p. 168.

[a]All figures are end-of-month. Statistics on unemployed for 1927–29 are based on recipients of support; those for 1930–33 on those classified as unemployed.

in the total unemployment figures (column 4), it appears that white-collar unemployment did *not* change drastically between 1927 and 1933. The average of
all percentages listed in column 4 is 8.9, which means that about every tenth
unemployed person was a salaried employee. According to the census of 1925,
however, the percentage of salaried employees of the total number of white- and
blue-collar workers was 19.5; that is, about every fifth person in the total was a
salaried employee. According to this rough comparison, unemployment of the
total workforce was twice as high as that of salaried employees.

Ludwig Preller has calculated that, of all white-collar workers, about 2.4
percent in 1927 and 13.6 percent in 1932 were unemployed.[17] But the crisis hit
blue-collar workers still harder. According to official statistics, unemployment
among blue-collar workers increased tenfold, between 1925 and 1933, compared
to only about fourfold among white-collar workers (see table 5.4). The figures
in Table 5.4 also show that male manual workers were hit much harder than
female workers, whereas white-collar women were unluckier than their male
counterparts. Finally, even the employees in leading positions were by no means
invulnerable to unemployment.

Although unemployment among both blue- and white-collar workers increased continuously from September 1928 to January 1933 (with one minor
exception in September 1932), blue-collar workers were additionally burdened
to a much greater extent than white-collar workers with seasonal fluctuations in
unemployment. Also, the business cycle increased unemployment among salaried
employees somewhat later than among the wage earners due to their different
termination periods. Conversely, because of the "rationalization" of office work,
white-collar workers became victims of technological unemployment in the 1920s,
while factory workers were spared.

Table 5.4: Increase in Unemployment, among Wage and Salary Earners, 1925–33
(1925 = 100)

	Total	Men	Women
Salaried Employees in			
Leading Positions	449.9	429.9	
Salaried Employees	424.2	401.8	475.0
Wage Earners	970.6	1042.8	674.7
Total Unemployed,			
Including Household Personnel	819.4	886.0	619.2

SOURCE: *Statistisches Jahrbuch für das Deutsche Reich*, 1934, p. 19.

Figures on unemployment among different types of white-collar workers shown in table 5.5 provide insights into structural changes that are obscured by the figures for the totals. Comparing the percentages contributed by various types of white-collar workers to total white-collar unemployment, the following picture emerges. Commercial employees and office workers (occupational groups 25 and, respectively, 26 in table 5.5) accounted for by far the greatest portion of

Table 5.5: Unemployment of Salaried Employees by Type of Work (percent of total white-collar unemployment)

		Unemployed Salaried Employees	
	Type of Work	Male	Female
December 1927	Commercial	68.4	82.1
	Office	16.4	16.0
	Technical	13.7	0.4
	Free Professions and Other	1.5	1.5
		100.0	100.0
December 1928	Commercial	66.3	81.5
	Office	11.9	17.0
	Technical	20.9	0.7
	Free Professions and Other	0.9	0.8
		100.0	100.0
December 1930	Commercial	64.8	80.6
	Office	9.8	17.1
	Technical	24.3	0.7
	Free Professions and Other	1.1	1.6
		100.0	100.0
December 1931	Commercial	62.5	80.9
	Office	8.7	14.3
	Technical	27.4	1.1
	Free Professions and Other	1.4	2.4
		100.0	100.0
December 1932	Commercial	63.3	82.2
	Office	8.9	14.3
	Technical	26.2	1.1
	Free Professions and Other	1.6	2.4
		100.0	100.0

SOURCE: L. Preller, *Sozialpolitik in der Weimarer Republik*, p. 169.

white-collar unemployment. This was a consequence of the fact that these two groups numerically dominated the category of salaried employed personnel (employed and unemployed). The share of female white-collar unemployment contributed by two occupational groups was especially high, never falling below 95.5 percent. By comparison, the percentage of male white-collar unemployment for which commercial and office personnel were responsible shrank steadily between 1927 and 1933, with the proportion contributed by male office workers decreasing by half.[18] At the same time the corresponding proportion for male technical employees increased steadily from 13.7 percent in 1927 to almost twice that (26.2 percent) in 1932.

White-Collar Workers and Entrepreneurs

The social esteem which salaried employees enjoyed and which was reflected in their privileges cost wage earners no more than annoyance and envy, but frequently saddled the entrepreneurs with a pecuniary burden. It was the entrepreneur, not the worker, who bore the costs of the employee's longer vacations, his longer termination periods, and his other privileges. Declining profits during economic crises intensified the entrepreneur's interest in regarding the white-collar worker as just another labor cost, and in neglecting, diminishing, or circumventing the privileges of his status.

Only the symbolic preferments that the entrepreneur granted to many employees—for example, distinguished forms of address ("Herr Mueller" in lieu of "Mueller"), special titles, and the like—cost nothing and yet brought him some gains. The same was true of the belief in opportunities for social advancement that was cultivated in factory papers and house organs by featuring the biographies of "deserving members of the 'family.' " Similar ends were also served by small presents, special decorations, favorable mentions, and other symbolic distinctions. The inventiveness of the superiors was nearly unlimited.[19]

Entrepreneurs voluntarily offered some preferments, despite their expense, in order to control office politics or to maintain useful distance between white- and blue-collar workers. For example, one of the largest firms in the electrical industry reimbursed members of the board of trustees who represented the white-collar workers for the cost of second-class railway tickets, whereas representatives of the blue-collar workers were entitled only to lower, third-class travel.[20] Many firms arranged occasional festivities and outings for their office personnel, during which time economic and social inequality was suspended. If only for an evening or afternoon, the section chief drank coffee with the commercial apprentice, the boss danced before all eyes with the secretaries, and the malaise of everyday life gave way to moments of fabricated happiness. This was a capitalist counterpart to the "safety-valve customs" (Thurnwald's "Ventilsitten"), by means of which rigid social hierarchies in all epochs and in many different cultures are ritualistically suspended or reversed for a time. Such arrangements by the firm were the Mardis Gras of the office, as it were. The absence of blue-collar workers on such occasions contributed to hardening the differences in social prestige. Management extended to white-collar workers preferences in social esteem that blue-collar workers were denied. All these measures were researched by specialized "psychotechnicians" and recommended because of their excellent effects on the "climate of the enterprise."[21] When the costs of their policy toward white-collar workers were still small compared to corresponding expenditures for blue-collar workers, many entrepreneurs were "glad to incur these costs voluntarily, in order to strengthen their position in relation to organized labor by means of the office personnel." In contrast, "the resistance of independent small merchants to social welfare measures for salaried employees developed quite early." Because most members of the old middle class employed salaried personnel exclusively, the costs of such measures weighed heavily with them.[22]

Before the passage of social insurance legislation for salaried employees in 1911, revealing conflicts developed over the value, aims, and determination of the preferred social policy. These conflicts involved all social strata—workers, salaried employees, entrepreneurs, and their representatives in the political parties and government. The basic issue was whether to extend to salaried employees the health and pension insurance originally created for the workers, or to create a separate insurance policy for them.[23] The most important concern for the overwhelming majority of white-collar workers was that their "service function" be recognized. They wanted an independent pension-insurance policy that would not only lighten their burdens as members of the labor force, but also testify to their superiority over manual workers. Thus, with the exception of a small minority consisting mainly of technicians, they rejected the recommendation of the workers' unions to extend the existing social insurance to cover salaried employees.

The attitudes of the entrepreneurs toward white-collar workers were no more unified than their diverse interests. The different aims that the entrepreneurs pursued with respect to white-collar workers were also influenced by general political considerations and expectations. For example, one might expect the entrepreneurs to have been interested in splitting the labor force by discrimination and hence to favor separate insurance for members of the new middle class, but this held true, initially at least, only for industrialists in middle-sized firms who voiced relatively liberal opinions. Gustav Stresemann, president of the Bund der Industriellen (BdI, League of Industrialists), advocated a policy that would unite industry, commerce, and the middle classes against the agricultural interests. At the same time, in his judgment, separate insurance should be created as "a bulwark against socialism."[24] A separate insurance plan, the BdI explicitly maintained, would fortify the separate consciousness of the white-collar "estate" and protect it from radical political and radical trade union views.

A very different set of opinions was expressed in the Centralverband Deutscher Industrieller (CVDI, Central Association of German Industrialists), especially by the big industrialists, who sought to obstruct the formation of separate state insurance for salaried employees. Although these industrialists, like the entrepreneurs organized in the Bund der Industriellen, were interested in curbing the influence of the radical trade union Butib, they felt that insurance plans organized by private enterprises would be more effective in splintering the labor force than would a separate state insurance plan. Thus, in responding to the arguments of the BdI in 1911, the *Deutsche Industriezeitung*, the organ of the CVDI, asked:

> Can one believe that employees organized in the Bund der technisch-industriellen Beamten (Butib) would change their views as members of the separate pension plan? . . . Can one no longer hope that the still moderate salaried employees in the general social insurance plans might exert a quieting influence on the manual workers through their contact? But these are pure speculations; the attitude of the CVDI toward separate pension plans was determined exclusively by technical-administrative considerations.[25]

In the industrial enterprises, the CVDI argued, the greatest difficulties would arise in the attempt to separate the more poorly paid employees from the workers, which would be necessary in a separate insurance scheme. Members of the workforce who received equal pay should qualify for the same social aid from the state. The considerations behind this attitude were evident from the CVDI's advocacy of restricting insurance payment obligations by narrowly defining the income groups that qualified for state insurance and by preserving the substitute private pension plans. Thus, its economic interest in the lowest possible cost of insurance for salaried employees was one of the factors that prompted the CVDI to temporarily prefer extending the existing social insurance.

However, during the period from 1911 to 1913 the arguments of the liberal BdI gained more and more adherents among members of the CVDI. For example, a CVDI resolution in 1913 stated that "the salaried employees, by education and economic function, form an intermediate link between entrepreneurs and manual workers and thus occupy a socially mediating position."[26] But during World War I those industrialists who regarded Wilhelmine society as the model for all social order again enjoyed an increase in power and influence.[27] Their ruthlessness in dealing with salaried employees, despite the declared social truce (Burgfriede), contributed to a certain radicalization of the new middle class during the war. Nor were the entrepreneurs inclined to improve the legal and social position of white-collar workers in the years following World War I. During the period of rationalization they proceeded to dismiss office personnel, and they opposed the law for the protection of the termination of employment (Kündigungsschutzgesetz) of 9 July 1926. The DHV lamented: "The fact that the law pertains to an especially valuable contingent of the labor force, the salaried employees, had no influence whatever on the entrepreneurial attitude of brusk rejection."[28] Finally, in the great economic crisis, the entrepreneur allowed white-collar workers to feel their economic dependence and misery to the same extent that manual workers did.

In the debates over separate social insurance for the employees the term "new middle class" (neuer Mittelstand, literally "new middle estate") became part of the German vocabulary. Many politicians spoke of the new middle class in order to receive electoral votes from the parties on the left. Conflicts of interest between the old, independent middle class and the economically dependent white-collar workers were obscured by the use of euphemisms, but the often repeated assertion that the middle class serves social reconciliation and peace—an idea that can be traced back to Aristotle—did not fail to have its effect. Inasmuch as the assertion assigned to the salaried employees a position morally elevated above the class struggle, it answered their wish to avoid sinking into the manual workforce.

However difficult it may be to distinguish accurately between the many political, economic, and bureaucratic interests which culminated in a special legal position for white-collar workers in Germany, there can be no question but that the existence of a radical workers' movement played a decisive role. In the Wilhelmine empire the workers were placed outside of society, and the so-called middle-class society was dominated by agrarian, feudal, and military interests and standards. The revolutionary rhetoric of the workers' movement inspired the state and the upper strata with fear. The more social weight they could provide to the new middle class, the less ominous the future appeared.

Not only were the white-collar workers' legal privileges supported by the policies of the non-socialist salaried employees' unions, they also intensified conflicts between white- and blue-collar workers in *all* trade unions, regardless of political orientation. This was true in both the empire and the Weimar Republic up to its decline.

VI Middle-Class Notions and Lower-Class Theory

In the Weimar Republic two different views of white-collar workers gained currency: the lower-class theory and the middle-class theory. The lower-class theory was advanced by socialist intellectuals and politicians and by the Afa-Bund, while the middle-class view enjoyed great popularity among white-collar associations not connected to the Afa-Bund—principally the GdA and the DHV, whose combined membership far exceeded that of the former. The middle-class view also found spokesmen among politicians in all political parties from the Democrats to the National Socialists. The most radical formulations did not originate with the members or functionaries of the associations, but with ideologists, whose center of work was neither the factory, the office, nor the shop, but the realm of political rhetoric. They wrote or spoke with passion, interpreting a reality they seldom knew through their own experience. What did Rudolf Borchardt, the poet, really know of the life of white-collar workers, or Ernst Jünger of the worries of laborers? What concrete observations lay at the bottom of Hans Freyer's fantasies about the "Volk"?

In examining the middle-class views I shall disregard the most extreme formulations for now, and return to them later in the discussions of nationalism in chapter 10. In all middle-class views, the salaried employees were assigned a position between the upper and lower strata, between the capitalists and the proletariat. It made no difference whether specific types of employees (commercial clerks, technicians) were singled out for special attention, as they were among the Christian-national organizations, or whether all the different types of white-collar workers were considered together as an "estate," as was characteristic of the GdA conceptions. Such divergent emphases reflected the different organizational principles on which the functionaries of the various associations formulated their "sociologies." They all agreed, however—and this is decisive—that white-collar workers belonged to an intermediate "estate."

The line separating salaried employees from the strata above them was always less distinct than the boundary separating them from those below. For example, advocates of the proletarian theory followed the example of both legal practice and official census categories in excluding employees with executive functions from the stratum of white-collar workers, considering them instead as "economically independent," while the middle-class theoreticians tended to designate such persons as salaried employees.[1] (A parallel may be seen in the independent artisan stratum. Attempts were repeatedly made to include semi-industrial large handicraft production as part of the handicraft economy, in consequence of which "handicraft" appeared to comprise a larger stratum than it actually did.) The lines of distinction that set white-collar workers apart from the lower strata, from blue-collar workers and employees operating office machines, were sharply drawn. The customary principles of this delimitation must be briefly considered.

Blue-collar workers were engaged mainly in production, white-collar workers chiefly in the distribution, planning, and preparation of work and in administration. Occasionally the social superiority of white- over blue-collar workers was derived from these functional differences,[2] but this derivation was generally untenable. Functional differences did exist between the two kinds of gainfully employed persons, but they were not always even recognizable in the activities of the individual employee or worker and therefore could not be the manifest basis of social rank. More importantly, economic function never determined social rank and prestige in society. If distributive functions had conferred superior rank upon those who performed them, the owner of a village dry goods shop, active in distribution, would have been superior to the artisan and even to the captain of industry, both of whom were active in productive functions. Social distinction could be conferred by the performance of distributive, planning, or preparatory functions only if they were superordinate to those which were exercised in the sphere of production. But inasmuch as economic necessity demands the co-operation of all these activities, and since none can be more easily dispensed with than any other, there simply is no autonomous rank order of functions. As a result, the different economic functions were not translated into a social hierarchy of the persons performing them.

The same reasoning applies to the notion that the distributive, preparatory, or administrative quality of their work helped to forge a special occupational consciousness among white-collar workers. Quite apart from the fact that such a consciousness would have been functional rather than occupational, the persons who performed white-collar tasks were not characterized by any special set of attitudes or distinctive social prestige. A broker, a woman selling flowers on the street, and a correspondent in a wholesale firm might share a general distributive function, but they differed widely with respect to rank, attitudes, and social consciousness. Social attitudes and ranks are evidently not grounded in economic functions, which are identified for other, analytic purposes, namely, the theoretical understanding of the larger economic process (distribution, production) or of the processes within the enterprise (administration, preparation of work). Even the negative definition—that the white-collar worker is in any case not "productive" like the blue-collar worker—is of little use, because many other social strata resemble white-collar workers in this respect without sharing their special rank or prestige. On the other hand, peasants and agricultural workers are productive in the same sense as workers without forming a social unit with them.

Of perhaps greater relevance, most salaried employees differ from workers in how their work activities are related to economic goods. The workers encounter goods as a concrete substance which they extract, refine, and transport. The salaried employee handles them in an abstract form as names or numbers, symbols or designs, measurements or patterns, or in their technical character or composition, or in respect to their economic cost, price, or profit. An important exception is the salesperson, but she or he distributes goods to people (customers) in a way the manual worker does not. This difference between salaried and manual workers did not confer a privileged rank on the white-collar worker. Indeed, no one could imagine that it did, except by erroneously equating it with the difference between physical and mental labor, and thus by disregarding the well-known difficulties in cleanly and serviceably distinguishing mental from physical work. This error was incorporated even into legal codes, which defined the salaried employee in terms of work activities that must not be "predominantly physical."[3]

The DHV always insisted that the work of commercial employees be regarded as "delegated" by the entrepreneur. As we shall see, this view came closest to a correct understanding of the superior rank occupied by the white-collar worker. The DHV claimed that commercial employees ranging "from the assistant bookkeeper to the responsible executive participate in the commercial direction of the enterprise."[4] And since entrepreneurs had delegated certain functions to these employees, they differed not only from manual workers but also from technical employees and foremen, whose work was thought "to resemble rather that of highly qualified workers."[5] Thus, the rivalry between commercial and technical employees within the enterprise was reflected in the opinions of their functionaries. A view from the employer's camp did not support the DHV:

In the large (industrial) establishments . . . the work of the engineers is valued more highly. In one establishment the technicians enjoy special esteem, in the other the commercial employees. In general, the higher esteem of the technician may be due to the fact that he is engaged in the primary activity . . . upon which the secondary, distributive function of the merchant is based. A contributing cause of his high esteem is the fact that the technician has acquired more knowledge through longer education. Finally, the fact cannot be disregarded that, in general, the scientific education of the merchant is concluded with his apprenticeship and his attendance at a commercial school, whereas the technician, owing to this activity, must continuously try to enlarge his scientific knowledge.[6]

The middle-class thesis that entrepreneurial functions were delegated to commercial employees was not generally tenable. J. Silbermann, in his own middle-class theory of salaried employees, objected that numerous artisans and merchants combined the work of entrepreneurs, white-collar workers, and manual laborers in their activities, and that even many blue-collar workers could regard their functions as part of the entrepreneurial function. The thesis of the DHV was therefore "neither complete nor correct."[7] This criticism was also supported by the fact that entrepreneurial functions had changed with the historical development of the economic system. Was the self-employed owner of a shop the prototype for the entrepreneur in trade and commerce? Did the large, lowest strata of salaried employees in industry perform functions which once were contained in the work of a master craftsman? If the DHV argument were valid, delegated entrepreneurial activity would be found not just in the work of the commercial employees, nor, as Silbermann added, in the activity of many blue-collar workers, but also in the activities of *all* laborers, including those of the lowest-ranking unskilled workers. But it was already stretching the point to describe the work of auxiliary bookkeepers, office-machine operators, card-file keepers, or money counters—in short, the work of the subordinate personnel in the office—as delegated entrepreneurial activity. The DHV explanation of social rank held neither for the workforce as a whole nor even for all salaried employees, but at best for only a small upper layer of white-collar workers.

The merit of the DHV thesis, however, is that it did not attempt to understand the white-collar workers' social privileges exclusively as a consequence of their economic tasks, but rather as a product of their ability to decide how these tasks were to be performed. This decision-making capability was actually controlled by those few persons who were dominant within the enterprise. The social rank, power, and prestige of white-collar workers were delegated to them by these persons. This derivation, which incidentally does not do justice to *all* principles of the social rank order, will be given more comprehensive and detailed treatment in chapter 7. Here it suffices to observe, in the interest of precision, that the issue is not one of delegated control but of the delegated prestige of the entrepreneur and employer—in short, of "the capitalist." In his entrepreneurial activities, the capitalist deals with such outsiders as competitors and consumers; as employer, he faces the employees within the enterprise. The capitalist (as a sociological type) thus derives his rank and prestige from both external and internal sources. Similarly, the rank and prestige of the salaried employee depends not only on his position within the hierarchy of the enterprise, but also on the importance of the enterprise in which he is employed. Thus, for instance, the bookkeeper in one of the many medium-sized enterprises is less highly esteemed—despite equal pay—than the bookkeeper who works for a "prominent" firm. The social self-esteem of the white-collar worker is also influenced by this difference.

The notion that commercial employees performed entrepreneurial functions was often closely associated with the view that they differed from manual workers in their possession of an occupation and a corresponding occupational consciousness. This view, however, could not provide the basis of a middle-class theory of white-collar workers.

A superficial effort was required to look for consciousness, pride, and honor of occupation among white-collar workers but not among laborers. In fact, for several reasons, consciousness and pride of occupation were more prominent among highly qualified workers than among clerks. For example, guild traditions had remained powerful in the occupations of various workers, because the corresponding craft participated strongly in the training of the young. Moreover, the organizations to which manual workers belonged originated as occupational associations, whereas the many associations of salaried employees had, from the beginning, an organizational basis that cut across several occupations. Finally, changing from one type of economic enterprise to another was a constant possibility for salaried employees because their function was not specifically confined to any single occupation.

Occasionally, the term "occupation" was used to convey a somewhat different meaning. In plans for an occupational restructuring of society, "occupation" was meant to convey an obligation to serve in a given type of enterprise without regard to its social rank. This and associated conceptions of "occupational estate" and the "occupational order of society" were of fascist origin and were no less opposed to the lower-class theory than was the middle-class theory of the white-collar workers. Yet, even working with the fascist conception of an occupational estate, the DHV attempted to justify the social privileges of white-collar workers by claiming that commercial clerks still constituted a special "occupational group."[8] Every occupation comprises people of different social positions and ranks, the DHV contended, including employers, white-collar, and blue-collar workers. If commercial and technical employees formed a special estate, it certainly was no occupational estate. Technical employees belonged to their "estate organization" not because of their occupation, but because of their social position within that occupation. Workers and entrepreneurs of the same occupation could not join. Werner Sombart was quite right in saying that an association of employers and an association of employees were not two occupational associations, but none at all.[9]

In modern society, with its highly developed division of labor, people engaged in the same occupational work seldom form a community. The content and form of social life are determined primarily by equality of occupation only in a few circumstances, which include continuity of work in a given occupation, apprenticeship leading to work as a skilled master, and the chance to tie the meaning of life to one's occupation. These circumstances did not exist for white-collar workers in the Weimar Republic, least of all for those of low and middle rank.

Every salaried employee was in danger of losing his job regardless of his performance, so that it was not possible to speak of the continuity of his work in a given occupation. Even the elite employees in executive positions were vulnerable to the business cycle. The decisive facts in their professional life, as in that of the mass of lower-placed employees from whom they tried to distinguish themselves,[10] were not merit and performance but the collapse or takeover of an enterprise, or a technical innovation. In 1929 Vela, the organization of executive employees, investigated the reasons for dismissal of 537 unemployed members. The causes in 174 cases were bankruptcy, liquidation, or closing; in 93 cases contraction of work or personnel; in 54 cases rationalization or reorganization; in 42 cases change of ownership, takeover; and in 102 cases such varied reasons as "too expensive," "too old," illness, or intrigue. Only 12 of 537 executive employees were dismissed because of dissatisfaction with their performance.[11]

A large majority of white-collar workers did only fragmented work, with the consequence that "he who performs only a small fragment of the work can hardly develop a lively interest in the whole work process."[12] The occupation had thus disintegrated. Nowhere was this fact more visible than in the professional training of the young. Only in exceptional cases were apprentices instructed in such a way as to become acquainted with all aspects of their occupation, and only in exceptional cases did they gain the ability to understand the work process as a whole.

In 1925 in Prussia, 9 percent of white-collar workers employed in industry and handicraft were apprentices, as were 14.5 percent of those employed in trade and commerce. In subsequent years significant changes occurred at the expense of adult workers. In 1930 one girl was employed as an apprentice for every adult female employed in trade; in small retail trade only every fourth salesperson was not a female apprentice![13] As the economic crisis deepened, the inclination grew stronger to regard the apprentice not as someone in training, but simply as someone who worked cheaply. In 1932 many smaller establishments had more "apprentices" than employees.

The DHV declared that the apprentice's familiarity with merchandise had decreased as the size of enterprise increased. A GdA survey in the fall of 1931 established that many apprentices were no longer trained in important areas of their occupation. The extent of their shortcomings was almost incredible, as table 6.1 indicates. It seems impossible in the light of these figures to regard apprenticeship as a time during which young people were trained to know their occupation and to recognize it as a lifelong task. The extraordinary efforts of the white-collar workers' associations to enhance the occupational training of their young members was always justified by pointing to the inadequacy of training on the job.

In sum, the middle-class theory could be derived neither from a special function in the economic process nor from occupational qualities. Even "delegated entrepreneurial activity" was to be found only among a small minority of white-collar workers. The stratum as a whole comprised many employees of very different ranks so that only those at the top were in social proximity to the entrepreneurs. Moreover, even the social prestige of this small minority at the highest rungs of the social ladder—like the prestige of the middle strata—had been founded only in part on the delegation of prestige in the enterprise.

Table 6.1: Training of GdA Apprentices in their Third Year of Apprenticeship

% Not Trained in	Retail Trade	Wholesale Trade	Industry
Simple Correspondence	77	47	29
Correspondence according to Dictation and Instruction	83	52	36
Simple Bookkeeping	84	66	63
Complex Bookkeeping	93	96	78
Treatment of Goods	58	42	31
Wage Calculation	95	96	52
Independently Serving Customers	13	—	—

SOURCE: GdA, ed., *Die kommende Angestellten-Generation*, p. 103.

Before turning to the bases of social prestige, we must still briefly consider the theory which attempted to explain the social prestige, political actions, and opinions of white-collar workers in terms of their class situation. This theory offers greater initial insight into the economic conditions of life of salaried employees than does the middle-class theory, but it encounters considerable difficulties in its explanation of the social prestige and political orientations of white-collar workers.

According to the lower-class theory, salaried employees are proletarians. Like blue-collar workers, whose social situation they share, they are forced to sell their labor-power on the labor market, their economic life is precariously dependent on the business cycle, their interests conflict with those of the employers, and any improvement of their wages, working conditions, and economic life prospects depends exclusively on vigorous collective action. Based on elements of Marxist class theory, this conception identifies white-collar workers not as an estate but as part of the working class. Since the last third of the nineteenth century, the economic situation of many white-collar workers had indeed approached the working conditions of manual labor. Achieving independence had become more rare, economic insecurity had increased, the functions to be performed at work had been increasingly specialized and soon were mechanized as well. The distance between the average employee and the entrepreneur was growing even as the employee's working conditions and life prospects came increasingly to resemble those of blue-collar workers.

After the revolution of 1918 the lower-class theory seemed to find strong support in the adoption of trade union practices by white-collar associations. Did this trade unionization signify the final liquidation of occupational politics and the acknowledgement of the class situation, that is, of the basic socioeconomic conflicts between salaried employees and the entrepreneurs? The middle-class conception of the white-collar worker as a private civil servant appeared to fade. A degree of organizational similarity even developed in all blue- and white-collar workers' unions, regardless of their political orientation. Although all of these trends might be seen as attesting to the growing insight of salaried employees into their own proletarianization, it must yet be emphasized that these new proletarians, despite their unionization, did not renounce their privileges in social prestige vis-à-vis the old manual-labor proletariat. Disregarding a relatively small, radical minority, unionization did not signify a turn by salaried employees to anti-capitalistic efforts and socialist aims.

First, in this connection, trade union efforts to increase wages and improve working conditions do not result in the socialization of the means of production and are not necessarily linked with the socialist demand to bring it about. On the contrary, before World War I the socialist idea had already been crowded out among the workers by the practical daily work of the trade unions. The pledge to socialism became a kind of rhetorical tribute functionaries paid to the reformist movement in order to remind Social Democratic workers of the political and moral dignity withheld from them by the state. Such reminders did not imply an obligation to promote social revolution, but increased solidarity in the struggle for social progress and Social Democratic seats in the Reichstag. Thus, even the old proletariat did not fight foremost for the realization of socialism but for raising the standard of living. It is possible to view this phenomenon as an aspect of the embourgeoisement of the old proletariat and then to ask why white-collar workers, in pursuing their interests, should have been less middle-class-oriented than blue-collar workers.

But the decisive problem for the lower-class theory was the undeniable fact that a large majority of the so-called new proletariat, despite its unionization, became politically active neither along with nor next to the old proletariat, but in fact emphasized their differences over their similarities. Despite their trade union activities, the majority of the white-collar workers continued to insist on their social superiority over blue-collar workers. They also detested and maligned the general political values which the majority of blue-collar workers in the Weimar Republic held dear, including democracy, parliamentarianism, reconciliation, and the desire to reach an understanding with the victorious powers following World War I. Like their views on social policy, the unionization of the middle-class associations did not at all mean they had abandoned their middle-class conceits. Instead, of the three types of unions that white-collar workers could have joined during the Weimar years only the "middle-class" organizations *gained* in size and importance. Toward the end of the Weimar Republic they emphasized the middle-class self-understanding of white-collar workers even more sharply than they had at its beginning. For example, in 1931 a programmatic publication of the GdA, which was politically more moderate than the DHV, stated that "the commercial clerk, the technician, the foreman, and the office employee in the past were miles removed from political thought and feeling. . . . War, revolution, and the postwar period have been unable to change anything in this innate attitude of the white-collar workers. On the contrary, today's salaried employee feels himself more strongly than ever to be a member of the 'new middle class.' "[14]

The lower-class theory explained the orientation of the white-collar workers' middle-class associations as the result of their "false consciousness." But how did it explain false consciousness? The evidence used by its adherents to demonstrate that nothing must exist in practice that did not exist in theory was deplorably scanty. False consciousness was usually presented as a symptom of a general retrogression. Different tempos in the development of the relation of production and of the conceptions which human beings form of them created the possibility of "inadequate," historically obsolete thinking. Also, the tradition of a non-proletarian, middle-class past remained alive among the salaried employees, and thus prevented their recognition of the current social situation. It was only a matter of time, however, before sociological enlightenment would illumine this situation darkened by wishes, memories, habits, and resentments.

In the most concise ideological critique, which was published prior to 1933, the history of white-collar workers was divided into three phases.[15] After attributing an ideal-typical ideology to each phase, each type of white-collar workers' association was located in its appropriate phase according to the ideology which best fit it. As a result of this procedure, all non-socialist associations could be viewed as living under the spell of the past. Only the free trade union Afa-Bund had reached the historical and ideological crest of the present. It alone offered the "true," correct consciousness, because only its conception of white-collar workers as "new proletarians" corresponded to the most recent economic situation. The result was the following scheme:

Social Position	Corresponding Ideology	Today's Organization
Phase 1: Assistant to employer	*Not yet* employer	Vela
Phase 2: New middle class	*Not* worker but *new* class between "the" classes	DHV, GdA
Phase 3: Salaried employee	*Not* worker, but part of the proletariat	Afa-Bund

This ideological critique, which summarizes what the lower-class theory has to offer with respect to the phenomenon of rank and esteem, does not excel in precision. Whether the notion that past traditions haunt the present can be reconciled with the categories of the class theory is at least questionable and in any case should be suggested only if it can be demonstrated that specific institutions and particular current social conditions sustain a consciousness that was based upon and corresponded to earlier conditions of production.[16] Without such a demonstration, the relationship between base and superstructure, or reality and consciousness, is destroyed.

Middle-class conceptions also derived the social consciousness of white-collar workers from their tradition,[17] which they valued positively, as opposed to the lower-class theory's negative valuation. Tradition was regarded not as a source of error but as an especially valuable testimony to social rank and esteem. The precision of this derivation again left much to be desired, but because the middle-class conceptions were not based on the methodological presupposition that consciousness corresponded to reality, their shortcomings may be more easily forgiven.

The proponents of the lower-class theory moved away from tradition with the speed of those who felt themselves to be in possession of the rational truth. Once they were engaged in a conflict with "ideologues" who derived the rank of the white-collar workers from traditions, they could no longer defend the rank of salaried employees against attacks that originated in the camp of manual workers. They did declare that the salaried employee, though a proletarian, was no blue-collar worker, but they never focused on the difference. When C. Nörpel,[18] a spokesman for manual labor, attacked the privileges of white-collar workers in his fight for collective labor legislation, their representatives could only parry with arguments closely akin to middle-class notions. Thus, when Nörpel declared that no fundamental difference existed between the labor of workers and that of salaried employees, and that the latter were only legally privileged, the representatives of the proletarian white-collar workers replied that the salaried employees performed "after all . . . special functions. . . . If a struggle against the existing law pertaining to salaried employees . . . had anything to do with socialism, then socialism would be tantamount to the equalization of all workers on the lowest level. Socialism is the precise opposite. . . . It is correct, isn't it, that socialism can be created only if the highly qualified strata of labor, i.e., the salaried employees, can also be counted on to support it?"[19] Regardless of whether this rejoinder was true or false, it was in any case not supported by the conception of salaried employees as proletarians. Instead, it relied on a modified class theory which presented the proletariat as hierarchically stratified.

The principles of this modification, however, were not closely considered. Such an effort would have involved an analysis of social rank, its significance, and its content, and this in turn would have forced a revision of the Marxist theory of true and false consciousness. In other words, in their reply to Nörpel's argument, the proletarian white-collar workers appeared suddenly as highly qualified workers. This made sense with regard to the relatively conservative foremen, but not to the average socialist member of the ZdA and the Butab, that is, the proletarian commercial and technical employees.

VII The Foundations of Social Rank and Respect

In order to understand more precisely the claims to rank and social respect advanced by the white-collar workers, it must be emphasized at the outset that Weimar Germany was a capitalist society overlaid with peculiarly German features. In this society a plurality of social valuations based on noble birth, wealth, state office (both civilian and military), education, religious denomination, and "race" competed with one another. Corresponding to these social valuations were different conceptions of domination, different ideals of the order of social ranks, different social distinctions and stigmas, and different styles of life.

These numerous valuations—the ethical foundations of the social order of ranks—were alien to one another. For example, the social respect which the civil servant claimed and enjoyed by virtue of his participation in the power of the state contradicted the valuations reflected in the social rank of the industrialist, inasmuch as the latter's prestige was based on wealth and economic success. The entrepreneur enjoyed respect because he owned capital. The respect of the civil servant was tied not to his wealth but to his service, although the higher civil servant received a relatively high salary. A lower civil servant was generally more highly regarded than a manual worker drawing equal pay, and among civil servants of equal pay the political civil servant (the so-called *Hoheitsbeamte*) was esteemed more highly than the economic civil servant (the so-called *Betriebs-beamte*) who worked for the state-owned railroad or a comparable enterprise.

Similar differences in rank existed within hierarchies formed on the basis of other valuations. Just as in the ancien régime the French *noblesse d'épée* (nobility of birth) were more highly regarded than the *noblesse de robe* (nobility of office), so in Germany old nobility and old wealth were more distinguished than the newer aristocracy and nouveaux riches. In the army social distinction was determined not only by military rank but also by the reputation of a particular regiment, which was manifested in, among other things, the percentage of noblemen among its officers. At the time of Wilhelm II, it was ironically said in aristocratic circles that "we have seven regiments of curassiers; the eighth is located in Cologne," where the sons of bourgeois magnates and industrialists did their service.[1] As regards social prestige acquired through education, the differing values placed on humanistic or natural science studies were sometimes reflected in distinctions of rank; beyond this, finer distinctions related to faculty and specialization. Generally, the social ranks of the officer and the educated person are not the same in all societies. Both the military officer and the university professor enjoyed higher respect in the German empire and in the Weimar Republic than, say, in the United States. The same held true of the civil servant and the salaried employee.

The social limits of the different valuations are never definitely drawn. Members of aspiring strata assert that the valuations on which their claims for rank and honor are based are morally superior to those of the ruling strata. The aspirants try either to devaluate and destroy the alien honor or to participate in it by virtue of intermarriage or individual ascent. The menaced strata in their turn may attempt either to limit the social field of their own valuation more strictly or to yield and broaden it. Thus, toward the end of the eighteenth century the German nobility began "to study with middle-class seriousness." They put— in the words of the non-noble A. L. Schlözer[2]—"a one in front of their birth-zero, maintaining thereby anew their old superiority over the middle class," that is, a nobleman's worth equaled zero, but through studying he could raise it to ten. He did so by following the principle of valuation that championed education over noble birth. Thereafter, especially in nineteenth-century Germany, the principles of valuation favoring wealth and education became closely allied. Similarly, before World War I more and more middle-class elements entered the officer corps, at first in those parts of the army where horseback riding was not of paramount importance and newer technical requirements had to be met (engineers, foot artillery).

A comparative historical investigation of social rank and honor would show that a social order comprising the whole nation exists only if either (1) a valuation has monopolistic status, that is, it is generally recognized and its representatives are at the same time its rulers, or if (2) a recognized rank order of valuations exists, so that a particular kind of rank and honor predominates, as it did under the feudal aristocracy in old Prussia. Only if one of these conditions exists will the people be sufficiently integrated to form a stable social order.[3]

For its part, the industrial labor force was ostracized for many years in Germany prior to World War I and was feared by the ruling classes because of its organizational success. The workers were not fully citizens, just as, in general, the idea and nature of responsible citizenship were both unpopular and unknown among the middle and upper classes in prewar Germany because of the authoritarian character of the state. Friedrich Engels still held the opinion that universal military service would weaken and eventually cause the class-based state to collapse because it incorporated young proletarians into the army, but his expectation was not fulfilled. Rather, school and military service contributed to the dissemination of notions that exalted disciplinary order. This fact benefited the trade unions and big economic enterprises, was romanticized in the life of voluntary associations, and later tempted adventurous intellectuals to assert a close connection between Prussianism and socialism. Prior to World War I some segments of the population regarded socialist workers as "scoundrels without a fatherland"—an evil phrase that became popular. The error of this opinion was revealed in 1914 as the international slogans of the German labor movement faded and Social Democratic functionaries and workers fought and died for the nation, which in peacetime had denied them political membership.

Despite the dictated peace of Brest-Litovsk, which ended the war with Russia, German military leaders lost the war. This notwithstanding, they advised the emperor to abdicate his political power, which they had already de facto wrested from him. The collapse was born of the military inferiority of the Reich, of political hubris, and of the social shortsightedness of the ruling classes. But this did not prevent those guilty of the defeat from circulating the legend of "the stab in the back," a myth designed to hold the republican caretakers of a bankrupt Germany responsible for its defeat and misery.

In the aftermath of the war the political and trade union representatives of the workers gained power and prestige, which frightened the middle class. Those strata which traditionally had been superior to the workers appeared to suffer losses of economic security, political influence, and social respect even as the workers—at least politically and socially—were ascending the social ladder. The result was doubly unbearable for descending groups. To their absolute deterioration was added the relative decline of their positions.[4]

Salaried employees were also drawn into the whirlpool of this social development. While a minority of organized white-collar workers became more class-conscious, the majority not only defended both their special legal privileges vis-à-vis blue-collar workers and the representation of their interests against the entrepreneurs, but also placed an especially high value on their rank and prestige in order to demonstrate continued social superiority over manual workers.

The German middle strata were neither rich nor aristocratic, their education left something to be desired, and, except for police, postal employees, streetcar conductors, firemen, and the like, they did not wear uniforms. They could share the social standards and rank of nobility, wealth, education, and civil or military state service only in one of four ways that were to some degree open to all underclasses:

1. through occasional individual ascent to the ranks of the highly regarded and socially privileged;
2. passively, through preference extended by members of the upper classes who after the model of a patron-client relationship grant certain social advantages or privileges over still lower strata;
3. actively, through admiration and emulation of higher styles of consumption if only in trivial substitutes and inexpensive ways—as was true, for example, of the eighteenth-century middle-class pattern of buying inexpensive silhouettes instead of more costly portraits painted for aristocrats in oil on canvas; and
4. through ostentatious disrespect—partly condescending and partly hostile—for those strata which, according to the traditional conception of upper-class standards and styles, did not deserve respect.

Of these four avenues of protecting and increasing social rank and prestige, the first two became increasingly blocked as the capitalist system was entrenched. Ascent to economic independence became even more rare. The claim of a private civil servant *(Privatbeamter)* to be close in social standing to the civil servants turned out to be illusory as the life of the white-collar worker became less secure. Neither the state nor entrepreneurial circles sought to assuage the class struggle by maintaining or enlarging middle-class privileges pertaining to social insurance and labor law. Instead, white-collar workers had to defend their privileges politically and with the help of their unions against the interests of the entrepreneurs. The economic and social interests of the salaried employees sometimes coincided with those of manual workers, but the white-collar workers highly valued a style of life which distinguished them from blue-collar workers, even if such a distinction was not supported by an inequality of income. Similarly, the majority of salaried employees did not welcome the workers' increase in power after the revolution, even though they also benefited from the government's recognition of trade unions. In general, most salaried employees continued to cherish a belief in their social, political, and moral superiority over the manual workers.

Not only did many white-collar workers retain their anti-proletarian attitudes and values despite their own proletarianization, they also maintained some positive commitment to middle-class traditions. Otherwise, those psychologists would have been right who, like Hendrik de Man, discovered in the attitudes of the middle-class employees nothing but the resentment of an "office slave" who, in the rationalized enterprise, mourned the passing of the velvety sofa and the family journal of his parents. Resentment might have played a role occasionally but it was not fed merely by nostalgic memories. The legal privileges of white-collar workers were partly responsible for distinguishing their political attitudes from those of manual laborers, as were some features of their working conditions that precluded their reception of socialist ideas. At least one such feature, that of "hidden class membership," will be discussed in some detail in chapter 8. Hidden class membership prevailed not among those employees who worked in a smaller enterprise and were therefore traditionally middle-class-oriented, if only by contact with the old middle class, but rather among their colleagues who worked in the larger enterprises. According to the lower-class theory, the salaried employees' working conditions should have made it more difficult for them to preserve their anti-proletarian inclinations. However, their hidden class membership provides an institutional explanation for their "middle-class" attitudes.

An attempt will also be made to determine more precisely the foundations of the white-collar workers' social rank and respect. Some portions of the salaried-employee stratum claimed and were granted their social rank and respect on grounds already mentioned and here repeated in summary form:

1. Due to delegated participation in the respect of those who dominated the enterprise,
   a. as assistants of the small entrepreneur, and
   b. as functionaries of the capitalist.
2. Due to education,
   a. by appreciating and acquiring products of culture, which the worker allegedly neglected, or
   b. by participation in knowledge offered by natural science and in technology.
3. Due to stressing nationalistic convictions,
   a. by devotion to pre-republican values of the state and the military, as expressed above all in service and discipline, or
   b. by devotion to anti-republican values as "warriors in civilian clothes."

These foundations of social rank and respect are not independent of one another in reality. The social rank of the white-collar workers can be traced to all three (and in addition to legal privileges). However, for sociological purposes they require analytic separation. Reality also favors such a separation, inasmuch as different white-collar groups based their claims to rank and esteem on different principles of respectability. Thus, principle 1.a pertained exclusively to (small-town) employees working in small enterprises, while principle 1.b was of greatest importance to employees in middle-sized enterprises. All employees may have gained in respect due to a liberal education (2.a), but since the spread of modern, specialized scientific education is an urban phenomenon, principle 2.b primarily helped white-collar workers in large cities. The claim to respect based on nationalist convictions and attitudes (3.a) was apparently widespread among all middle-class groups, whereas (3.b) pertained mostly to ideologues, functionaries, and members of the DHV.[5]

VIII The Hierarchy within the Enterprise and Masked Class Membership

The hierarchy within the enterprise, in which white-collar workers in middle- and large-sized enterprises are placed, is not adequately reflected in titled positions like president, vice-president, treasurer, section chief, and so forth.[1] It reaches much further down into the enterprise than the system of titles would suggest. In the private firm, as distinct from governmental bureaucracy, only the upper ranks are distinguished by titles. Neither is organizational refinement accurately reflected in salary differences. These merely approximate the hierarchy but do not coincide with it. Not all typists, draftsmen, or auxiliary bookkeepers receiving equal pay are also of equal rank. By contrast, the power to give orders, which spreads downward from top management in ever smaller allotments, is a more precise index of hierarchical position. The hierarchy of persons and the distribution of power to give orders may be represented by pyramids that resemble one another, except that the second stands on its head: the greatest concentration of power is at the top of the hierarchy. More power to give orders is therefore an indication of greater proximity to top management. Not only is the degree of delegated power to give orders an index of hierarchical position, it is also the most important principle of hierarchical stratification; it flows from the domination of the enterprise. Frequently but not necessarily connected with the power to give orders is responsibility.[2]

Another possibility for attaining higher rank, one associated neither with the power to give orders nor with responsibility, is the organizationally conditioned relationship to persons with power to give orders. For example, the private secretary, because of her "confidential position," is superior not only to the typists, but frequently also to higher employees. It is also possible for a "private" relationship with persons wielding the power to give orders to enhance one's rank within the hierarchy. To be sure, this private relationship—with a friend, comrade in the same regiment, member of the same lodge or student corps, or partner in a love affair—must be known in the enterprise in order to result in further distinction.

The capacity to enhance rank must also be attributed to education. For example, among employees of equal rank the "doctor" (Ph.D.) is distinguished, as is the working student who eats at the boss's table in the office dining room. In Anglo-Saxon countries enhancement of rank owing to education is somewhat less effective, if only because non-medical academic degrees do not entitle the holder to be addressed as "Doctor." *(Herr Doktor)*.

Even efficiency can be a distinguishing factor among employees of equal rank. The best draftsman is a bit ahead of other draftsmen receiving the same pay; the fastest typist rises in prestige above equally paid typists. Possibly, this advantage may be traced to the assumption that the most efficient employees possess better chances of promotion and of resisting economic adversity.

Finally, experience in the enterprise or length of service can enhance hierarchical rank. The apprentice in his third year is superior to the first-year apprentice, and if higher age carries no stigma—which it often does in times of crisis—the eldest in any given rank enjoys certain advantages.

Examined closely, all these foundations of distinction can be reduced to participation in the power or prestige of those who dominate the enterprise.[3] The authority to give orders, responsibility, a special relationship with a superior (whether it originates within the enterprise or is of a private character), and length of service—all these constitute the means by which an individual can participate in the power and prestige of management. The same holds indirectly true of education, inasmuch as its acquisition depends, as a rule, on the prerequisite of an advantaged social origin, that is, on social proximity to the rulers of the enterprise. Finally, efficiency can also entitle one to ascent within the hierarchy, either actually or according to widely held expectations.

The captains of enterprise determine the specific content of respectability, inasmuch as their publicly recognized leadership, which is proclaimed by ideologues, also serves to legitimate the respect of subordinate persons. In principle, the same observations also hold true of societies with nationalized economies, in which leadership over specific enterprise is executed by persons who owe their office to the decision of political power holders. In this case, respect, and the efforts of subordinates to gain it, are permeated by military, precapitalist, or anticapitalist valuations, depending on how claims to legitimacy by the ruling class are publicly justified. Although rights of co-determination given to the lower ranks can reduce abuses of the authority to give orders, they cannot abolish either the indispensable hierarchical relations within the enterprise or the differences in social respect to which those relations give rise.

If it were possible to flatten out the hierarchy completely, and thus to abolish the institution to which respect and power are owed, the social respect of the white-collar workers would disappear. More precisely, since the social respect of salaried employees may also rest on other foundations, that social respect which is "produced" within the enterprise would disappear. Nowhere, of course, is the hierarchy completely flattened out, not even in giant enterprises,[4] but its effects have been modified by the depersonalization of control. Furthermore, because of the increasing size of the enterprise and the growing refinement of its hierarchy, those who occupy the lowest levels have increased in greater numbers than those at the top. As a result, an egalitarian situation has been created at the lowest levels of the hierarchy. The mass character of white-collar workers at the lowest levels enfeebles the hierarchical principle. Quite rightly, the dependence of "the" white-collar workers has always been demonstrated with reference to these employees holding the lowest hierarchical positions. Because they no longer participate in the power and respect that accrues to higher positions in the hierarchy, lower-level white-collar workers recognize more readily the proletarian features of their situation than do other salaried workers, among whom those features are less pronounced. The visible equality of their powerlessness and the absence of prestige privileges condemn them to be the inevitable victims of the hierarchy.

The hierarchy within larger enterprises must now be considered in another perspective. Not only does it serve as a foundation of white-collar prestige by allowing employees to participate in the power and respect of management, it also aids in masking their class affiliation.

In the large enterprise the capitalist is but a shadowy figure. As a person, he is invisible. The employee never meets him, but instead meets many people to whom functions of the capitalist have been delegated. Most, if not all, of these functionaries are employees. In the small and, to some degree, the medium-sized enterprise, employee and employer meet as persons. As the enterprise grows in size, however, the class affiliation of the superior is increasingly hidden.

The social appearance of any individual employee is determined by the observer's vantage within the hierarchy. Thus, depending on the observer's own position, an employee may appear as a superior with authority to dispose, manage, give orders or control, or as a subordinate who follows orders, or more simply, as a giver or taker of work. Simple reference to the hierarchical stratification of the functionaries inadequately comprehends this phenomenon, for the decisive fact is that a single person possesses both proletarian and capitalist qualities. The correspondent who is subordinate to and receives directives from the chief of his section also transmits them to the secretary who takes his dictation. For her he is the boss (and she frequently calls him that). She, in turn, may function as a superior to the messenger, as, for example, when she orders him to have the typed letters signed or to discreetly fetch her a glass of water from the fountain. The employee who calculates the cost of filling an order reports to the chief of the bureau of calculations. In large enterprises, especially in cases of mass production, it is possible to separate out the mere arithmetic aspects of the work and have them done (with the help of machines) by less qualified persons. In relation to them the calculator functions as superior, especially when mistakes are discovered. He does not supervise the manager and the foremen, but they are nevertheless "forced to respect him, because he can—and even must—look into their cards."[5]

The last illustration indicates that the phenomenon of hidden class membership is ubiquitous. It pertains not only to employees who have authority, however limited, to give orders to subordinate employees, but also to persons who work in other bureaus on the same level of the hierarchy and who perform one-sided or mutual-control functions within the organization. Thus, a study suggests: "The bureau of calculations always fights the engineer in charge of time studies, because he gives the impression that the bureau's employees are weak in arithmetic."[6] Indeed, even subordinate employees can perform functions of employers in relation to "superior" employees. The girl who wraps the merchandise in the department store "controls" the work of the salesgirl; typists paid according to piecework or receiving premiums "pressure" their superiors, the correspondents, toward rational distribution and circumspect preparation of work, thereby increasing the "higher" performance that is not paid by piecework. These subordinate personnel perform as if on behalf of the invisible capitalist.

It is not at the hand of the capitalist, therefore, that many employees directly experience exploitation. Rather, it is at the hand of one another. The messenger boy is exploited by the typist who rushes him; the typist is exploited by the correspondent, who determines, within limits, her immediate workload; the correspondent is exploited by his section chief, to whom he reports; the manual worker is exploited by the foreman; workers and foremen, among others, are exploited by employees in the bureau of calculation and in the office controlling production deadlines; these are exploited by their immediate supervisors, and so on. In short, the experience of the employee points not to capitalists and class enemies, but to other employees who act like capitalists even though they do not own the means of production. Taken at its extreme, this situation seems to prove B. Traven's anarchistic contention that the worker's greatest enemy is the worker. This, however, would be going too far, for workers are enemies only where they compete with other workers.

The phenomenon of hidden class membership produces the fetish of the superior and engenders moral confusion. The fetish of the superior is fundamentally important not only in the large enterprise but in modern society at large: the less comprehensible the total fabric of social life, the more difficult it becomes to locate the individual who is responsible for mishaps. Accountability in fact becomes anonymous because everyone can rightly claim to have performed only his or her required function. Every superior follows the instructions of his superior. Even the president of a large corporation depends upon a board of trustees or upon bankers who grant him loans, and even they are not "free." The lack of freedom that almost everyone seems to bewail is very real and, apparently, very difficult to endure. Life pulsates between people, not between people and institutions. For this reason, human actions and reactions are characterized by an irremediable immediacy. They may be theoretically "false" to some intellectuals, but they are quite real to the people involved. Thus, workers who had beaten up a white-collar employee declared that "the gentleman is a matter of indifference to us, we only wanted to hit the directorate."[7] Similarly, the poor person typically directs his envy not at the millionaire, who is mythical to him, but at the neighbor who is only a little less poor but whose relative affluence he can see. The rage of a laid-off employee can often find no concrete object other than the hapless employee who works overtime at the unemployment office, is not highly paid, and certainly does not represent the capitalists. Animosity against the means test is directly expressed against the person who administers the test, even though he is not responsible for this requirement. Finally, hatred against the state has always been directed foremost against policemen, who represent the power of the state to its subjects.

According to Marx, the struggle of workers against individual capitalists (as, for example, in the uprising of the Silesian weavers) is the product of an early, inchoate stage of capitalism, in which labor lacks both mass character and insight into the "real" structure of the system. Marx was theoretically correct in arguing that the dependence of wage earners upon the capitalist cannot be suspended by the destruction of machinery and by action against individual entrepreneurs. But even though the real structural relationship between capitalist and wage earner is abstract and nebulous, the workers' need to find some specific individuals responsible for their situation remains strong enough to continually disturb the circles of abstraction.[8]

The phenomenon of hidden class membership demonstrates the inadequacy of any sociological approach that simply regards salaried employees as proletarians, for such a categorization fails to comprehend their situation in the large enterprise.

Consider the correspondent in the large enterprise. His colleague in a small enterprise works without assistants and under the direct supervision of the entrepreneur. He is more difficult to replace than the correspondent who is only one among many in the large establishment, for his experience in the enterprise carries more weight. Disregarding the different resiliencies of small and large enterprises during an economic crisis, the more independent correspondent in the small establishment is clearly less proletarianized than his colleague in the large firm, no matter how their wages compare. Although the correspondent in the large enterprise is objectively more dependent than his small firm counterpart—because of the division of labor—he possesses the authority of a superior in relation to the typist and other assistants, whereas his colleague does not. Moreover, he wields this authority despite his greater dependence and despite the narrower range of his work. Considering his greater authority, then, the correspondent in the larger enterprise is less a member of the proletariat than his colleague in the small firm who completely lacks the employer's authority. This example merely points to the social consequence of the division of labor, which has made possible the increase of white-collar workers in relation to the total workforce.

The phenomenon of hidden class membership has a neutralizing effect upon social conflicts. The industrial employee not only encounters the phenomenon, he personifies it. He is continuously entangled in a living contradiction: as employee he must pursue his employer's interests or else risk failure as an employee. This inevitable dilemma is created in the middle-sized enterprise as capitalist power is delegated to the salaried employee. In the big enterprise the same tendency prevails, but the division of labor is more elaborate and the delegation of managerial functions is restricted to ever more modest quantities of power and respect. Salaried employees in these large enterprises are left with nothing to value apart from internal order. Inasmuch as they contribute to the orderly functioning of the establishment, they are perhaps inclined as good Germans to idealize the discipline to which they are subjected.

To some degree, blue- and white-collar workers are equally exposed to the hidden class membership of the superior. Like the salaried employees, manual workers never meet the capitalist, and they encounter in the superior a "false" social quality. That is, they fail to see the foreman, the section boss and his assistant, the time checker, as the employees they are. They do see themselves "correctly," however. In the shop the manual workers are mostly in touch with other workers, with people whose social quality is unambiguous and cannot be distorted because they have little authority to give orders to others. If the manual laborer does encounter the phenomenon of hidden class membership, it is usually in salaried employees rather than in other manual workers. Moreover, the authority exercised by these employees is frequently associated with some legal privileges. This connection is significant in furthering solidarity among manual laborers and in impeding their solidarity with white-collar workers.

Salaried employees in large enterprises encounter false class membership far more often than do manual workers, for they more frequently meet people whose social character changes with the level of the hierarchy from which it is observed. They are also more likely to encounter colleagues whose social position is subject to false assessment, because an uncommon capacity for objectivity is required to look beyond their social position and recognize the character of their labor, their replaceability, and the insecurity of their lives.

Only certain strata within the enterprise are so situated that they can easily look through the veils of hidden class membership. This is especially true of the very lowest strata, who lack even the least significant capitalistic functions. Thus, alert, observant messenger boys, who are in contact with many salaried employees of different rank, are often able to offer insights that are astonishingly free of distortion and that can contribute to a concrete sociology of the enterprise.

Only the lowest ranks of white-collar workers are, like manual workers, exposed to the phenomenon of hidden class membership without embodying it themselves. For various reasons, however, even they do not fully avail themselves of the chance to be free of illusions. At least three of these reasons deserve mention.

A large number of these unqualified employees consists of women who leave employment earlier than men and who therefore think more optimistically of the future if they think of it at all. Their attitudes and opinions are influenced not only by work experiences but also by their anticipated gender experiences (marriage, child-rearing). It is perhaps possible to trace the sober, trade unionist orientation of technical personnel, as well as their coolness toward the middle-class ideal of compromise, to the fact that even the lowest positions are held by men rather than women. Of course, the more radical orientation of the technical employees must be attributed to other causes as well.

As has already been pointed out in chapter 1, in retail trade the salesperson's illusion of freedom—that is, his or her representation of the enterprise in contacts with customers—reduces the psychological impact of economic insecurity.

In the giant enterprises of industry, however, the discipline governing personnel is even more exacting than it is in commerce. It reaches down to the last anonymous employee who services the office machines, and it is unmitigated by personal contact with "undisciplined" people who do not belong to the office—that is, with customers. The lowly worker can choose either to criticize the discipline to which he is subjected or else to endow it with an ideology. He usually does the latter, for otherwise, instead of participating as a co-worker in the order which has seized him, he falls victim to loneliness.

IX The Function of Education

Those who viewed the salaried employees as part of a new middle class explained their special character with reference to their social proximity to the entrepreneurs, to the quality of their service, or to the nature of their occupation. But the Great Depression weakened the validity of these explanations by increasing the insecurities and jeopardizing the privileges of white-collar workers. As many employees saw their situation approach that of the workers, they opposed all the more vigorously the dreaded notion that they might indeed belong to the proletariat, as the lower-class theory insisted. Especially as the most important middle-class associations of salaried employees began to resemble workers' organizations by pursuing their interests like trade unions, it became doubly important to rid the concept of "the proletariat" of its ominous Marxist connotations. This could be done either by embracing a voluntaristic definition of the proletariat or by stressing the "education" of white-collar workers in order to distinguish them from the proletariat.

According to the voluntaristic definition of the proletariat, peaceful workers had been victimized by radical intellectuals, who had tricked them into believing that they belonged to the "proletariat." In fact, however, the "proletariat" was an "obsolete" concept. Such conceits were, of course, not shared by all white-collar workers or by all organizations representing them. They were confined to those salaried employees and their functionaries who struggled against the political aims of the Afa-Bund, the SPD, and the KPD, and to those anti-democratic intellectuals who furnished the slogans for that struggle. For instance, the confused writer Ernst Jünger, a favorite among Germans, wrote: "The proletariat . . . is a mass of the old style, just as its individual physiognomy is that of the bourgeois without a stiff collar. It presents a very flexible economic-humanistic concept." Jünger considered "sentiments of the heart and systems of the mind" to be "refutable, whereas a thing is irrefutable, —and the machine gun is such a thing."[1] Another treatment of the issue was both less skillful and more nebulous:

What are today the old conflicts between capital and labor, bourgeoisie and proletariat? No longer the thread [!], along which thinking is forced mono-moniacally to proceed. . . . Instead they are either solved, obsolete problems, that have passed away with the century that created them. Or else they are the interior aspects of a whole [!], which, it is true, has a vital interest in reconstructing its social order, but is fully affirmed as a unit, because it represents the historical principle, which is the future of all.

Professor Hans Freyer bears responsibility for this miserable style.[2] A. E. Günther,[3] who later boasted that he had publicly burned the Weimar constitution in 1930,[4] was more malicious: "Marx constituted the proletariat as a secularized ghetto and implanted in it the subversive character which operates in the class struggle." August Winnig offered a similar point: "Not the journeyman Wilhelm Weitling, but the revolutionary, Jewish, litterateur Karl Marx became the baptist of the German labor movement. This is the great catastrophe in whose shadow not only our labor movement but our entire German life has existed up to the present."[5] All these writers, so well versed in demagoguery, were close to the DHV, and many of their books were published by the Hanseatische Verlagsanstalt, the publishing house of the DHV.

With regard to education as the distinguishing mark between white- and blue-collar workers, the most blatant formulation best reveals the real intent behind the words: "If we fail to succeed in becoming personalities," a declaration of the DHV announced, "all our work leads only to the vision of the garbage collector."[6] This vision was the target of all the efforts by members of the labor force to attain "less work—more wages." Although the DHV thought "the liberal cult of the personality conceded the capacity to become a personality to anyone short of being feeble-minded,"[7] it celebrated education—the liberal principle of social prestige—as a means of elevating the salaried employees above the worker. Education was to render proletarianization irrelevant. By arguing that an educated proletariat did not rank as proletarian, it became easier to admit one's own economic insecurity without consequence for rank and prestige: "Even for the most capable clerk the economic possibilities are limited. . . . Only he can maintain the value of his personality who has developed in himself a realm of values independent of the ups and downs of economic success."[8]

At the Dresden meeting of the DHV in 1928, "The Calling of the Clerk: National Education"[9] was discussed in detail. The speaker pointed out that, because the modern economy was depersonalized, human beings performed only a depersonalized function within the firm, were "replaceable at any time," and were no longer fulfilled as persons. "In the development of our personality," he went on to ask, "is it possible for us to evade this process of dehumanization or are we subjected to it also in this sphere?" "We do not want that!" he answered. "He is a proletarian who wants to be one." This had been the famous formula of Möller van den Bruck, whose treatise *The Third Reich*, in the opinion of the DHV, "ought to be made the drill book of German politics."[10] Education, the speaker declared, was to be the means of relieving "the tensions between de-humanizing working conditions and the striving for personality" as well as of fortifying the anti-proletarian will.

This thesis was buttressed by historical references. The middle strata had also been the bearers of national culture in the nineteenth century. Over time, however, not only did the character of these middle strata undergo change,[11] so also did the content of their education. Their primary cultural values had been "the cosmopolitan humanism" of the German classics and "the sciences," even though "a passionate partisanship for political values" was already noticeable in Treitschke's historical writings. By the time "technology and progressing capitalism descended upon the scene," the old education had "crumbled." Today, the eco-nomically leading strata are no longer capable of setting an example for the commercial clerk to follow. The upper strata began to read slick magazines instead of family journals and discussed films instead of Goethe's *Faust*. To be sure, the cultural values of the nineteenth century were by no means fully used up. (The German Middle Ages and German prehistory were, for instance, still "unexploited as elements of national education.") It was in the modern stratum of salaried employees, however, that the nation gained "a fresh middle stratum" thirsting for education and suitable as a carrier of culture.

Precise information about the educational interests of the salaried employees is scarce. However, the following tendencies seem to exist: (1) the larger the size of the city in which white-collar workers reside, the greater is their urge to acquire knowledge; (2) white-collar workers are less interested in the natural sciences than blue-collar workers; (3) the most proletarianized white-collar workers are most interested in sociology and least concerned with philosophy. But for those who are more favorably situated, these preferences are reversed.[12] The education of salaried employees can be properly evaluated only when their typical schooling is known. According to relatively comprehensive figures contained in the GdA survey of 1931, 59.1 percent of the male white-collar workers and 65.8 percent of their female colleagues had gone only to elementary school, that is, until age fourteen.[13]

Consideration of the social function of education created less confusion than questions regarding its desirable content. That education enhanced social prestige was clearly realized if not openly admitted. Thus, argued the DHV, "To us it seems to be a question of the mental health of our nation and of the balance of its composition that besides the millions of people who are unable or unwilling to rise above a purely instinctual life, and besides the few ten thousand political soldiers of fortune and economic climbers, there stands a strong social stratum which knowingly bears responsibility for the national destiny in all its heights and depths."[14]

Contained in this apologetic yet bombastic presentation is an idea that, if modestly advanced, accurately testifies to the power of the mind. That is, misery and persecution have little power over the rare person who leads a life of the spirit, for he defies misfortune. But to allow "the instinctual life" to serve as a background for one's own social prestige is to misjudge the differences between exceptional individuals and ordinary people. It is, in addition, a rank defamation of the many who live in misery. Ultimately, it reveals a preference for the self-interest of a social "estate" over the often-evoked "common interest" of the people.

The historical perspective of DHV ideologues was also defective. The decline of classical education was caused not so much by the politicization of the bourgeosie at the time of Treitschke as it was by the increasing social importance of technical knowledge and by the enrichment of the bourgeosie after the Franco-Prussian War of 1870. (The *nouveaux riches* were honored by the imperial court and given special titles, for example, *Kommerzienrat* [literally, 'commercial councilor'] corresponding to the *Geheimrat* [literally 'privy councilor'] of the governmental bureaucracy.) The associated decline of culture was given its most biting treatment by Theodor Fontane in his Berlin novels, especially in *Frau Jenny Treibel*. In a letter to his son Theo in 1888, Fontane described the history of this *Frau Kommerzienrätin:* by continuously singing a favorite sentimental song to a circle of acquaintances she acquires "a claim to 'higher things,' which are really only things associated with her husband's title, i.e., much money means 'the higher things' to her. The purpose of my story is to show the emptiness, the cant, the lying, the superciliousness, and the heartlessness in the attitudes of the bourgeois, who speak of Schiller and mean Gerson"[15]—the name of a well-known Berlin department store.

The DHV explicitly justified its motive for embracing education, the liberal principle of social esteem, by pointing to the increasing dehumanization of office work. This was not quite so absurd as it appears, for the descent of the average white-collar position in the hierarchy of the enterprise—the result of a progressive division of labor—was accompanied by a higher level of education. In the past, before the proletarian situation of the salaried employees was fully developed and the clerk could still assume broad responsibilities and anticipate a brighter future, the level of his education was considerably lower than in the Weimar Republic. As late as the turn of the century lack of education was an almost universal characteristic of commercial clerks.[16] This deplorable situation was largely a consequence of the inadequate performance of elementary schools and partly also the fault of the principals responsible for training apprentices. As late as the 1890s in Prussia and Baden, the specialized occupational schools were not much better than the elementary schools.

Commendable exceptions, however, existed in Saxony, where the commercial schools were associated with the general school system, and in the city of Hamburg, as a result of the educational institution founded as early as 1868 by the Association 1858.[17] The occupational associations fought indefatigably for many years to elevate the educational level of salaried employees. But to see this struggle exclusively as an expression of responsibility toward national culture is to misjudge its nature, for it was also a concentrated effort to limit the supply of clerical labor in much the same way as other "estates" had done. The educated person has better chances in applying for a job than the uneducated. The educated person has more prestige. In German society it has been true not only of the salaried employees that "the education is remarkably strong in forming society and 'estates.' "[18] Treitschke had already pointed out that in Germany one could find "the differences of social stratification" in education. The difference between the educated and the uneducated, acknowledged by everyone, had also served the organization of the civil service: "a mental division, the examination, separates the higher civil servant from the inferior one who has not studied."[19] After the reforms by Scharnhorst at the beginning of the nineteenth century, entry into the officer corps was also dependent "upon proof of a certain kind of knowledge." And indeed, in the era of Wilhelm II, one-year service in the army and advancement to the rank of reserve officer were dependent on six years of education at a secondary school (after three years of elementary schooling), attendance at which involved paying a monthly fee. Ordinary recruits had gone to a lower school without fee and served for two years. Even in the Weimar Republic the sons of workers were virtually excluded from studying at a university.[20]

The function of education becomes especially apparent if the procedures for elevating educational levels are considered. They did not affect the objective proletarianization of white-collar workers. Formal education could even be dispensed with in many cases because the required skill was developed by performing the function on the job—something that happened all the more frequently as the division of labor progressed. At the same time, the more cheaply education could be acquired, the more its social value was diminished, and the cost of education fell as its content and the methods of teaching it were adapted to the practical needs of the economy. Commercial and language skills could be acquired cheaply and were therefore available to some extent to members of social strata who had been barred from this kind of education in earlier generations.[21]

This development had two consequences. First, employees with relatively higher educational qualifications increased in number, which enabled entrepreneurs to demand high qualifications as a prerequisite for a job even where it was objectively unnecessary. Such practices counteracted the tendencies toward enfeeblement of the social hierarchy that are inherent in the democratization of education, for higher qualifications are expensive and consequently an index of higher social prestige. Second, the competition of new job seekers from socially lower strata aroused the endangered members of the labor force to seek a curtailment of competition by insisting on yet higher educational qualifications. Their insistence was not in the common interest of the people or nation but in the special interest of those who were privileged by their "better" social origins.

Thus, the DHV seriously demanded examinations for clerks even though the introduction of office machines had lowered the position of the average commercial employee in the social hierarchy and led to increased unemployment. The DHV was at least partly successful. The GdA also took the position that educational work was "the carrier of anti-proletarian forces"[22] in the movement of white-collar workers, but this union opposed the introduction of examinations for commercial clerks "simply after the model of the crafts."[23]

The demand for examining clerks served the same purpose, or at least the subsidiary purpose, that most of the commercial associations had pursued before World War I in their fight against working women, namely, that of preventing the "hunger competition" of cheap labor. The foremen favored higher education for the opposite reason. Since 1925 the DWV had devoted special attention to the professional education of foremen in an effort to improve their position relative to that of their *theoretically* educated competitors, who threatened to win out against the practical experience of the foremen in the plants.[24] No doubt the foremen acted more prudently than had the socialist white-collar trade unions in the prewar period. They consciously neglected professional education for the same reason they distrusted the creation of special sickness insurance for trade union members because instead of strengthening class consciousness these measures actually promoted awareness of separatist prestige. In this regard, the contrast between the Deutscher Bankbeamtenverein (DBV) and the radical Allgemeiner Verband der Bankangestellten is especially interesting: the former excelled in its educational efforts, the latter rejected professional education.

Finally, the educational aims and activities of the individual associations were closely related to their respective ideologies. The target of the DHV's educational efforts was "the personality of the entrepreneur in the best sense of the word." The work of the GdA was founded on "a compromise with life" and "an acceptance of the hard facts." The ZdA changed its educational orientation from "occupational usefulness to a concern with society at large." The Afa-Bund afforded the best training for activity in the shop councils, the DHV continued to cultivate its traditional civic education toward an heroic ideal, and the members of the GdA were strongly interested in travel literature and other avocational topics.[25]

In the educational history of the white-collar workers, which can be only scarcely sketched in the present context, the connection between education and social prestige is quite evident. Especially significant in this regard was the development of technical knowledge. The social prestige of German technicians was quite low in the middle of the last century, for only those who were humanistically educated were regarded as educated. Members of the higher social strata therefore did not become technicians. In Germany at that time, unlike in France and England, the technician was regarded

> as an elevated craftsman, the civic engineer as a scientifically tinted bricklayer or carpenter, and the machine technician as no more than a refined locksmith. All were assumed a priori to have correspondingly narrow judgment and poor intellectual vision. These views had so misled public opinion that the attributes by which the technician inspired confidence in his competence included one-sided ambition, a deficient general education, and a neglect of social appearance and form.[26]

At the turn of the century the first club-like associations of technicians were formed. Their purposes were not sociopolitical but were exclusively related to professional training. These associations were the breeding ground for the new scientific intelligentsia, which subsequently advanced a threefold claim for social prestige.

First, the claim was directed against the bearers of humanistic education. In the course of the nineteenth century the technical intelligentsia made considerable gains in prestige, perhaps even attaining complete equality with its rivals. This gain in social prestige was founded upon the engineer's creation of the technological prerequisites of high capitalism and upon his emergence as the social representative of the popular ideology of progress, whose flowering coincided with the withering away of the classical humanistic idea of cultural progress. The gain in social prestige corresponded to the social differentiation of technical personnel in industry. Not all bearers of the new knowledge were able to register additional social prestige. Such gains were reserved for an upper layer entrusted with the more difficult and prestigious tasks that arose with the increasingly scientific character of the mode of production. Joining this upper layer presupposed a relatively costly education and hence a high level of parental affluence.

Second, the claims for social prestige were directed against those technicians who were not educated at a technical university. These claims were rooted in the general principles that governed the rank order in society, but until the postwar period they had to be asserted against the view that creative technical achievements were not necessarily the fruit of academic education.[27] The middle-school technicians, who had *not* met the requirement of ten years of schooling necessary for one-year service in the army,[28] could not become reserve officers. The education they had acquired at a special technical school did not count, and those who met the requirement on the basis of the "special skill paragraph" (*Kunstparagraph*), that is, §589, section 6 of the law of the military establishment (*Wehrordnung*) were too few to matter. In 1899 engineers with an academic diploma (so-called diploma engineers) gained the right to acquire the degree of doctor of engineering, which implied both formal equality with the academicians of older faculties and a mark of distinction over the middle-school technicians. In the Weimar Republic, during the Great Depression, the diploma engineers suffered a high rate of unemployment. As a result their social distance from the middle-school technicians was actually narrowed even though their advantages of prestige, derived from their social origins, persisted. Thus, for example, the holders of certificates issued by (most of the) higher professional schools were admitted (after 1921) as members of the Verein Deutscher Ingenieure after only five years of employment as engineers, whereas ten years of employment were required for the holders of certificates from other (lower) technical schools. The Depression did not alter this pattern of discrimination.

Third, the prestige claims of scientific intellectuals, and especially technicians, were directed against the monopoly of legal education in the administrative service. Here they encountered the strongest opposition and did not prevail. The monopoly of legal education in the administrative service was based on an instruction dated 23 October 1817. At that time Freiherr von Hardenberg pushed through the reforms that led to the replacement of the old cameralistic practice with legal studies as the new basis of education.[29]

Despite the very different educational efforts and ideas supported by commercial employees, foremen, and technicians, in each case education furnished the opportunity to attain or enhance their social prestige. The decline of classical, humanistic education is traceable to this opportunity. It also eased the efforts of those who felt superior to the merely "instinctual" life to release the tensions "between their working conditions and their ideal of becoming personalities" by acquiring the "unconsumed" educational treasure of Germany's distant past. They overlooked the fact that the development of these tensions was associated with the destruction of the humanistic ideal of education by the specialized intelligentsia of the capitalist age,[30] whose representatives included themselves. Nor could this development be reversed by politicizing the contents of education.

X Nationalism

Soldiers and Warriors in Civilian Clothes

It is impossible to offer easy generalizations about the predominant political orientation of white-collar workers in the Weimar Republic. Like their functions and work experiences, their political views were not uniform. A wide spectrum of political opinions may be gleaned from programmatic statements of their various trade unions, which differed according to the general type of employee they drew as members. The average member of the Afa-Bund was no nationalist, for example, and the average "clerk" in the DHV no Social Democrat. The extreme nationalism of white-collar workers in the Weimar Republic was centered in the DHV and not in the Afa-Bund. Even the GdA failed to reach the extremism of the DHV.

Even more hazardous than generalizations about the political views of salaried employees are general assertions about the middle strata. After World War II, M. Rainer Lepsius investigated the nationalist convictions and pronouncements of various social strata during the Weimar Republic. He attempted to identify the nationalism of the middle class (*Mittelstand*), which he distinguished perspicaciously from that of the peasants, the workers, and the Catholics. Lepsius contended that "the self-portrait of the middle class contains not only the demand for privileges but also a constitutive claim of national honor and esteem, a claim to represent and administer the normal morality of society."[1] In some respects Lepsius's views of the middle class and its "characteristic nationalism" resemble the opinions set forth in this chapter, which originated in the years preceding Hitler's assumption of power. However, Lepsius's views are in need of supplementation. When Lepsius speaks of the middle class (*Mittelstand*), his focus is entirely on the so-called old middle class, that is, small independent merchants, craftsmen, "provincial members of the middle class," and the like. Since the majority of German white-collar workers regarded themselves as part of the middle

103

class, it is reasonable to ask whether or not Lepsius's statements also pertain to these employees and to the civil servants of middle and lower rank. Lepsius asserts that the social morality of the middle class is a "pre-industrial relic" which even "today is still firmly embedded in the national culture" because its transfer from generation to generation is institutionalized in the school system. These statements are not altogether plausible with reference to salaried employees. They do pertain to many employees in small towns, but to say of DHV members that their anti-semitic nationalism contained a claim to "normal morality" would entail consequences which Lepsius hardly intended.

Furthermore, the nationalistic sentiments of the middle and higher salaried employees in big enterprises cannot be readily understood as a "pre-industrial relic." Urbanization and the expansion of enterprises have influenced the opinions and feelings of this white-collar stratum. The division of authority and the discipline experienced in large firms presumably weakened the pre-industrial component of middle-class nationalism in favor of more modern political passions. Of course, the intensity of nationalism did not lessen for this reason; the reverse seems to be closer to the truth. Furthermore, Lepsius does not mention the disciplinary-military component of middle-class nationalism. Many observers have noticed its significance for the structure of the big German enterprise and for German society at large. This military component of German nationalism demands attention also in the nationalistic orientations of the new middle class.

The way in which an employee is integrated into an economic enterprise is not unequivocally determined by the form of the organization. Rather, the spirit which animates these forms characterizes society at large. For example, shortly after the revolution of 1918 German foremen pointed out that no longer was the foreman to be "a factory policeman." The former military system, it was said, had its redeeming features, but its weakness was evident in the fact that the "spiritual interests" of the laborers were not satisfied at their places of work, but only outside of the factory. Now the foreman would have to make an effort to educate his workers to become conscious of the need for cooperation; he ought to be their "adviser and helper, and if need be [!] their comrade."[2]

This self-criticism was interesting because it was a confession: it supports the view of Goetz Briefs "that in Germany the barracks and the elementary schools formed social categories in the economic establishments. . . . The direction of the enterprise from the top of the hierarchy down to the foreman evidently imitated the military model."[3] In Holland, where the army enjoyed the kind of social prestige which in Germany was granted to fire brigades, the quoted opinions of German foremen would have sounded absurd, because any corresponding Dutch experience was lacking. As early as the 1920s in the United States, the foreman was expected to have the qualities of a "human engineer," who treated his men with prudence and circumspection in the interest of high productivity. For a superior to model his action on the military sphere was German, or more precisely, Prussian. Following militaristic tradition in such a way could meet with approval only in a society which offered social models bearing military features. Correspondingly, that "the extraordinary moral power" of the foreman be strengthened by "not imposing upon him conflicts with the workers, his partners—which in the long run is simply unbearable" was a demand that, as late as 1922, could be characterized as "fundamentally new" only in Germany.[4]

At the same time, the overwhelming majority of the unionized foremen were members of the "free," that is, socialist, trade unions. These former workers were moderate Social Democrats rather than early National Socialists. If they voted the SPD ticket they often followed a trade unionist family tradition, and their votes did not change and were not intended to change the organizational spirit reigning in the big enterprise. Indeed, they participated functionally in maintaining these organizations.

In Germany and especially in Prussia, the model of discipline and hierarchical order was the army. After defeating Austria in 1866, Prussia's ruling nationalist orientation assumed a military character. It has often been pointed out that in Germany even the organization of the trade unions betrayed the military training of the people. How much more justified is this statement when applied to the large industrial enterprise! The immediate guardians of military spirit in industrial offices after 1918 were demobilized officers in the preferred position of personnel director. Next to them was the staff of academic adjutants, who carried the esprit de corps of their fraternities into the firms. They also disseminated this spirit as alumni by recommending and preferring members of their fraternities for appointments to vacant positions. It was considered exemplary for the leading salaried employees to feel a moral responsibility to cultivate an esprit de corps among their subordinates. The superiors were thereby assured that they did not sacrifice more "than does the general who feels like a comrade of the younger gentlemen in the corps of officers and maintains comradely relations with them without losing any of his superiority in service or any command authority."[5]

The remainder of the hierarchy felt obligated to "intelligent obedience" (Spengler), because it was the prerequisite for advancement. Only he who could obey was permitted to command, and he who wanted to command had to obey. The big German enterprises were not governed by parliaments. "Out of the will to achievement and responsibility of so many who are called to fit into a hierarchy of responsible order, there grows the power . . . to remain independent of the considerations of the soul of the masses, which is fed by the fleeting sentiments of the day." With these bombastic words Max Habermann, a leader of the DHV, characterized the spirit of his organization in 1931. Characteristically, his talk bore the title "Speech to the Young Soldiers of the DHV."[6] The young clerks, who considered their organization as the "barracks grounds of their estate's honor,"[7] may actually have believed that Habermann presented an inspiring account of their office experiences.

During the first years of the Weimar Republic nationalism still pointed back to the militarism of the empire. It was reactionary and oriented toward the social models of the Kaiser's era, to the officer, the reserve officer, and the fraternity student. Among the nationalistic white-collar workers, the inclination to cultivate prewar customs surfaced especially in their styles of sociability. It began at the "beer evenings" of the DHV locals in the small towns and ended with the large festivities of the organization or with the Festive Dance of the Clerks in the big cities. Student customs also shone brighter as they too reflected the brilliance of military representation. The corps of officers and the corps of students were thus complemented by the corps of salaried employees. The similarity can be demonstrated down to the lovesongs intoned at social gatherings. To the tune of a well known student song ("Keinen Tropfen in Becher mehr": "Not a Drop Left in My Glass"), the members of the DHV sang a ditty whose last stanzas treated the commercial clerk as follows:

> In the notebook of the heart
> he has forever written down
> the names of many young ladies!
> In the account book of the heart
> he has listed also many
> kisses of his ladies!
> In the main book of the heart
> he often enters only one!
> She alone he loves.
> But I must confess that
> many a man has on the side
> *contis pro diversi.*
> Were one to wish to see all accounts
> more than a small hour
> would be needed.

Here a pair of blue eyes,
there some curly blond hair,
there some rosy lips.
DHV, at any time
you were ready for battle,
fighting for your rights!
But at the same time you don't reject
the wondrously lovely
sex of Madame Eve.

In the songbook of the DHV these stanzas faced a poem by Matthias Claudius, one of Germany's foremost lyric poets.[8] All twenty-one editions of the songbook were edited not by some low functionary of the association but by the leader of the movement.

In 1918 the national idea and those who embraced it were humiliated by the forced disarmament of Germany. Both military power and the visible representatives of the national idea vanished from the social stage. To be sure, nationalistic, anti-pacifist, anti-parliamentarian, anti-semitic, anti-socialist, and anti-feminist white-collar workers in the DHV tried to cling to their national ideals, but they succeeded only in changing them. The organization of the big German industrial enterprises, whose spirit was not decisively changed by the law concerning shop councils, was helpful to them in this regard. Discipline in the enterprise functioned as a substitute for military discipline. W. Stapel, according to Max Habermann "one of the best educated Germans of our day," wrote the following about the social classes in his pamphlet *Prussia Must Be*. The first estate is formed by the warriors, the second by the civil servants ("civilians to be sure, are a little comical, but they too have a place in this world"), the third estate is formed by the peasants, and the fourth by the industrial and commercial merchants, who must be tolerated because they are important for the finances of the state. The journal of the DHV rejected the evaluation of civil servants and compensated for the neglect of the salaried employees as follows: "It is possible to compare objectively the warrior and the merchant, but not the warrior and the civil servant if the comparison is to do justice to their qualities of character and their contributions to the whole. The enterprising merchant with his assistants represents a battle unit in the . . . struggle for life of the nations—according to his qualities and his task he is a warrior in civilian clothes."[9]

The absurd designation of the merchant and his white-collar assistants as "warriors in civilian clothes" was based on extravagant conceits which spread among middle-class youth, including young white-collar workers, in the Weimar

Republic. These conceits falsified the traditional meaning of the "military" profession. Far from demonstrating a commitment to Prussian values, they had originated in the fantasies of literati who spoke of "Volk" rather than the "nation," of "warriors" rather than "soldiers," and of adventures rather than work. During the Weimar Republic, Ernst Jünger, the most influential of these literati, expressed enthusiasm about the "steely thunderstorms" of the lost world war and despised the "normal morality" of the "middle class."

The social origin of Jünger's views did not lie in the fixed, immovable battle lines of 1914–18, when the fronts froze in a hail of bombs and Europe's soldiers were devoured as cannon fodder. Rather, this new heroism exalted the experiences of the shock troops, the hard-trained volunteers who were called upon for dangerous special attacks and, if they survived, were withdrawn from the front until ordered back for the next attack. They were a highly paid elite of specialists in violence, estranged from the mass of ordinary soldiers. In Germany the astonishing popularity of this adventurous warlike spirit *after* the war was rooted in malaise over the tedium of civilian existence, with its dry work and bitter unemployment, over the absence of risk in everyday life, and over the lack of tradition in citizenship.[10]

The warlike component of extreme nationalism between the world wars was not confined to Germany. "War is for the man what motherhood is for the woman," said Mussolini. As Henry A. Turner has shown, the heroic ideal "has been more fundamental for the popular cultures of Europe than has been generally acknowledged."[11] Many observers have traced the prototypes of "utopian anti-modernism" (Turner) in Germany back to the nineteenth century,[12] although neither the fatigue with being European nor the distaste for industrial society were confined to German literati and artist circles.

DHV and NSDAP

That the anti-modern adventure ideology of the warlike, non-bourgeois life enjoyed some popularity in the Weimar Republic cannot be satisfactorily explained as a consequence of either economic misery or parliamentary paralysis. Nor was it engendered by National Socialist propaganda and terror. The victory parade of extreme nationalism and the glorification of violence could not have occurred without the disorientation of large numbers of people, including many intellectuals.

The disorientation was partly the result of shattered traditions. Traditions in which the ethos of society finds expression offer intellectual and moral orientation. In the German empire the three traditions with the broadest base in the population were military, Catholic, and proletarian free-unionist. Various special investigations have proven that when National Socialism entered Weimar politics on a broad level, it was least successful in the Catholic parts of the country and in the industrial centers of the free trade unions in large cities.[13] Catholicism and proletarian consciousness were the strongest bulwarks against extreme nationalism, a fact demonstrated in every election until Hitler assumed power.[14] By contrast, the Protestant-military tradition was shaky after 1918. It could muster little support against the storm of new nationalism because nationalist propaganda fulminated against the usual foes of respectable, old German politics: the class struggle, parliamentarianism, free trade unions, Social Democracy, and Communism. Military and reactionary circles were shocked not by Hitler's civil war tactics, but rather by the demands of his plebeian paramilitary organizations. The "Führer" would demonstrate soon after gaining power—in the bloodbath of 30 June 1934—that nothing could make him pause to show respect for the bearers of military tradition.

As for the racist, anti-semitic component of the official NSDAP ideology most Germans either accepted or belittled it. Prior to 1933 and during the first few years of the Third Reich, even many German Jews assumed the anti-semitism of the NSDAP to be a tactical device for attracting votes and thus failed to take it seriously. To the members of the DHV it was nothing new. Although the racist anti-semitism was a more recent phenomenon, the association had long cultivated a *Volk* tradition. People with deep-seated prejudices have little trouble overlooking or even approving of terror, brutality, and murder so long as the victims of such "excesses" are the objects of their prejudices.

During the initial years of the Weimar Republic most DHV representatives in parliament found their preferred forum in the German National People's Party (Deutschnationale Volkspartei, DNVP). When the DNVP was founded in November 1918, it attracted the supporters of all conservative prewar parties. In the elections of May 1924 it almost doubled its seats in the Reichstag, which led to an increased representation of the "all-German" (extreme rightist) and "economic-harmony" (anti–trade unionist) interests in the party. Conflict with the representatives of the DHV, which had adopted a trade union orientation in 1918, was merely a matter of time (see chapter 12). In June 1928 Walter Lambach, a member of the DHV and a Reichstag deputy for the DNVP, attacked the "monarchism" of the party. This led to bitter fights within the party and, after Hugenberg's election as its chairman, to the resignation from the DNVP of Lambach and other representatives of the employees.

Shortly thereafter a similar development took place in the right-wing, though less extremist, German People's Party (Deutsche Volkspartei, DVP). After Gustav Stresemann's death in October 1929, the entrepreneurs gained at the expense of more liberal elements in the party. As a result of this development, Thiel and Glatzel, who represented the DHV in the Reichstag group of the DVP, met with increasing difficulties. Under the leadership of Dingeldey the party became more and more reactionary. In a critical vote of confidence on 16 October 1930, the DVP in the Reichstag opposed Chancellor Brüning, but Thiel and Glatzel broke party discipline to vote for him. When Dingeldey announced early in 1932 that his reduced party would cooperate with the DNVP in the forthcoming elections, Thiel and Glatzel left the party.[15]

After the open conflict with reactionary forces, the leadership of the DHV sought to promote a "folk-conservative" orientation in German politics. On the one hand these efforts were directed against the reactionary forces, on the other hand they were "folk-national" *(völkisch)* but more "civilized" than the *völkisch* movement of the NSDAP. The leaders of the DHV seriously hoped for a Brüning-Hitler coalition government. Wilhelm Stapel was the main spokesman of the folk-conservatives on cultural policy and Max Habermann was their most prominent political sponsor among the DHV leadership. Nazi rhetoric which claimed to "transcend" the class struggle appealed to Habermann, who enjoyed a close connection with Brüning that had begun when the latter was manager of the Christian trade unions. Habermann overlooked the excesses of the Storm Troopers and had even less comprehension of Hitler's unlimited appetite for power than he did of Hugenberg's and Dinkeldey's reactionary aims. In the opinion of Albert Krebs, a leading Nazi in the DHV, Habermann regarded the NSDAP as "a political party like all other parties." He "had no access to the realm in which unbridled and unformed feelings, lusts, instincts, and longings reign. . . . Even ten years later, he did not understand . . . the wild fanaticism that had seized the men in the innermost circle of the party—without regard for any traditional moral order."[16]

Habermann and Krebs arranged the first conversation between Brüning and Hitler in the fall of 1930. Then, after an article by Habermann, entitled "Brüning and Hitler," was reprinted many times in the German press, Gregor Strasser arranged for an exchange on 6 November 1931 between Bechly and Habermann of the DHV and Hitler, Hess, and Gregor Strasser of the NSDAP.[17] Habermann believed that a Brüning-Hitler alliance—that is, between the Christian trade unions and an anti-liberal, anti-Marxist mass movement—had assumed its "live form" in the forty year history of the DHV.[18] However, despite Habermann's "optimistic" view of the exchange with Hitler, the encounter failed. Through the so-called Harzburger Front, Hitler sought contact with the reactionary and capitalistic circles of the DNVP, and rejected a connection with Brüning, the Catholic Center Party, and the Christian trade unions. When Bechly and the administration of the DHV publicly supported the reelection of Hindenburg, the break with Hitler was complete. Only the connection between Habermann and the "revolutionary" Gregor Strasser lasted until the latter's "liquidation" on 30 June 1934.

Max Habermann overestimated Brüning and failed to recognize Hitler for what he was. His efforts to protect the DHV against the Nazi movement were concerned not with "the racist-nationalistic conception as such,"[19] but with sectarianism, with "jealousies" among the leadership, and with questions of economic and social policy. When he, Bechly, and other functionaries of the DHV claimed leadership of the trade unions, they always meant only the Christian-national Deutscher Gewerkschaftsbund (DGB), of which the DHV was a part, and not the powerful free trade unions. They had the "national myth" in mind—and evoked it often—rather than republican civic virtue when they spoke of the "folk-organic democracy of the masses" (whatever that meant); and they considered the SPD, the free trade unions, and Hugenberg more dangerous than the threat of Hitler. The parliamentarian cross-connections of the association reached to the NSDAP, but not to the SPD. No leading functionary of the DHV ever objected to the ridicule heaped upon parliament, fought against anti-semitism, warned against the exploitation of nationalistic sentiments, or publicly condemned the terror of the SA. Only their opposition to Marxism and to the most supercilious reactionary forces was really serious.

The corruption of nationalism among DHV leadership was manifest not only in their tactical efforts to move closer to Hitler but even earlier in their silence on the referendum against the Young Plan. The predecessor of the Harzburger Front was the Reich Commission for the German Referendum against the Young Plan, created on 9 July 1929, in which the DNVP, the NSDAP, the *Stahlhelm*, and other patriotic associations collaborated. The Reich Commission proposed a law which would declare all representatives of the Reich who opposed its views on either the Young Plan or refusal to recognize the German war debt as being guilty of high treason and therefore subject to imprisonment. The DHV leadership, despite its concern over the cooperation between Hugenberg and Hitler, did not take sides on the issue of the referendum, but members of *Fahrende Gesellen*, the youth organization of the DHV, joined the Nazis in demonstrations against the Young Plan.

The attempt of DHV leaders to find a national compromise between reactionary and extremist policies, between Hugenberg and Hitler, disturbed the
members of the association. Bechly's and Habermann's policies were bitterly
criticized and noisily opposed within the organization, especially by younger
members. Members who criticized the policy of the DHV too forcefully or vo-
ciferously were expelled.[20]

The elections of September 1930 revealed the miserable failure of Habermann's political hopes. The number of Nazi deputies in the Reichstag rose spec-
tacularly from 12 to 107, while the folk-conservatives, DNVP, and DVP suffered
catastrophic losses. Habermann had been wrong not only about Hitler but also
about the Germans. He finally offered resistance to Hitler only after the collapse
of the Weimar Republic,[21] an event which the DHV had helped to bring about.

In the Weimar Republic the publishing activities of the DHV were not
unimportant in destroying a sense of measure, clarity, and open-mindedness and
in preparing an intellectual menu according to the folk-conservative cultural
diet. Along with various journals designed for members and for the "young soldiers" of the DHV, the publishing enterprises of the association—Deutsche
Hausbücherei, Hanseatische Verlagsanstalt, Georg Müller, and Albert Langen—
published authors whose writings reached out to readers beyond the DHV membership in order to aid in "the erection" of an intellectual "front." In Stapel's
vocabulary even belles lettres was described in military language. No recognition
was reserved by readers of these "frontal" books for authors who did not write
völkisch or volk-like. For example, Georg Büchner and Georg Christoph Lich-
tenberg were probably unknown to the DHV readers, and they certainly had not
heard of Friedrich Georg Forster. Heine was "alien" (artfremd). Fontane was
probably little read anyway—he was published by S. Fischer—and if some of
his opinions about Bismarck had been known, DHV readers would certainly
have considered him to be "alienated from the Volk" (volksfremd).[22] Instead,
the publishing houses of the DHV disseminated works of nationalist, anti-semitic,
and anti-parliamentarian authors, including Grand Admiral von Tirpitz, Werner
Sombart, Walter Lambach, Moeller van den Bruck, Wilhelm Stapel, Hans Blü-
her, Adolf Bartels, Werner Jansen, August Winnig, Ernst Jünger, Erwin Guido
Kolbenheyer, Hans Grimm, Hanns Johst, Hermann Ullmann, Albert Erich
Günther, and Wilhelm von Polenz. Older German authors who, like Gustav
Freytag and Wilhelm Raabe interlaced anti-semitism in their prose, were also
included in the list of DHV publications.[23] The yearbooks of the DHV contained
references to many völkisch authors. And of course, Theodor Fritsch's "Handbook
of the Jewish Question" (in its thirty-first edition in 1932) was prominently displayed in DHV bookstores.[24] In short, the DHV distributed books that sold well

to the half-educated members of the German middle classes. They were not burned during the Third Reich.

In the winter of 1933–34 Max Habermann wrote an unpublished history of the DHV, containing an estimate that no less than half the members of the DHV voted the Nazi ticket as early as the Reichstag elections of 14 September 1930.[25] And the GdA? It was usually considered democratic, that is, close to the Deutsche Demokratische Partei (DDP), but as early as 1931 large parts of its membership were captured by the NSDAP. According to a survey of the GdA, no less than one-third of approximately one thousand functionaries were National Socialists, about one-third were Social Democrats, and the remainder were committed to other political parties.[26] In the last elections held during the Weimar Republic, the percentage of DHV, GdA, and unorganized white-collar workers who voted for the Nazis was presumably much higher than is indicated by the estimate of 1930 and 1931.

According to frequently quoted figures compiled by Hans Gerth, salaried employees comprised more than one-fifth (21.1 percent) of NSDAP members in 1933, but only one-eighth (12.5 percent) of the gainfully employed.[27] Like other middle strata—independent persons and civil servants—they were over-represented in the party, while the reverse was true of manual workers. Wolfgang Schäfer has compared the social stratification of the party with that of German society at large for the year 1930.[28] If the percentage of each occupational stratum in the total labor force is taken as equal to 100, the index number for the percentages of blue-collar workers in the Nazi party is only 61.2, of white-collar workers, however, 213.5. This index of overrepresentation was exceeded only by independents (230.0) in 1930, but not by civil servants (162.7) or farmers (132.0).

Research on the elections held in the Weimar Republic corroborates the vulnerability of white-collar workers to the appeals of National Socialism. The party received its weakest support from blue-collar workers, its strongest from independents and especially, in the cities, from those independents in commerce and trade. White-collar workers and civil servants were not far behind, however.[29] Alexander Weber's detailed investigation of communities in Baden and Hesse confirms this social stratification of the NSDAP voters.[30]

"Volk"

The nationalism of white-collar workers also served to emphasize their social claim for prestige. In his essay "Of That Which Someone Represents" Schopenhauer said of national pride that it betrays in its possessor the lack of individual qualities of which to be proud, otherwise he would not embrace that which he shares with so many millions. He who possesses personal distinction will clearly recognize the faults of his own nation, for they will be constantly before his eyes. But every miserable simpleton who has nothing in the world of which to be proud avails himself of his last chance: he is proud of the nation he happens to belong to and this makes him feel good.[31]

Schopenhauer's views do not afford any immediate insights into the social function of nationalism, but they do stress the fact that national pride makes the lack of praiseworthy personal qualities more bearable.

In the empire, the nationalism of the German middle strata was marked by socially discriminating features. In the Weimar Republic it provided, in addition, compensation for social disadvantages which the middle strata believed they unjustly suffered in relation to blue-collar workers.

German nationalism before World War I was socially discriminating. Thus, for example, nationalists felt morally superior to Social Democratic workers who were regarded as internationalistic and as lacking a fatherland. The workers, who distrusted the state, were not thought even to belong to the nation. The poor in the middle class sought to avoid being identified as proletarians by stressing their national convictions. Socially discriminating prejudices are always articulated by marginal strata, even though they tend to be close to the victims of their prejudices. Examples are abundant. Thus, converts discriminate against members of their former religious community; assimilated Jews in the Weimar Republic were prejudiced against "Eastern" Jews; "poor white trash" despised blacks in the United States; new wealth always spurns the group of its origin; partly assimilated immigrants discriminated against later immigrants (for example, the Huguenots in Prussia against the French immigrants after 1789); the blacks who settled early in American cities fought the arrival of new settlers from rural areas; and to some extent, the Germans who migrated to America after 1933 were not always friendly toward the Austrians who escaped somewhat later.

The social discrimination and loss of status imposed upon the German workers was hardly diminished by the social "truce" declared during World War I, when socialists and nationalists alike defended the fatherland. Following the revolution at the end of the war, discrimination again increased. Even when the workers in the SPD voted for Hindenburg in the presidential elections, extreme nationalists accused them of lacking patriotism. But the political purpose of nationalism during the Weimar Republic was not to display nationalist convictions, as it had been during the empire. Unlike the conservatives, National Liberals, and anti-semites before the war, nationalists could no longer believe that their views helped to preserve the state, for they now sought the destruction of the existing, newly established political regime. Neither the reactionary DNVP nor the NSDAP had any scruples about spreading pernicious lies and poisonous propaganda concerning the causes and consequences of Germany's defeat in World War I, and both parties heaped calumnies upon republican politicians. Even at the beginning of the Weimar era, the nationalists were shocked less by the frequent political murders and other proofs of the barbarianization of political life than by democratization. Especially provoking to nationalists were the political and status gains that the workers and their organizations had scored in the Weimar Republic. The political function of nationalism had gained a social component.

The German middle classes were embittered when they compared their situation to that of the workers. Because the prestige and status of the workers had improved after the revolution, the middle classes grew increasingly dissatisfied with their own social situation. As a result their nationalism added a new compensatory function to its old discriminatory function of the prewar period.

The nationalism of most white-collar workers was sharpened by a series of economic and social events, including inflation, rationalization, and after 1929, the economic crisis with its attendant disappearance of interest income, diminished chances for social advancement, mass unemployment among salaried employees, and salary reductions among the employed. The majority of white-collar workers rejected the Afa-Bund and its policies, and their determination to stay out of the proletariat remained inflexible. Indeed, their claim to social superiority over blue-collar workers only grew more urgent in response to their pressing insecurity and to the simultaneous increase in the power and prestige of the workers. In the course of economic and political developments after 1918, however, the nationalistic convictions of the anti-socialist white-collar workers were divided into two factions: the economically powerful reactionaries who sought only to restore the past, and those such as the clerks, who were equally hostile toward the reigning parliamentarian system, but who were economically dependent upon and therefore locked in economic conflict with the entrepreneurs. This second faction insisted that they were not part of the proletariat. Rather, because they had lost their capitalistic rank as a result of their proletarianization, but had remained non-proletarians by virtue of their nationalist convictions, they claimed to belong to the "Volk." The "Volk" did not include the capitalists, just as, before the war, the "nation" did not include the proletariat.

In capitalist societies the typical representative of the people—"the honest man and child of the people" as the court preacher Adolf Stoecker introduced himself to Berlin workers in the *Kaiserreich*—is a member of the lower middle classes, who are distinguished by neither wealth nor education. The aristocrat stands above the people, and the educated person is readily suspected of estrangement from the people, but the capitalist and proletarian appear to destroy the unity of the people so long as they are engaged in the class struggle. By rejecting participation in the class struggle, the middle strata could regard themselves as more genuine representatives of the people, that is, the *Volk*, than those strata that not only participated in the struggle but saw in it a moral mission consistent with socialist ideology. Despite pursuing their economic interests through trade unions, white-collar workers who were not organized in the Afa-Bund strictly rejected the international class struggle. Accordingly, they regarded the conception spread by the Afa-Bund of a transformation of the capitalist system by means of class struggle as proletarian, immoral, and harmful to the welfare of the German people.

In the DHV *völkisch* ideas had been part of the official ideology since the 1890s. Members were well prepared for the infusion of the *völkisch* idea with the anti-modern pseudo-mythology of blood and race, which found so much enthusiastic support during the last years of the Weimar Republic. They were also receptive to Stapel and Habermann's folk-conservative ideas, and especially to the political falsification of the *Volk* concept, which, like the falsification of the meaning of "military," was accomplished by eager writers. In 1931, for example, Professor Hans Freyer in his influential pamphlet *Revolution von rechts* (Right-Wing Revolution), designated the *Volk* as the agent of a "revolutionary" [!] break from class society to a vague but enthusiastically annunciated classless future. "After society has become wholly society," he wrote, "and has comprehended and recognized all forces as interests, all interests as reconcilable, and all classes as socially necessary, there appears in it that which is neither society, nor class, nor interest, hence irreconcilable, but abysmally revolutionary: the *Volk*."[32]

In this manner, the class struggle was rejected as obsolete, social compromise was devalued, and political compromise calumniated. According to Hans Freyer the *Volk* was "the counterpart of industrial society, the only one which history has readied for it. It is the only legitimate asker of the question: for whom? For the answer, which it gives itself, is: for me."[33] In his enthusiastic muddleheadedness, Freyer emphasized, to top it all, that it is "strictly prohibited" ("schlechterdings verboten") "to attempt to theoretically comprehend" the *Volk*, this "new subject of history," "with the formulae of the old world." To inquire "as to which form it will assume when it reaches the end of its movement" is "not only false but also cowardly."[34] This nonsense, which contained the echo of Nazi rhetoric, was taken seriously by half-educated middle-class youth, including young employees, and was considered respectable because it originated not in the mind of an ambitious politician but in that of a scholar.[35] None of this had much to do with "normal morality," for which it was much too extravagant, consisting as it did of babble rather than reasonable speech. Nonetheless, toward the end of the Weimar Republic it had become a part of middle-class nationalism in Germany.

The nationalism of white-collar workers, which served their claims to social prestige, was not a coherent ideology nor was it evenly embraced by members of this social stratum. Rather, it shone in many colors. Moreover, the component features of this ideology cannot be correlated with particular years or with distinct parts or layers of the salaried stratum. However, by claiming to be members of the Volk, white-collar workers could appear to be "moral" and at the same time advance their claims to social prestige in several ways: (1) by evoking the spirit and using the organizational form of the social structure which, prior to 1918, had embodied the old nation and which had lent power to those social models in which the Volk recognized its integration into the social order, that is, the army and its leaders; (2) by falsification of the military, and especially Prussian tradition, that is, by creating the myth of the "warrior" in contrast to the despicable figures of the civilian and citizen; (3) by rejecting the merely reactionary nationalism of the entrepreneurs, the opponents of the Volk and their ideologies; (4) by rejecting liberal-democratic ideas, which "atomized" the Volk in a disorderly manner; (5) by combatting the Marxist idea of the class struggle, which seemed to threaten the Volk; and finally (6) by sanctifying the race, in which the conflicts of interest that were suspended or hidden in the Volk appeared to be reconciled.

XI White-Collar Organizations until 1918

This section and the remaining chapters present a brief history of white-collar associations through their disintegration in 1933.

In the second half of the nineteenth century salaried employees began to form associations on the basis of occupation. These associations did not serve to obtain any social or economic advantages for its members, but were primarily devoted to convivial ends and to self-help. Membership was also open to economically independent persons. For example, the Association for Commercial Clerks of 1858 (Verein für Handlungs-Commis von 1858) held "that a divided pursuit of occupational interests *[Standesinteressen]* must be avoided at all costs by both sides in the best interest of the entire merchant class. We want to promote the closeness of our ties, not their dissolution."[1] The Association of German Clerks in Leipzig (Verband Deutscher Handlungsgehilfen zu Leipzig, VDH), founded in 1881, also recommended that "the occupational work *[Standesarbeit]* be oriented not toward hostile conflict between the two groups [principals and clerks] but toward sustaining a feeling of solidarity and toward striving as much as possible for mutual understanding and compromise."[2]

Around the last decade prior to the beginning of World War I the associations evinced a growing interest in the creation of legal privileges in relation to the workers, especially in the areas of social insurance and labor law. Some entrepreneurs supported these privileges; others opposed them. At that time commercial clerks did not yet have anything to do with trade union aims to increase wages and improve working conditions. Such collective methods were used by organizations of blue-collar workers, who at least rhetorically connected them with socialist ideas about the transformation of capitalism. The first salaried employees to adopt such notions were those who worked most closely with manual laborers and who did not rely upon a confidential relationship with the principals, as did the commercial clerks in small firms. Specifically, the first white-collar workers to adopt trade unions methods were technical employees, including foremen, and the poorly paid, lower commercial employees who experienced increasing insecurity.

In 1884 the German Foremen's Association (Deutscher Werkmeisterverband, DWV) broke away from the consolidation of local associations. The financially potent DWV worked for the extension of protective laws for commercial employees to cover technicians as well. Although most of the foremen came from the working class and were trained in trade union work, the DWV was relatively moderate and later settled on the conservative wing of the free trade unions.

The early organizations of technical employees in the sixties were also small, local associations. They were finally consolidated in 1884 as the German Association of Technicians (Deutscher Technikerverband, DTV) with five hundred members. The DTV organized an auxiliary health insurance plan and devoted itself to the protection of inventors, but despite its interest in social legislation, it valued its character as an occupational organization. In this regard it resembled the associations of engineers, architects, chemists, iron-works employees, and so forth, some of which had been founded as early as the 1850s.

The first radical trade unions of technical employees and foremen originated only after the turn of the century. They were the Association of Technical-Industrial Employees (Bund der technisch-industriellen Beamten, Butib), founded in 1904 in Berlin—renamed in May 1919 the Association of Technical Employees and Civil Servants (Bund der technischen Angestellten und Beamten, Butab)—and the German Association of Mine Inspectors (Deutscher Steigerverband), founded by mine inspector Georg Werner in 1907. Both associations were sharply opposed by the entrepreneurs. Members were punished, persecuted, and placed at a disadvantage when applying for a job. In 1911 Butib organized the first strike of technicians—nearly 250 designers in the iron industry. As members of the German Association of Mine Inspectors, the inspectors who determined the piece wages in mining declared their solidarity with the miners. They were thereupon terrorized by the mining officers. Functionaries of the association were prosecuted in many criminal cases. Finally the association, which at first had grown despite all persecution, succumbed in the fight against the entrepreneurs.[3] In 1918 it was transformed into a special branch of Butib.

The first weak signs of a trade union orientation among commercial employees came from the Association of German Merchants (Verein der deutschen Kaufleute), which had been founded in 1884. The association formed an alliance with the liberal workers' organizations by joining their central organization. Moreover, beginning in 1906 it accepted female employees as members with equal rights. Despite its declared political neutrality, it was close to the liberal Progressive Party (Fortschrittspartei). The influence of the association among commercial employees was relatively weak. In 1913 it had 20,300 members, less than one-sixth of the white-collar workers organized in the DHV.

When the German commercial employees lost their sense of occupational community with the independent members of the old middle class and were exposed to economic insecurity, they slowly began to pursue their own interests collectively. The old "harmony associations" were inhibited from turning to energetic activity by the membership and influence of the principals. The repeal of the anti-socialist law in 1890 encouraged the emergence of local commercial trade unions, which were consolidated in 1897 in the Central Association of Male and Female Commercial Employees (Zentralverband der Handlungsgehilfen und Handlungsgehilfinnen, ZdH).[4] Because this organization considered salaried employees to be no more than proletarians, it rejected the idea of an independent, white-collar workers' movement and joined the General Commission of Free Trade Unions.

Like the technicians in Butib, the members of the ZdH "had to battle for two decades through a flood of employers' terror, persecution and punishments."[5] The ZdH stood for socialist principles and as early as 1911 advanced a thesis, widely discussed *after* World War I, that the introduction of office machines was equivalent in principle to the introduction of machines into the factory.[6] Members of the ZdH, however, were recruited from the young, lowest-paid personnel in commerce and consisted (after 1904) mainly of young women. The ZdH enjoyed no large success before World War I. By professing socialism the commercial employees would have risked adding to their economic insecurity the social stigma of proletarian membership. Their old, shaken, middle position between the classes disposed them to reject the reputedly anti-national proletariat and socialism. In 1912 the ZdH had still fewer members than the Association of German Merchants.

Leadership of the commercial employees who had begun to notice the opposition between their interests and those of the principals was assumed not by the ZdH, whose leaders quoted Karl Marx, but by the German National Association of Commercial Clerks at Hamburg (DHV), whose intellectual creators were Adolf Wagner and the court preacher Adolf Stöcker. The association was founded in 1893 to oppose the Social Democratic agitation among commercial employees. According to paragraph 1, section 5 of its constitution, the association's mission was "to resist the entry of Social Democracy into the commercial occupation."[7] In waging this fight, however, the anti-semitic leaders of the DHV had to adopt many of the social policy aims of the SPD and ZdH, including, for example, the legal determination of a maximum working day, legal establishment of a free Sunday, legal notice of job termination, regulation of apprenticeship training, and so forth.

The DHV exerted a remarkable attraction over the German white-collar workers by combining radical, sociopolitical aims with loudly professed anti-semitism, anti-feminism, nationalistic-*völkisch* views, and constantly repeated claims to social respect, that is, to social and moral superiority over the socialist blue-collar workers. The salaried employees dreaded proletarianization and despised Social Democrats and Jews. From the beginning the DHV battled the SPD and ZdH with words that would appear a generation later in Streicher's NSDAP paper, *Der Stürmer*. Thus, in an 1895 broadsheet titled "A Word to All German Commercial Clerks," the anti-semite Johann Irwahn spoke of the necessary "relentless struggle of labor against capitalism. . . . Everywhere we can see the consequences of this struggle; we observe how the clerks are being increasingly pushed out of the middle class and into the ranks of the proletariat." To justify his agitation against female employees, who could acquire membership in the DHV as easily as "Jews and persons proven to be descended from Jews" (paragraph 2 of the DHV charter), Irwahn readily resorted to innuendo. It was well known, he wrote, that in shops with female employees some merchants would "secretly introduce for their private use a certain Oriental institution, which is prohibited with us; see the cases of Rosenthal, Singer, Tietz, Gattel, etc."[8]

The DHV was very successful not only because of its streamlined organization and energetic representation of the occupational interests of its members but also because of its political orientation. In 1905 it was the largest organization of white-collar workers in Germany. By 1912 it had 130,000 members. Despite a temporary decline after 1918, it maintained its dominant position during the Weimar Republic.

The main characteristic of DHV ideas and policy was their linkage of anti-proletarian and trade union views. Although the DHV accepted principals as members until 1918, it nonetheless represented the interests of commercial employees against entrepreneurs who acted "anti-socially." Even so, however, it also sought to maintain the social distance between white- and blue-collar workers. In this way the association constructed a national policy which could incorporate its commitment to A. Stoecker's "pure socialism," that is, a socialism freed "of all Marxist dross."[9]

The Christian-Social movement, which Stoecker had tried to launch among Berlin workers during the crisis that followed Germany's unification in 1871, quickly foundered because of Social Democratic resistance. Johann Most, a man of the proletariat, demagogically advised Stoecker, the child of the people, to settle his account with heaven and not with the workers. In a modified form, with even stronger emphasis on anti-semitism, Stoecker's ideas proved influential within the middle class.[10]

The founders of the DHV had realized "that Social Democracy would undoubtedly prevail among the commercial clerks if it continued to be the only expression of trade union thought. In order to compete with Social Democratic ideas, the DHV founders countered with anti-semitism, which eventually proved superior in its appeal to the commercial employees. No matter how repugnant it may seem today, anti-semitism was ideal for use in unionizing the commercial clerks."[11] From the beginning, the DHV attracted anti-semitic male clerks. Its leaders also came exclusively from anti-semitic political parties and from the youth leagues. The DHV sought with increasing urgency to influence social policies that benefited commercial employees, in order to compete with the ZdH. As a result its trade union activities became more important. To be sure, until the post-World War I period these activities were mitigated by some concern for the interests of social strata that did not belong to the working class, but they were at the same time facilitated by the conviction that in economic policy the solidarity of interests between white-collar workers and entrepreneurs was stronger than that between white- and blue-collar workers.

Before 1914, in many white-collar organizations that accepted principals as members, the interest of commercial capitalists in free trade was compatible with the consumer interest of the salaried employees in low food prices. Accordingly, these organizations opposed agricultural tariffs prior to World War I and reproached the DHV because its functionaries in the Reichstag supported protectionist policies to the detriment of salaried employees. Bechly, the leader of the DHV, rejected these attacks in 1911 by alleging first that the DHV was not interested in economic policy, and second that economic policy had to be judged in the following terms: "Are commerce and industry capable of increasing the employees' share in the profits [sic] derived from increased capital gains . . . ? I believe we can answer this question in the affirmative. But if we do, are we then to demand that the whole economic policy be fundamentally changed only to obtain for the salaried employees a less expensive food basket?"[12]

A trade union ideology, essentially different from that of the DHV, did not take root among commercial employees in Germany. In 1908 Butib made a futile effort to organize commercial employees in industry into a trade union that would be neither anti-semitic nor organizationally allied with the labor movement, but would instead follow the trade union principles of Butib. The effort failed because it was opposed, although for different reasons, by all white-collar workers' associations, including the ZdH.[13]

Until the outbreak of World War I only a narrow segment of white-collar workers underwent radicalization. Most salaried employees, including the large majority of those organized, rejected any solidarity with blue-collar workers. In the endless debates over the 1911 law that dealt with social insurance for salaried employees, the middle-class character of white-collar workers received frequent emphasis. This view was taken not only by salaried employees adhering to an anti-proletarian orientation, but also by politicians and government officials hoping to make white-collar workers indebted to the state through special welfare measures, and by those entrepreneurs who wanted to prevent solidarity of blue- and white-collar workers by means of a special social insurance for the latter.

World War I stimulated unionization to some extent. This was due in part to the economic and social deterioration of the conditions of life, a development from which salaried employees suffered more than workers. In part, the so-called "limited slide to the left" by the white-collar workers was a manifestation of war-weariness and of the political exasperation which spread increasingly to large portions of the German people.[14] The revolutionary events in Russia, military defeat, and, above all, the political collapse of the empire, all contributed to a structural transformation of the employees' movement and, for a while, to a veritable boom in unionization.

While the overall costs of living increased by about 30 percent between the outbreak of the war and the end of 1915, even the nominal salaries of employees decreased by comparison with the wages of workers. Neither the absolute deterioration of white-collar workers' income relative to higher prices nor its relative deterioration compared with the average income of blue-collar workers was a passing phenomenon—like the mass unemployment among salaried employees shortly after the outbreak of the war. The economic insecurity of white-collar workers continued until the end of the war to impair their traditional notions of themselves as assistants to the principal in smaller firms and as private civil servants in larger enterprises. Also, their labor conditions were more proletarian than they had been prior to the war because the entrepreneurs relentlessly exploited both their low levels of unionization and the rifts between existing associations. Entrepreneurs reduced the real income of white-collar workers and abolished many of their privileges in the office. Because they paid lower salaries to female employees than to their male colleagues, the increasing employment of girls and women appeared inevitably as a means of lowering incomes. Employers did little or nothing to alleviate concerns over re-employment after the war among salaried employees who had been drafted. Many white-collar workers sank down below the economic level of the workers. Thus, a restructuring of the labor force occurred at the expense of the employees and in favor of manual workers. This was especially true in the war industries, but it was not confined to them.

The measures that the employees' associations adopted to counter the economic hardships of their members began to jeopardize their traditional, trusting relationship with employers in the middle-class associations and at the same time led to a noticeable growth in membership of the real employees' trade unions, especially Butib, the ZdH, and the Verband der Büroangestellten. From 1913 to 1918 the Afa associations increased from 80,000 to 146,000 members, whereas the total membership of middle-class commercial associations decreased from 450,000 to 437,000.[15]

White-collar workers demanded minimum salaries and cost-of-living increases, collectively petitioned over the food situation, and supported common resolutions on the application of the auxiliary service law. To be sure, radical workers sharply opposed the compulsory character of this law by mass actions, although the majority parties in the Reichstag and the top functionaries of the workers' unions were convinced of its necessity. Also, the rejection of strikes, which the middle-class employees' organizations had guarded as being in bad taste, had already been weakened during the war due to the intransigence of the employers. Finally, organizational consolidations countered the splintering division of the employees' movement into many associations.

The Study Group (Arbeitsgemeinschaft), founded as early as 1913 to promote a unified law for salaried employees, united the small, radical associations of white-collar workers and became the forerunner of the free trade unionist Afa-Bund. In the middle-class camp, the DHV and the Verein für Handlungs-Kommis von 1858, the two largest associations, concluded an agreement in May 1915 that ended their competition and jurisdictional disputes. In July 1916 a unified organization for the labor exchange of commercial clerks was created and, finally, on 8 October 1916 the great Arbeitsgemeinschaft der kaufmännischen Verbände was founded. It comprised eleven associations with a total of 600,000 members[16] and served the large majority of commercial employees not only vis-à-vis the organizationally solidified interests of the employers but also in dealing with the mass organization of manual labor.

Beginning on 15 October 1917 Hans Bechly of the DHV served as president of the Arbeitsgemeinschaft. During its first nationwide meeting on 10 March 1918 he delivered his programmatic speech against the SPD's endeavor "to pull us down into the mass (of workers)" and against the organized entrepreneurs who treated the salaried employees as though they were laborers.[17] A unanimous resolution was passed calling upon employers to lift the salary levels of white-collar workers "so that it will be possible for the salaried employees to maintain their bourgeois middle position in economic life." Despite the considerable shrinkage of income and despite the refusal of industrialists to negotiate with the Arbeitsgemeinschaft—as they did with the labor unions—those attending the meeting jointly declared that: "We shall not need to change our tactics for this reason. We do not want to chase utopias and, conscious of our responsibility, we refuse to turn violently against the present circumstances by transferring the workers' tactic to the movement of salaried employees. After all, this is not yet how matters stand in our profession."[18]

The entrepreneurs nonetheless tried to arrest the collective efforts of salaried employees during the war by various means, including disciplinary punishments, dismissals of organized employees, and, above all, by supporting existing company unions or founding new ones in order to further the interests of capital under the guise of an alleged compromise between employers and employees.[19]

But the radicalization of some white-collar groups during World War I cannot be attributed exclusively to economic and social causes. General political developments also had a destabilizing effect upon German society. Despite patriotic exuberance at the beginning of the war, weariness spread throughout the nation when victory and peace disappeared from view. Discontent with coal, clothing, and food shortages was especially high in the large cities, a condition made worse by domestic mismanagement and the enemy blockade. In addition, bitter controversies were expressed over war aims and the electoral reform in Prussia, where voting rights still depended on income. The big cities suffered a shortage of edible fats, while on the farms axles were being greased with butter. However, the enmity between city and countryside, which surfaces in all emergency situations of industrial society, embittered the masses less than the political controversies, which suggested to them ideological resolutions derived from the familiar model of class struggles. Peace by victory and social exploitation appeared to belong together, just as a negotiated peace seemed to belong with social reform. Labor organized in the free trade unions was close to the SPD, but the leaders of the SPD and the trade unions were impeded by patriotism, the proclaimed social truce, office, and age from transforming the discontent of the masses into radical action.

Some elements of the labor force, including the functionaries and members of the ZdH, were attracted to the more radical USPD. In large political strikes not called for by trade union leaders, they dragged blue- and white-collar workers into the streets despite the proclaimed social truce. On 28 June 1916, the day of Karl Liebknechts' court-martial, a one-day protest strike took place for the accused. He had won the hearts of many workers and employees, who had no sympathies for the Spartacus League but were taken by Liebknecht's intrepid advocacy of peace. By the end of 1916 discontent with the auxiliary service law had increased among blue- and radical white-collar workers, and in May 1917 200,000 workers struck in Berlin to protest the inadequate supply of food. At the same time the demands of strikers in Leipzig, where the USPD was strongly represented, pertained not only to economic matters—inadequate supplies of food and coal at lower prices and repeal of the auxiliary service law—but also to important political aims, including "a government declaration of its readiness to conclude peace immediately and renunciation of any open or hidden annexation, . . . repeal of martial law and censorship, . . . the immediate lifting of all restrictions of the right to assemble and to form associations and coalitions, . . . universal, equal, secret, and direct franchise to vote for all public corporate bodies in the Reich, the states, and communities."[20] Five of the seven items in the strikers' program referred to political reforms. In July 1917 the majority in the Reichstag passed its resolution on peace.

Following the October revolution in Russia, hundreds of thousands of workers struck in Vienna, Budapest, and other industrial cities of Austria-Hungary. Despite military censorship the excitement seized German workers as well. On 28 January 1918 400,000 workers in Greater Berlin ceased to work. The next day the number of strikers exceeded a half million. The strike spread to so many other big cities that the USPD finally estimated the number of strikers to be above one million. The program of the strike coincided with the demands in Leipzig in 1917, the only new demand being "participation of representatives of labor from all countries in the peace negotiations." This new demand can be explained by the fact that socialists were part of the government in England, France, and Belgium, whereas Germany was ruled by a military dictatorship. Although the still less-than-revolutionary strike demands did not differ from the political aims of the SPD, which together with the USPD was represented on the action committee, the strike was ruthlessly crushed by General Ludendorff. Mass arrests were made, seven large enterprises in Berlin were put under military management, thousands of workers were called up for military service, and meetings were dissolved by the police. On 3 February 1918 the strike collapsed. It was a severe defeat for the majority in the Reichstag, but a triumph for Ludendorff and the supporters of peace through victory.

All things considered, "the limited slide" of white-collar workers toward the left during the war must not be understood as a consequence of economic hardships, but as part of the general political scene. Germany waged war with a feudalized heavy industry and a pre-industrial social structure. In the bitter debates over war aims, the imperialist desires of the ruling strata for annexation were opposed not only by the yearning of the masses for peace, but also by the death that democratically embraced the whole nation on the battlefields of an undemocratic social structure.

In evaluating the slide toward the left by the salaried employees it must also be emphasized that theirs was a split movement. Associations such as the ZdH and Butib were class-conscious and socialistic. In party politics they stood to the left of the SPD, stressing the social similarity of blue- and white-collar workers. For these associations the slide toward the left by the salaried employees meant primarily an increase in membership. In the middle-class associations, however, limited radicalization did not mean greater closeness to manual labor. Instead, functionaries and members of these associations believed as strongly as ever before that they would be able to eschew proletarianization and were obligated to fight socialism.

XII White-Collar Unionization in the Early Weimar Republic

Genuine unionization of salaried employees occurred only as a consequence of the November revolution in 1918. On 15 November 1918 the German employers' associations, including those in heavy industry, reached an agreement with the German Commission of Trade Unions and with the most important remaining trade unions. This agreement established parity in labor relations; the entrepreneurs no longer insisted on being masters of the house. Fearing the chaos of the revolution, they sought to assuage the trade unions and receive their protection by accepting their principal demands. The trade unions were recognized as parties to labor contracts and the "yellow" organizations were no longer to be supported by the employers. Working conditions were to be established through collective bargaining, and the eight-hour working day was introduced. Also, demobilization and maintenance of economic life were to be regulated by a central committee established on the principle of parity.

On 4 December 1918 the Central Commission of Industrial and Commercial Employers and Employees was established. Soon thereafter, on 23 December, the Council of People's Delegates announced the legal validity of collective wage agreements, and finally, the Weimar constitution secured the right and ability of all unions to bargain collectively (article 165, section 1, second sentence).

In view of this social upheaval, on which the power of trade unions in the new state was founded, the middle-class associations of white-collar workers faced three possibilities for political action.

First, had they tried to maintain their traditional form of organization and continue their middle-class policy in a non-union manner, white-collar workers would have lost all influence in society. They would have relinquished initiative to the free trade unions, and soon would have atrophied to the status of convivial clubs with a small membership.

Second, it was at least theoretically possible for salaried workers to adapt to the new circumstances by abandoning their middle-class character to pursue trade union aims and even by accepting the political leadership of the free (socialist) trade unions. In this case, unified trade unions would eventually have emerged as happened under a different political label and in perverted form in 1933.

Both routes were impassable, due partly to the inertia that is characteristic of all social structures and that can be overcome only by force or catastrophe, and partly to the deeply rooted aversion of most salaried employees to the radical free trade unions. The latter appeared to reject middle-class, white-collar claims to prestige and privileges. They spoke instead of class struggle and nationalization, although despite the increase in their power they were unable to transform society in a revolutionary way.

Third, the middle-class associations were thus left with a compromise as their third possibility of reorientation: adaptation to the new circumstances, that is, unionization, but with a continuation of their anti-socialist policy and tenacious, ongoing struggle for the privileged status and social esteem of white-collar workers. Although unionization of middle-class organizations did not prevent them from pursuing their old social goals, it nonetheless was the tribute they paid to the new political conditions in order to protect their own interests and those of their members. Functionaries of middle-class associations openly conceded that their unionization was an adjustment to prevailing political conditions rather than economic and social deterioration. Thus, the first annual report of the GdA said of the Arbeitsgemeinschaft kaufmännischer Verbände (Union of Commercial Associations), which all important middle-class organizations, including the DHV, had joined, that "the union was forced by the direction of change to alter its organizational base and to make a clear distinction between genuine salaried employees' organizations and the associations which admitted principals as members."[1] Many white-collar workers of lower and intermediate rank probably welcomed unionization when confronted with the political upheaval that followed four years of war. The situation was different, however, for employees of higher rank and for academicians.[2] Even the non-executive white-collar workers in the DHV and GdA rejected political radicalism, despite their own unionization. This rejection was pressed less aggressively by the GdA than by the DHV, but even the GdA energetically pursued the preservation of the salaried employees' superior social prestige.

The political upheaval led to consolidations of both right-wing and left-wing organizations of technical and commercial employees, and to a massive influx of previously unorganized white-collar workers into the left-wing associations united in the Afa-Bund. For example, Butib increased its membership from 30,000 near the end of 1918 to 48,000 on 1 April 1919. In May 1919, after merging with the Deutscher Techniker Verband, it changed its name to Butab and advocated "the economic liberation of the entire working class."[3] Due partly to the merger and partly to new membership, its ranks swelled to 100,000 by the fall of 1919.

Equally remarkable was the growth of the ZdA. Its membership had increased somewhat during the war, but in the first quarter of 1919 it shot up from 66,000 to 138,000 persons.

Many young male and, even more noticeably, female white-collar workers joined free salaried employees' associations, while the two other umbrella organizations newly formed in 1919 and 1920—the Christian-Social Gesamtverband Deutscher Angestelltengewerkschaften (Gedag) and the GdA, which was close to the Deutsche Demokratische Partei (DDP)—initially lagged behind the Afa-Bund. It is impossible to determine whether this radicalization was more attributable to economic and political developments during the war or to the revolution, which was itself caused by these developments as well as by military events and the course of foreign policy. In any event, the great majority of the joiners were undisciplined in trade union affairs and quit the radical associations during the next few years. Nevertheless, enthusiasts in 1919 believed that strata awakened from political indifference—"youth," railwaymen, agricultural workers, salaried employees—were "the standard bearers of the revolution."[4]

Among people who were influential in the trade unions or in politics, all associations that still followed the old middle-class style by accepting principals as members were now termed "yellow." As a result, the middle-class associations of white-collar workers decided to acknowledge that their members were indeed members of the labor force—something they had not only previously denied, but sometimes denied in a doctrinaire manner. The organizational focus of the associations was changed accordingly. Economically independent persons could no longer acquire membership in the harmony associations of prewar days. Collective salary agreements (instead of individual contracts) and even strikes were now defended and justified by associations that had been intransigently middle-class in character.[5] Associations that had restricted membership to specified highly qualified employees now admitted colleagues from the lower ranks. Thus, the Deutscher Techniker Verband, even prior to its fusion with Butib, extended its membership roster beyond middle-school technicians to include draftsmen and technical office employees, who had been excluded before the revolution. Emil Lederer, the most qualified, contemporary scientific observer of the white-collar workers movement, considered this democratization of the association a more important innovation than the acceptance of the right to strike, "which had risen in rank, as it were, during the war and could no longer be dismissed contemptuously as a 'proletarian weapon.' "[6] The DHV, which now excluded entrepreneurs from membership, did not push democratization to the point of accepting women, Jews, or colleagues descended from Jews as members. Women's work in particular led to "the deterioration of the race," according to the DHV journal in July 1919.[7]

It appeared to the middle-class associations that in 1919 the strike "lost its stigma for the first time in the history of the movement of white-collar workers."[8] The first important strike of salaried employees took place in the metal industry of Berlin from 2 to 19 April 1919, and was fueled primarily by the demand that white-collar workers share in decisions to hire, fire, and give notice. The Afa-Bund and, in retrospect, the GdA as well, spoke of the "industrial agitators Borsig and v. Siemens," who opposed this demand.[9] The strike of the bank employees from 8 to 19 April was based on similar demands.[10]

Big strikes also took place in other cities, such as Lübeck, Mühlheim-Ruhr, Leipzig, Ludwigshafen, Mannheim, and Hamburg. "Alle Räder stehen still, wenn dein starker Arm es will" (All wheels stand still if your strong arm wills it)—in these words the journal of a nationalist employees' association celebrated the strike[11] as a new weapon which, it proclaimed, would be effective against the entrepreneurs in the prevailing situation.[12] The employees' strike in Lübeck was against twenty-five firms, that is, almost all of industry. After three days the entrepreneurs had to tell the blue-collar workers that their continued employment was impossible. Employees in the central German mining industry had similar experiences. Thus, in addition to being successful vis-à-vis the entrepreneurs, the strikes by salaried employees seemed to contain an important lesson regarding the relationship between white- and blue-collar workers. This lesson was especially welcome to middle-class employees. Their functionaries had spread the view that social power had passed during the revolution from the entrepreneurs to radical labor. "The salaried employees only exchanged one dependence for another. Yes, they changed a pressing dependence for a more pressing one."[13] Bechly, the president of the DHV, was of the opinion that the revolution had replaced "the old state of social classes" not by a people's state but by another "one-sided class state of the Social Democratic workers. . . . The pursuit of their own advantages by the classes, that happen to have political power, is much, much more shameless, than before."[14]

Indeed, blue-collar workers adhered noticeably to their old distrust of white-collar workers. As the law on shop councils was being prepared, blue-collar workers demanded the right to co-determine the hiring and firing of salaried employees. They sought to consolidate white- and blue-collar social insurance programs, and tried in the National Assembly to delay extending the salary limit on the employees' social insurance, which was to secure its financial viability. They wanted to abolish the independent health insurance of the white-collar workers in order to force them into the public health insurance program. Spokesmen for the middle-class employees admitted with remarkable candor that "the main obstacles to the full socialization of salaried employees, which their enemies strive for, are the social insurance created for the salaried employees and the specific stipulations in various insurance laws that take account of the special characteristics of the salaried employees."[15]

Even the Austrian socialist Karl Renner once declared in a speech to white-collar workers that

> the intellectual workers [needed a militant organization] (1) vis-à-vis the state and its legislation, (2) vis-à-vis the organized entrepreneurs, and (3) in relation to the workers." [He added,] "You may be surprised that I, a Social Democrat, say this. But as a Social Democrat I am far removed from onesidedness. . . . Organized labor is strong, the organized entrepreneurs are strong. You are in the middle and therefore have the right to be equally organized and in every respect be so strong that you will not be ground down between two millstones.[16]

Salaried employees provided confirmation of this opinion in judging their own strikes shortly after the revolution. They triumphantly concluded from their experiences in Lübeck "that the strike by salaried employees is a sword which simultaneously hits the employers to the right and the workers to the left"![17] "We need no other proof in order to know that salaried employees and [in particular] commercial employees can also assert and maintain themselves today in the midst of all turmoil if they act in solidarity."[18] Such utterances came close to praising the "class struggle"—between white- and blue-collar workers!

When labor reproached middle-class employees for standing in the camp of the class enemy, the middle-class associations pointed out that radical white-collar workers, many of whom supported the USPD and whose radicalism often surpassed that of labor, pursued the aims of manual workers and not of salaried employees. The conflict defied a political solution. Whichever political alternative was selected by the employees and their associations, they stood to be accused of social treason. Their decision would be taken either as acceptance of capitalist domination or as unconditional solidarity with the workers. Although independent employees' associations did exist, they differed from those of manual labor and, with the principle of harmony abandoned, also kept their distance from the entrepreneurs. Any political or economic decisions were made in the shadow of the old social conflict between capitalist and anti-capitalist forces. This conflict split the body of employees because their social characteristics did not generate any politically integrative forces. The salaried employees did not find a political position of their own because they were too socially heterogeneous and too numerically weak to act independently. Bound by tradition to middle-class thinking and to the capitalist economy, they were, when they did break away from tradition, either irresistibly attracted or deeply disturbed by the socialist workers' movement and its utopian conception of the future.

In domestic policy the difference between organized white- and blue-collar workers became unmistakably clear soon after the revolution. The DHV was a prominent social conduit for the stab-in-the-back legend,[19] which traced responsibility for Germany's defeat in the war not to fighting at the front but to radical opposition at home. This legend undermined the authority of the new German republic and its government. The GdA was more moderate than the DHV, but it also showed its lack of commitment to the Weimar Republic when Wolfgang Kapp attempted to restore the monarchy by a coup d'état (the Kapp Putsch). Whereas the free trade unions of blue- and white-collar workers called a general strike in order to fight this reactionary peril, the GdA left action to its members.[20]

In the debates over nationalization and the law concerning shop councils—the two most important economic policy struggles to emerge shortly after the revolution—the middle-class employees affirmed their commitment to capitalism and thus weakened the fight against it. In the debates on nationalization they participated only by warning and procrastinating. Circumstances demanded that they do more than reject every proposal, but even their counter-proposals contained more criticism of plans for trenchant economic changes than they did constructive suggestions. In their search for arguments with which to defend the interests of white-collar workers against nationalization, they happened upon two ideas in the storehouse of liberalism: that the bureaucratization of the economy posed a general danger to white-collar interests, and most especially, that salaried employees' chances for social ascent would be considerably diminished by nationalization. Their confidence in capitalism was stronger than their reservations over a promised future about which only one thing was certain: that the workers fought for it. The opportunities offered by the private economy had the advantage of familiarity, and the memories of imperial Germany did not fade at once.

Many free employees' associations joined the workers in supporting nationalization. The radical proposal number one, that coal mining be fully socialized, was co-signed by Werner and Kaufmann, the representatives of Butab.
Werner was supported by the Afa-Bund,[21] although the DWV, the free association
of foremen, remained reserved.[22] Except for the ZdA and the Allgemeiner Verband der deutschen Bankangestellten, the commercial employees' organizations
opposed nationalization. The DHV tried to discredit it as mechanical interference
with the organic structure of the economy, seldom disagreeing much with the
entrepreneurs in general debates on economic policy. In a carefully formulated
assessment, the DHV pointed out that "commercial employees who hitherto
had had rather good chances for advancement in industrial firms would have to
face barriers in the socialized enterprise." The DHV feared not only bureaucratization but "a complete change in the mentality of the salaried employee."[23]

Similarly, the GdA, which was not represented on the Commission on
Nationalization, rejected both moderate and radical proposals of the commission.
This association also pointed to the danger of bureaucratization and to the fearful
risk that chances for advancement and independence would be diminished.[24]
Wilhelm Bergmann, a member of both the GdA directorate and the seven-man
Commission of the Reich Economic Council charged with examining proposals
for nationalization, advanced a substitute proposal of his own on "the imple-
mentation of taxation" in relevant cases.[25]

The concern expressed by employees in the debate over nationalization
were repeated to some extent in the fight over the law on shop councils. The
law's advocates and opponents came into especially sharp conflict over two points.

First, the middle-class associations considered matters of social policy to be
of primary importance in a law on shop councils. In accordance with their support
of "a social, just capitalism," they understood the right of the shop councils to
co-determination as a protection against autocratic behavior by the employer.

After it was passed, the law on shop councils was so quickly obscured, distorted, and partly destroyed by the administration of justice that it scarcely remained recognizable. Had it been fully implemented, it would have weakened
the economic power of the entrepreneurs. The law on shop councils had emerged
from the struggle of socialist employees against the government and the entrepreneurs: strikes had provided the final impetus to legal regulation.[26] Strengthening
the economic-policy function of the law was possible only from a radically socialist
perspective inasmuch as it presupposed both recognition of a fundamental opposition between entrepreneurs and employees as well as the will to overcome
this opposition.

The attitude of middle-class employees' organizations toward placing shop-council members on the board of directors testifies to their rejection or mis-understanding of the potential economic consequence of the law and to their appraisal of its sociopolitical value alone. The attitude of Gustav Schneider, leader of the GdA, was typical. Schneider was especially active in the National Assembly on the law concerning shop councils, whereas the DHV had virtually no influence, for its representatives sat on the benches of the rightist political parties, which rejected the law on shop councils altogether. Important leaders of the Afa-Bund belonged to the USPD, which worked in vain for a more rev-olutionary legislation and eventually rejected the whole law because of the com-promise it represented. It is impossible to say how far Gustav Schneider, as a member of the DDP, was also restricted by consideration for the wholesale trade interests in his party. On 18 January 1920, the law was passed with 213 votes against 64 dissents. Except for two stray deputies, the German National Party (DNVP), the People's Party (DVP), and the radical socialists (USPD) voted against; the SPD, the Catholic Center Party and the Democrats (DDP) voted for the law. Of the Democrats, however, only 39 percent of the deputies were present when the votes were cast, as against 66 percent of the Center Party and 73.5 percent of the entire house.[27] In any event, because of the prevailing coalition in the assembly, Schneider's influence upon the law was much greater than the im-portance of the GdA indicated.

According to Schneider, something could be said in favor of the entrepre-neurs' reservations about representation of the shop council on the board of directors.[28] The board represented capital, he said, and it was doubtful that an addition of labor representatives was "the organic way leading to the contact of both interest groups, desirable as such contact was in principle." Moreover, he continued, the relevant regulations invited entrepreneurs to evade the law and could lead to a deterioration of business morals. Moreover, "every unnecessary impediment" to industrial activity could inflict serious damage upon the total economy and therefore upon the employees. The DDP proposed that, instead of sending shop-council members to the board of directors, the shop council be given the right to have board meetings convened by the chairman of the board. In such meetings complaints about management and organizational questions concerning the firm could be discussed in the presence of one or two shop-council members possessing the right to vote. This proposal, like Schneider's critique of §70 of the law on shop councils, would relinquish the employees' activities in the field of economic policy. The whole problem was decided as one of social policy from the vantage point of "contact" between the two interest groups. Schneider expected that the boards of directors would find means of weakening the consequences of the law in economic policy, and he proved to be correct. Certain negotiations were relegated by the boards to committees from which representatives of the shop councils were excluded.[29]

The second point causing sharp conflict was that, owing to pressure exercised by the middle-class organizations, and again especially to Gustav Schneider's initiative, the salaried employees were protected by the law on shop councils from being permanently at the mercy of blue-collar majorities on the councils. Special councils of salaried employees, which were not included in the original bill, were established. Again, the efforts to attain them were directed against both the entrepreneurs and, with no less resoluteness, against manual labor. For example, in the first agreements between the Reich Labor Department and the Action Committee of the General Strike in Central Germany, the organizations of employees and the representatives of the employers (4 and 5 May 1919 in Weimar) arranged for shop councils to be elected by blue- and white-collar workers together. In this way those salaried employees who were politically distant from the workers could be neutralized. Opposing these plans, Schneider and the GdA, which was bypassed in the original negotiations, demanded that shop councils be composed according to a principle of parity. In effect, "parity" meant superimposing the qualitative significance of the salaried employees in the economy on the democratic principle of voting. In addition, the GdA demanded separate elections for blue- and white-collar workers. The workers' distrust of salaried employees found extreme expression in their demand that the employees join "the old proletariat" in principle, but the middle-class white-collar workers' associations were joined by the socialist Afa-Bund in objecting to this "craze of leveling on the part of manual labor."[30]

The first draft of the bill drawn up by legal reporters abolished the old committees of salaried employees. The middle-class associations of white-collar workers passionately demanded their preservation and enlargement. However, not only the socialists but also the Center Party deemed Schneider's demands unreasonable because they amounted to a multi-voting right for salaried employees in the shop council elections, that is, to the establishment of "potential equality" of blue- and white-collar workers, much like the concept of equality with which the Prussian Department of the Interior had attempted to solve the problem of political elections during the war. Schneider emphasized that salaried employees must be treated not according to their numbers but according to their economic contribution. It went without saying "that the salaried employees in an establishment were of precisely the same importance to the firm as the manual workers.

By striking, manual labor can render the salaried workers in a firm unemployed, but conversely, the salaried employees, by laying down their work, can prevent the workers from working. (Shout: You're doing it already!) That too has happened. In the Central German mining industry."[31] Deputy Koenen (USPD) had polemically pointed out before that Schneider, like "the gentlemen on the extreme right, who so favor the 'divide and rule' strategy," consciously or unconsciously furthers "the interests of the entrepreneurs."[32]

Inasmuch as the prevailing social stratification had influenced the structure of the legislating body, it also was reflected in the law on shop councils. For a correct appraisal of the social forces which influenced the origin and content of this law, the role played by representatives of the white-collar workers must be considered. The law had become a compromise and was therefore regarded differently by the various employees' associations even within the Afa-Bund, that is, as "tremendous progress" by the DWV, and as "a demagogic, botched piece of work" by Butab.[33]

Despite unionization, the middle-class associations tried not to depart too far from their middle-class orientations during the sociopolitical struggles of the postwar period. Often they pressed for the maintenance of old privileges, the establishment of new ones, and the prevention of equalization with manual labor. Occasionally they failed because of resistance by the political left. Frequently they succeeded, because of parliamentary cross-ties with representatives of the entrepreneurs. Two more important examples may be cited as illustrations.

When the 1922 law on labor exchanges was debated, two views clashed both in the Reich Economic Council and in the Reichstag. Free trade unions and the SPD considered it appropriate to include white-collar workers in the public monopoly of the labor exchanges. Large portions of the salaried employees joined the employers in either rejecting this regulation in general—for example, the academicians—or in demanding at least the continued independence of professional labor exchanges run by the associations. The DHV was especially active in supporting the professional exchanges.[34] Der Arbeitgeber, a journal of the employers, wrote, "Thus it was inevitable that many regulations were incorporated into the law against the will of the Socialists."[35]

In 1927, when the law on unemployment insurance was passed, the old struggle flared up again.[36] The middle-class associations, united in the so-called Committee of Seven, demanded that the auxiliary insurance plans (of the associations) be admitted into the state-run unemployment insurance program. The Afa-Bund and the ADGB were sharply opposed to this idea. The middle-class associations countered by contending that almost all special institutions and regulations favoring salaried employees had resulted from struggles against free trade union representatives, including the special insurance for salaried employees in 1911, the employees' councils in the 1920 law on shop councils, the employees' departments in the 1922 law on labor exchanges, and the 1926 law for miners.

The great crisis did not draw blue- and white-collar workers together into a community of interests over auxiliary unemployment insurances. The GdA and DHV were indefatigable in demanding them, basing their arguments primarily on the financial necessity of keeping the better insurance risks of salaried employees separate from the worse risks of blue-collar workers.

Finally, an example may serve to demonstrate the efforts of middle-class associations to use their arrangements for self-help in order to maintain the social superiority of white-collar workers. The health insurance programs of the associations competed with the general public health insurance.[37] They took from it relatively good risk groups and emphasized the social separation of white-collar workers from manual labor. In a small advertising pamphlet for its health insurance, the DHV presented two contrasting photographs. The first showed a man wearing the characteristically wide trousers of a carpenter facing the entrance of a "General Hospital." The second showed a gentleman, who could be identified as such by his pressed trousers and by the attaché case under his arm. With all signs of alacrity, an assistant physician in a white frock was opening a portal on which a sign visibly announced "Private Clinic Professor Dr. med. . . ." The worker on the first photo had to open the door himself. Written propaganda for the special health insurance of the DHV offered similar encouragement for the clerk to join: "Among others, the greatest thinker of our nation testifies to the fact that intellectual work can be stymied by illness. In one of his works he reports that a catarrh combined with headaches had disorganized him, as it were, for mental work, or at least had made him weak and dull." The pamphlet was referring to Immanuel Kant!

For enlisting new members the associations offered prizes in the form of books, other goods, and cash. The GdA introduced a special point system for this purpose. It credited the recruiter with two points, equaling RM 2 for every new member, but three points for every new applicant to join its health insurance. The DHV also rewarded successful recruiting for its health insurance. Indeed, its propaganda for health insurance was a more urgent concern than its recruiting propaganda. Thus, what unionization amounted to was revealed in the point system. Even the free, socialist employees' associations cultivated their health insurance plans, if only because they had to compete with other organizations. The ZdA especially incurred difficulties in this competition because a relatively large proportion of its members were enrolled in the public health insurance system.

Between 1918 and 1919 membership in the DHV increased from 148,000 to 208,000. The increase in Afa-Bund membership was even more impressive, quadrupling from 94,000 to 366,000. The revolutionary boom did not last for the Afa-Bund, however. Only two years later, in 1921, the middle-class associations (DHV and GdA) had 565,000 members, whereas only 313,000 white-collar workers were members of the Afa-Bund. Soon thereafter the DHV regained its old absolute numerical preponderance in the movement of Germany's white-collar workers.

The DHV's organization was efficient. Its political power rested on parliamentary cross-connections reaching from the Center Party to the NSDAP. For example, in September 1930 representatives of the DHV were well distributed in the Reichstag with Stöhr and Forster from the NSDAP, Lambach from the Conservative People's Party, Rippel from the Christian-Social Party, Thiel and Glatzel from the DVP, and Gerig from the Center Party. After the DHV stopped supporting Hugenberg's reactionary DNVP, its deputies in the Reichstag, the parliaments of the *Länder* (states), and the communal bodies decreased in number. In 1926, of the DHV's 1391 parliamentarians, 302 were members of the DNVP, 291 belonged to the DVP, 101 were members of *völkisch* parties, and 98 belonged to the Center. By the end of 1931 the total number of DHV parliamentarians had been reduced to 1078, but the NSDAP members had more than doubled to 210. DHV representatives at the DVP had declined to 118, a reduction of almost two-thirds, while its representation at the DNVP had been reduced to zero. The number of DHV members who had become parliamentarians through votes for consolidated lists of various middle-class parties had dropped from 745 in 1926 to 451 in 1931.[38] The DHV reached a large population beyond its membership through its public relations work, which was distributed by journals and large book publishing houses.[39] Its economic power resided in a concern that comprised banks, insurance companies, book publishers, and other enterprises.[40]

In short, the salient feature of the unionization of salaried employees at the beginning of the Weimar Republic was not their proletarianization. Nor was it the fact that the overwhelming majority of organized white-collar workers now used trade union methods to improve their situation in the capitalist economy. Similar efforts were undertaken by the foremen, most of whom were organized in the Afa-Bund, by many of the workers organized in the ADGB, and by members of the other two umbrella organizations of the workers. Only a small radical minority wanted to replace capitalism by a socialist order instead of reforming it. The politically decisive feature of white-collar trade union activity in the Weimar Republic was its animating purpose: to preserve the status and esteem of salaried employees vis-à-vis blue-collar workers. A strong, militant minority combined this trade union activity with anti-proletarian, anti-democratic, anti-semitic, anti-republican, and anti-feminist views. In 1929 the president of the DHV thundered against "the pacifist, Jewish and philistine exploiters of the Revolution on the left."[41]

While critics were aroused by the embourgeoisement of the workers and their functionaries,[42] they did not clearly recognize the political alienation of large parts of the new middle class from the institutions of the republic. One could term this phenomenon of alienation "debourgeoisement." But the salaried employees had really been subjects rather than citizens of the empire, and although they pursued their interests in the republic as trade unionists, many of them now were enemies of the state whose constitution guaranteed the power of trade unions. They despised the state and knew too little about the morality of citizens.

XIII White-Collar Associations in the Late Weimar Republic

Before the trade unions were destroyed in 1933, the following umbrella organizations of white-collar associations existed:

1. The Christian-national Gesamtverband der Angestelltengewerkschaften (Gedag) contained the DHV and VwA as its largest member associations. The associations united in Gedag formed together with the Christian trade union of the workers the Deutscher Gewerkschaftsbund (DGB).
2. The Liberal-national (Hirsch-Duncker) white-collar, blue-collar, and civil servants' associations were consolidated in the Gewerkschaftsring Deutscher Arbeiter-, Angestellten- und Beamtenverbände (Gwr). The largest association of the Gwr, and in fact, the largest of all the salaried employees' associations, was the GdA. The GdA was a "unified trade union" that, unlike the DHV, accepted female white-collar workers as members, and, unlike all other associations, comprised salaried employees of all kinds, including commercial and office employees, technicians, and foremen. In addition, the DBV and the AVV, the largest associations of bank clerks and insurance employees, respectively, played an important role in the Liberal-national Gwr.
3. The free associations of salaried employees were unified in the Allgemeiner Freier Angestelltenbund (Afa-Bund), which was consolidated in a cartel with the ADGB and the Allgemeiner Deutscher Beamtenbund. According to membership figures, the ZdA and the DWB were the most important associations in the Afa-Bund, but they were outstripped in importance by the numerically smaller Butab. The distribution of the organized white-collar workers among the three kinds of trade unions is shown in table 13.1.

In addition to these umbrella organizations of the trade unions and to the numerous, small, independent associations of salaried employees, two associations

of executive employees also existed. These were the Vereinigung leitender Angestellter (Vela) with about 30,000 members, and the Reichsbund Deutscher
Angestelltenberufsverbände with 47,964 members; the latter was relatively unimportant.

A survey of employee associations toward the end of the Weimar Republic
is an invaluable aid in understanding the political and ideological differentiation·
of the labor force (see table 13.1).

First, white-collar workers were proportionate to their total number more
organized than blue-collar workers. Disregarding both the independent associations to which about one-sixth of all organized salaried employees belonged
and the much less important independent, "yellow," and revolutionary associations of manual labor, almost 1.5 million white-collar workers confronted 5
million blue-collar workers organized in the three large trade union movements.
This means that about every third manual worker was organized, as compared
to 37 percent of the salaried employees.

The second major impression to be gleaned from table 13.1 is the appeal
of the socialist unions among the workers and the contrary preference for non-
and anti-socialist associations among the salaried employees. Of every ten or-

Table 13.1: Organizational Preferences of Salaried Employees and Workers, 1931

	SALARIED EMPLOYEES			WORKERS	
	Total Salaried Members	Female Members	% of All Salaried Employees	Total Worker Members	% of All Workers
Christian-National	593,800	93,432	34.1	689,472	13.2
Liberal-National	392,850	117,060	22.6	181,000	3.5
Free Trade Unions	465,591	109,331	26.8	4,104,285	79.0
Total Organized Employees & Workers	1,452,241	319,823	83.5	4,974,857	95.7
In addition:					
Communist, Syndicalist and other Revolutionary Unions	—	—	—	35,774	0.7
Neutral ("yellow")	—	—	—	123,083	2.4
Independent	286,530	66,472	15.5	62,034	1.2
Total	1,738,771	386,295	100.0	5,195,748	100.0
% of Organized Labor Force			25.1		74.9

SOURCE: *Statistisches Jahrbuch für das Deutsche Reich*, 1932, p. 555.

ganized blue-collar workers, eight belonged to free trade unions. Of every ten organized white-collar workers, approximately seven belonged to Christian-national and liberal-national associations, thus demonstrating their opposition to the free trade unions and to socialism. Contrary to labor, white-collar workers were inclined toward the Christian-national orientation. This fact assumes greater importance considering that the Christian workers were almost exclusively Catholic and constituents of the Center Party, whereas only a minority of the Christian-national white-collar workers were Catholic and most were politically allied with parties to the right of the Center.

Although it did not quite match their membership levels in the free trade unions, the proportion of white-collar workers to join liberal-national associations was almost seven times as high as that of laborers. Of the latter, only a small minority were members of liberal-national unions. White-collar workers even enjoyed an absolute numerical dominance in these unions, whereas blue-collar workers overwhelmed them with about nine times their numbers in the free trade unions.

The significance of the liberal-national unions of white-collar workers may be gleaned from their history. Their largest organization, the GdA, originated in 1919 in a merger of so-called harmony associations, to which most salaried employees belonged before the war. Similar origins are responsible for the high percentage of salaried employees in independent associations. Before the war a large number of small organizations had existed basically as clubs or as associations that comprised independents and the employees of small occupational groups.[1]

The weak position of the free trade unions—that is, the disinclination of salaried employees to accept socialistic ideas—becomes fully apparent once the ideological kinship of all other organizations is considered. All adhered to a more or less consistent middle-class doctrine. About three-fourths of all organized salaried employees were found in the middle-class camp. Thus, white-collar workers displayed a pattern of affiliation roughly opposed to that of workers. Measured by their membership in free trade unions, only a minority of the salaried employees embraced the proletarian conception of their position and of the capitalist social order.

Curiously, the picture is further clarified by examining the organizational affiliations of various occupational groups of salaried employees (tables 13.2–13.4). The middle-class, anti-socialist associations were strongest among commercial employees, while the free trade unions attracted primarily technicians and foremen. Proportionately, foremen were more highly organized than any other occupational groups. The non-radical DWV, which was affiliated with

Table 13.2: Unions of Commercial and Office Employees (end of 1931)

	Total		Female	
1. Christian-National				
German National Association of Commercial Clerks (Deutschnationaler Handlungsgehilfen-Verband, DHV)	409,022		—	
Association of Female Business and Office Employees (Verband der weiblichen Handels- und Büroangestellten, VwA)	92,390		92,389	
National Association of Office Employees (Reichsverband der Büroangestellten)	12,677		—	
TOTALS	514,089	47.4%	92,389	29.9%
2. Liberal-National				
Commercial Employees in the Federation of Salaried Employees (Gewerkschaftsbund der Angestellten, GdA)	298,500[a]		103,078	
German Bank Employees Association (Deutscher Bankbeamtenverein, DBV)	39,700		6,972	
General Association of Insurance Employees (Allgemeiner Verband der Versicherungsangestellten, AVV)	18,405		4,600	
TOTALS	356,605	32.9%	114,650	37.1%
3. Free Trade Unions				
Central Federation of Employees, (Zentralverband der Angestellten, ZdA)	203,489		102,007	
Central Association of German Bank Employees (Allgemeiner Verband der Deutschen Bankangestellten)	9,635		—	
TOTALS	213,124	19.7%	102,007	33.0%
CUMULATIVE TOTALS (1–3)	1,081,560	100	309,046	100

SOURCE: *Statistisches Jahrbuch für das Deutsche Reich*, 1932, p. 558.

ªThe figures for the DHV and the ZdA are taken from H. Hamm, "Die Wirtschaftlichen und sozialen Berufsmerkmale der kaufmännischen Angestellten," p. 44. The figures pertaining to the GdA are rough estimates. I have arrived at them as follows: of the 122,974 people included in the survey of the GdA of 1929, 111,180 were commercial and 5,796 were technical employees; 4,736 were foremen, and 1,262 were pharmacists. This means that approximately 91% were commercial employees (including pharmacists), 4.9% technicians, and 4.1% foremen. If these percentages are representative of the composition of the entire membership, it follows that, of the 328,000 salaried employees in this organization at the end of 1931, there were approximately 16,000 technicians and 13,500 foremen. The remaining 298,500 members therefore, were commercial or office employees. According to information furnished by the GdA, about 25,000 of these were employed in government and social security offices, and from 16,000 to 17,000 were traveling salesmen and agents, that is, 8.4% and 5.5%, respectively, of the non-technical category. With the exception of pharmacists, the other groups are not distinguishable. The pharmacists constitute 0.4% of the non-technical employees. Inasmuch as the Gwr, to which the GdA belonged, included both a separate union for private insurance employees as well as the DBV, which represented bank employees, it follows that the GdA had only a small membership among these two business groups. For this reason I have placed the figure 1.7% for the DHV under the heading "Private Insurance", and 1.1% under "Cooperative Societies table 13.5." A higher percentage for the GdA is unlikely, since the ZdA is the leader here. The estimates for industry and commerce were derived as follows: a comparison of the findings of the DHV and the ZdA shows that, of the polled members, 51% were in industry and mining, 29% in wholesale, and 14% in retail business (Table 14 of the DHV survey). The corresponding figures for the GdA members are 45%, 22%, 22%, 12%. (Cf. pp.84ff. of the GdA survey.) According to the surveys, in other words, the GdA had relatively fewer members in the enumerated branches of the economy than the DHV, 10% less in industry and mining, 30% less in wholesale trade, and 10% less in retail. These fractions have been deducted from the DHV figures in table 13.5. 20% remain under the heading "Others," of which 5.6% are agents.

Table 13.3: Unions of Foremen (End of 1931)

	Total		Female
1. *Free Trade Unions*			
German Foremen's Union (Deutscher Werkmeisterverband, DWV)	120,117		400
Amalgamated Construction Work Foremen (Polier-, Werk- und Schachtmeister Bund für das Baugewerbe Deutschlands)	12,189		—
Foremen's Union of the Shoe Industry (Werkmeister Verband der Schuhindustrie)	2,910		123
TOTALS	134,216	82.4%	523
2. *Christian-National*			
German Foremen's League (Deutscher Werkmeisterbund, DWB)	15,039		—
German League of Building, Mine, and Brickyard Foremen for the Building, Brick, and Allied Industries (Verband deutscher Polier-, Schacht- und Ziegelmeister für das Bau- und Ziegelgewerbe sowie verwandte Berufsarten)	375		—
TOTALS	15,414	9.4%	—
3. *Liberal-National*			
Foremen in the Federation of Salaried Employees (in the Gewerkschaftsbund der Angestellten, GdA)	13,500[a]		—
TOTALS	13,500	8.2%	
CUMULATIVE TOTALS (1–3)	164,130	100%	

SOURCE: *Statistisches Jahrbuch für das Deutsche Reich*, 1932, p. 559.

[a]See also note [a] to table 13.2.

the Afa-Bund, nearly monopolized their organizational commitments by containing more than 80 percent of all organized foremen.[2] Among the technicians no middle-class organization could compete with Butab. Hoisting engineers also were nearly all members of free trade unions.[3] However, the 9,000 members of the Association of Railway Engineers (Fachverband der Eisenbahner) belonged to the right-wing Christian-National Gedag.

The only other group whose membership was monopolized by the free trade unions was the artists, who belonged to the Genossenschaft Deutscher Bühnenangehöriger (Society of German Actors and Stagehands) or the Internationale Artistenloge (International Artists' Lodge).

Among commercial and office employees, however, the anti-socialist organizations prevailed, comprising no less than 80 percent. The DHV and its

Table 13.4: Unions of Technical Employees (End of 1931)

	Total		Female
1. Free Trade Unions			
League of Technical Employees and Civil Servants (Bund der technischen Angestellten und Beamten, Butab)	63,115		434
German Association of Hoisting Engineers (Deutscher Fördermaschinisten Verband)	1,970		—
Association of Cutters and Designers (Verband der Zuschneider und Zuschneiderinnen und Direktricen)	2,800		200
Association of German Captains and Helmsmen (Verband deutscher Kapitäne und Steuerleute)	2,000		—
Merchant Marine and Deepsea Fishing Association of German Ship Engineers (Verband deutscher Schiffsingenieure)	3,700		—
TOTALS	74,585	61.0%	634
2. Christian-National			
Association of German Technicians (Verband deutscher Techniker)	14,258		106
Academic League of the Technical Science Professions (Bund angestellter Akademiker technisch-naturwissenschaftlicher Berufe)	6,979		—
Association of German Captains and Ship's Officers (Verband deutscher Kapitäne und Schiffsoffiziere)	5,354		—
TOTALS	26,591	21.7%	106
3. Liberal-National			
Technicians in the Federation of Salaried Employees (Gewerkschaftsbund der Angestellten, GdA)	16,000[a]		—
Reich League of Female Technical Assistants (Reichsbund technischer Assistentinnen)	2,300		2,300
Association of German Seamen and Helmsmen (Verband deutscher Seeschiffer und Steuerleute)	1,012		—
Association of Technical Ship Officers (Verband technischer Schiffsoffiziere)	1,568		—
Professional League of German Air Pilots (Berufsvereinigung deutscher Flugzeugführer)	247		—
TOTALS	21,127	17.3%	2,300
CUMULATIVE TOTALS (1–3)	122,303	100	

SOURCE: *Statistisches Jahrbuch für das Deutsche Reich*, 1932, p. 559.

[a]See also note [a] to table 13.2.

sister organization for female employees, the VwA, were especially predominant. Table 13.5 shows that the free trade union of commercial and office employees, the ZdA, competed successfully with the middle-class organizations only in certain occupational settings, such as in retail stores—especially department stores and one-price stores—cooperative societies, government offices, and similar agencies.

It bears repeating that 66 percent of the members of the ZdA lived in cities of more than 100,000, as compared with only 41 percent and 56 percent of DHV and GdA members, respectively. Furthermore, commercial employees were more numerous in middle-sized firms than in large enterprises (see table 1.1). Thus, despite the figures in table 13.5, the ZdA appears to have been more strongly represented than the DHV and GdA in the large urban industrial enterprises. The ZdA's substantial female membership also suggests its greater appeal among low-ranking commercial employees in the large enterprises.

The formation of umbrella organizations for the salaried employees was essentially the result of the revolution of 1918. The revolution concluded the first phase of a development, which even prior to World War I had pointed toward a unification of the many white-collar workers' associations. In connection with unionization in 1918–19, organizational ties also developed between white-collar associations and blue-collar organizations in all three types of unions—free, liberal-national, and Christian-national. These ties had been the subject of heated controversy before the war. The tensions between white- and blue-collar workers' continued to find considerable expression in their organizational relations, but they were perhaps most intense *within* each of the three union branches.[4] This resulted from the different interests that existed within the labor camp, from the legal inequality of white- and blue-collar workers, and from the social esteem and prestige privileges that salaried employees claimed and enjoyed regardless of their union affiliation.

Table 13.5: Percentage of Union Membership by Occupation (End of 1931)

	Industry	Mining	Wholesale Trade	Retail Trade	Cooperative Societies	Private Insurance	Social	Gov't	Others	Total
DHV (male)	36.2	1.6	19.6	15.3	1.1	1.7	2.3	—	21.9	100[a]
ZdA (male)	24.5	1.0	8.5	8.1	10.7	4.2	13.2	22.0	7.7	100
ZdA (female)	15.6	—	6.8	33.3	27.4	1.5	3.0	5.2	7.2	100
GdA[b]	(34)		(17.6)	(13.8)	(1.1)	(1.7)	(11.8)		(20)	100

SOURCE: Figures for the DHV and ZdA are taken from H. Hamm, "Die wirtschaftlichen und sozialen Berufsmerkmale der kaufmännischen Angestellten," p. 44.

[a]See also note [a] to table 13.2.

[b]Male and female commercial and office employees.

Tensions were especially strong in the Christian-national wing of the unions, where religious differences aggravated sharp social conflicts between miners who demanded nationalization of the mining industry and commercial clerks whose functionaries enjoyed social contact with the exclusive, conservative *Herrenclub*. The very small Catholic minority in the DHV could not prevent Protestant intellectuals close to the association from evoking Luther and promulgating a militant theology of nationalism. Catholic critics, however, occasionally did charge them with conjuring up the spirit of Bismarck's conflict with the Catholic Church.[5] Not surprisingly, after the Nazi victory in January 1933 the DHV stressed that, unlike the Christian labor unions, it had never really been "Christian-social," but "national-social."

By appointing Catholics as functionaries in Catholic regions, the DHV managed to reduce the aggravation that its extremist Protestantism caused Catholic members. Moreover, the ideologized chasm between the DHV and the Christian labor unions was bridged in part by their joint interest in common economic enterprises.

Among the free trade unions, conflicts between Afa-Bund and ADGB were clearly evident, though less intense than those between white- and blue-collar organizations within right-wing trade unions. Within both left- and right-wing organizations, however, the salaried employees and their functionaries were politically more radical than the manual workers and their functionaries. The DHV was much more anti-Marxist than the Christian labor unions, and the Afa-Bund was more deeply interested in nationalization than the ADGB. In general, the much discussed theory of economic democracy was primarily a theory of the free blue-collar labor unions, and was treated with noticeable reserve by the Afa-Bund, whereas the action program of the free trade unions in 1932 came closer to the aims of the Afa-Bund than to those of the ADGB. Thus, in times of economic prosperity, ideological leadership of the free trade unions tended to be exercised by the blue-collar workers; but as the economic crisis increased in severity, the more radical activities of the white-collar workers gained in public significance.

This tension, aggravated by the sharp competition between different political types of salaried employees' unions, was reflected in the different compositions of their functionaries. The leaders of the Afa-Bund were younger than those of the ADGB, and a larger proportion of them were academically trained for their tasks of formulating and implementing economic and social policies. Younger, more radical intellectuals of the Afa-Bund confronted the more experienced practical men of the ADGB, who were more readily inclined to compromise.

The DHV also had entrusted much work on broad, general tasks to academic functionaries, whereas the ideological leadership of the GdA was exercized by older, practical men possessing a slightly provincial intellectual orientation. Perhaps it is for this reason that many of the GdA's publications were more boring than the writings published by the DHV or the Afa-Bund.

XIV The Disintegration of the Trade Unions, 1933

After Hitler seized power on 30 January 1933, it was no longer possible to mobilize the workers against National Socialism. The last chance to block the dictatorship by a general strike had been missed on 20 July 1932, the day of the coup d'état against Prussia. On 30 January 1933 the fate of the Weimar Republic was sealed, although many people entertained illusions that the new regime would be short-lived. These optimists included well-known industrialists, bankers, generals, church leaders, heads of trade unions, and leaders of all political parties from Hugenberg on the right to the Communists. In his foreign policy, too, Hitler was soon successful, which helped to entrench his power in Germany. Stalin quickly recognized de facto Hitler's regime by renewing the 1926 Treaty of Berlin in May 1933. This treaty, which Stresemann had negotiated with the Soviet government along the lines of the Rapallo Treaty of 1922, obligated each signatory to consult the other in times of crisis and to remain neutral in the event of an attack upon the other. Furthermore, beginning in early March, Hitler and Papen attempted to reach a concordat with the Holy See and used these efforts to weaken the resistance of German Catholics.[1] And on 17 May the Social Democrats voted for the resolution sponsored by the NSDAP, DNVP, Center Party, and Bavarian People's Party (BVP) supporting Hitler's peace declaration in the Reichstag (the SPD vote was in part influenced by the arrest and torture of party comrades).

If Hitler feared trade union action against the new government, it was soon evident that he had no reason for concern. The trade unions were not endangered by the feeble organization of National Socialist cells within the enterprises (NSBO), but they were weakened by the international economic crisis, unemployment, and shrinking membership and funds. Moreover, their leaders were men of the past who, engrossed in notions of legality, failed to comprehend the onslaught of unbridled violence into politics. Despite the terror of the SA, SS, and NSBO, which spread quickly after Hitler's takeover, the leaders of all three

151

kinds of trade unions believed at first that they could preserve their organizations by adjusting to the unfamiliar political scene. Their attempts to compromise with the new power holders accelerated the demoralization and Nazification of labor and the disintegration of their associations.[2]

Leaders of the Christian and liberal associations participated even more actively in their own destruction than those of the free trade unions, although leading functionaries of the ADGB were not far behind. Predictably, the middle-class associations of salaried employees were especially quick to try and be chummy with the Nazis, who did not need drastic measures in order to break up a unified trade union movement. Only the Afa-Bund was a notable exception. Its president, Siegfried Aufhäuser, who had fought the ADGB tactic of adjustment from the beginning, resigned his office on 28 March. A successor was not elected and, on 30 April, the Afa associations decided to dissolve their umbrella organization.

By that time the other trade unions had been thoroughly distracted. As early as the middle of March, the Christian associations declared themselves to be apolitical. Together with representatives of the liberal unions, they formed a delegation that visited Goebbels in order to negotiate the participation of the union members in the new state. In the same month, Theodor Leipart, the president of the ADGB, attempted to save the free trade unions. In two letters to Hitler he stressed the unions' separation from the Social Democratic Party and offered cooperation with the entrepreneurs.

In the camp of the white-collar workers, the DBV was pressured by its Nazi members to negotiate with the NSBO. The presidium resigned and the most important functions were assumed by Nazis. At roughly the same time, the GdA presented Hitler with the "GdA plan to unify the German trade union movement," and soon thereafter "coordinated" itself by electing a Nazi president. The Christian unions also adopted Nazi views. On 22 April Gedag and DHV left the Christian DGB. A week later the DHV followed and by means of "coordination," openly joined the Nazi camp. The name it had preserved in the transition from imperial Germany to the republic was now changed to "Deutscher Handlungsgehilfen-Verband," dropping the word "national," evidently in order to reject any suspicion that it once might have been close to Hugenberg's German National People's Party.

The Nazis were clever in appropriating alien feelings and symbols for purposes of political exploitation. Applications of this technique ranged from transforming favorite melodies into Nazi songs by furnishing National Socialist lyrics for them to the hypocritical honor bestowed upon Hindenburg in order to cheaply, ostentatiously, and without further obligation satisfy the traditions of the officer corps and of the conservative nationalists. For the workers, 1 May was a socialist holiday of great symbolic significance, but they had failed to have it recognized by the state even in the Weimar Republic. Following a masterful propagandistic proposal by Goebbels, a law on the introduction of a Holiday of National Labor was promulgated on 10 April 1933. The memories and feelings that workers associated with 1 May thus appeared to be honored but were actually appropriated by the Nazis. The day after the law was instituted, representatives of the Christian unions went to see Goebbels and offered to trade their participation in the celebrations in return for his consideration of their organizations. In his diary Goebbels described them as "harmless naive chaps."[3] On 15 April the ADGB welcomed 1 May as a people's holiday and four days later recommended the participation of the free unions. The international press of the trade unions was outraged. On 22 April the ADGB and the International Trade Union Organization broke off relations and the latter moved from Berlin to Zürich. According to well-prepared plans, the SA and SS forcibly occupied the trade union buildings on the morning after the Holiday of National Labor.

The destruction of the German trade unions occurred in two phases. First, all blue- and white-collar workers' organizations were integrated into two big umbrella organizations. Subsequently, eighteen Reich Shop Communities (Reichsbetriebsgemeinschaften) and two Reich Economic Branches (Reichsfachgruppen), with both employers and employees as members, were integrated into the German Labor Front (Deutsche Arbeitsfront, DAF).

The creation of the DAF abolished the old conflicts between the three types of unions. Three factors stand out when the new form of organization is compared with the old one it replaced: the rationalization of the associational structure, political unification, and the imposition of the leadership principle.

Concerning organizational rationalization, the roughly one hundred white-collar associations listed in the 1931 Statistical Yearbook were replaced by nine associations. United in the Gesamtverband der deutschen Angestelltenverbände (Umbrella Organization of German Associations of Salaried Employees) under the leadership of the National Socialist DHV functionary A. Forster (Danzig) were the following associations:

1. Deutscher Handlungsgehilfenverband (commercial clerks)
2. Verband Deutscher Techniker (technicians)
3. Verband Deutscher Werkmeister (foremen)
4. Verband Deutscher Büro- und Behördenangestellter (bureau and office employees)
5. Verband Deutscher Land-, Guts- und Forstwirtschaftsangestellter (agricultural employees)

6. Verband angestellter Ärzte und Apotheker (employed physicians and apothecaries)
7. Verband Seemännischer Angestellter (employed seamen)
8. Verband der Weiblichen Angestellten (female employees)

This reorganization of the associations was accomplished within a few weeks. The newly sanctioned political ruthlessness eliminated all resistance and at one stroke completed a development that would have required decades of evolutionary changes. Several smaller associations of foremen had belonged to the former Afa-Bund rather than to the DWV. Before 1933 their consolidation in the larger DWV had been attempted many times, but had always failed because of resistance by shoe-industry foremen in the city of Pirmasens, who, out of loyalty to their occupation, did not want their small association subsumed by the DWV. And this effort to preserve organizational autonomy occurred within the camp of free trade unions, where one association, the DWV, occupied a dominant position among the foremens' organizations concerned. By contrast, the other groups of salaried employees, especially commercial white-collar workers, were organizationally divided into numerous associations possessing different trade union and anti–trade union orientations. Their evolutionary unification would have been considerably more difficult if not impossible.

The rationalization of the associations, which, incidentally, A. Erkelenz had unsuccessfully promoted for very different reasons in 1932,[4] required not only political "coordination," that is, the reconciliation of different political, social, and trade union orientations, but also overcoming the resistance of each organization. For example, Erkelenz's proposal to unify the trade unions was doomed if only because the free unions had no interest in "swallowing" the liberal workers, who were disproportionally old and had especially high pension claims. The GdA also opposed unification, which would have undermined its leading position as an umbrella organization. Its high functionaries would have risked not being received in the Department of Labor or other forms of cooperation with state officials. In some respects, merging modern trade unions is not unlike merging economic enterprises. In particular, the difficulties arising from the necessity of balancing various economic enterprises run by different trade unions could hardly be overcome in a non-revolutionary manner, for they involved a new delineation of jurisdictions and a redistribution of the income received by leading trade union officials.

In reorganizing the white-collar associations the Nazis initially showed little intransigence in pursuing the aims of their anti-union policy, but were apparently content to take account of the character of existing organizations. Female white-collar workers were assigned to a special association without regard for their occupation. The DHV continued to exclude women as members, but accepted male commercial employees of any occupation. Separate organizations for bank clerks, and for employees in insurance, the book trade, and so forth were no longer guaranteed a niche in the DAF. Male members of the DBV were transferred to the DHV so they might find "their trade union home" in the "Reich Group Banks" (Reichsfachgruppe Banken). Female members had to transfer to the VwA.[5]

The associations which survived the reorganization, at least at first, were those which since 1918 had most ardently fought parliamentarianism, Marxism, and the free trade unions. The leading organizations in the new umbrella association were the DHV and its sister organization, the VwA. In a letter to the president of the DHV, published in the press on 4 May 1933, Dr. Robert Ley furiously, if ungrammatically declared, "As a sensible man I will not go and impose an organization crowned by failure, such as the Afa-Bund, upon the excellent association of the DHV, but on the contrary, I ask you and your entire association to assume the leadership in the newly-to-be built column of salaried employees. I am convinced that this will take a great weight off my shoulders."

The victory of the anti-socialist associations was based on their unqualified assignment of leadership functions to National Socialists, and upon their neglect of all functionaries who, in the previous years of parliamentary cross-connections, had worked in political parties other than the NSDAP. Within the DHV this "coordination" was most forcefully expressed by the resignation of Bechly who, despite considerable internal opposition, had sponsored the reelection of Hindenburg in the last presidential election.

At the First German Congress of Salaried Employees on 15 May 1933, A. Forster (Danzig), leader of the white-collar workers in the DAF, said that agreement between the individual organizations and the government was necessary, for these organizations must be not ends in themselves, but exclusively means toward the end of national resurrection.

The political unification of the organizations was guaranteed by the Führer principle. Its realization is shown in table 14.1. In no organization were any votes cast. Rather, leaders were appointed—the provincial leaders by leaders of central organizations, the district leaders by provincial leaders, and the local leaders by district leaders. The top leader of the central organization appointed all members of the Consultative Council, the representatives in the Central Associations, as well as the chairmen and the steadily employed specialists of working

Table 14.1: The German Labor Front (Early 1933)

Leader: R. Ley

Directorate: Central Bureau

Small Labor Convent (14 members)	*Large Labor Convent* (60 members)
1 Leader of Labor Front (R. Ley)	1–14 Members of the Small Labor Convent
2 Leader of Central Association of the Workers (R. Schumann)	15 B. Otte
	16 J. Kaiser
3 Leader of Central Association of the Salaried Employees (A. Forster)	17 T. Brauer
	18 T. Behrens
4 Leadership (R. Schmeer)	19 A. Fultin

Directors of Offices

5 Social Questions (E. Stöhr)	20–60 Directors of the main occupational groups and the main economic branches and other representatives of the trade union movement
6 Organization (R. Muchow)	
7 Propaganda and Press (H. Biallas)	
8 Tariffs	
9 Law	
10 Occupational Estates (M. Fraunhofer)	
11 Education (O. Gohdes)	
12 Economic Enterprises (K. Möller)	
13 Finances (P. Brinckmann)	
14 Youth	

The Two Columns

I Central Association of Workers Associations	II Central Association of the Associations of Salaried Employees
Leader: R. Schumann	Leader: A. Forster
	Manager: G. Schloder
	Council to the Leader
	Central Representation: Representatives of the nine associations
	Working Committees: Directors and Specialists
	Provincial Leaders
	District Leaders
	Local Leaders

committees. He was himself the legal representative of the central organization and exercised his leadership "supported by the advice and succor of the Council to the Leader." He belonged to the governing body of each affiliated organization, was entitled to participate in meetings and conventions of all their organs, and could demand that such meetings be held and table motions. Finally, he was authorized to raise objections to measures taken by the organizations or to prohibit their implementation, and he convened the "total representation." In short, he and the manager, who was the Leader's representative, held unlimited power over those below them.

In its final form the DAF had about 25 million members, almost half the German people. The social differences between employers and employees, as well as those between salaried employees and workers, had become organizationally irrelevant. Shop councils and trade unions had lost their functions as a result of various laws and edicts as early as April 1933. As a result of the law concerning the order of national labor of 20 January 1934 and further governmental measures in March 1935, the DAF became the compulsory organization for all "soldiers of labor." An association tied to the NSDAP, it primarily served as a conduit for the will of the party leadership.

Reich leader of the DAF was Dr. Robert Ley, a half-educated party hack who, unlike Gregor Strasser, owed his power to services rendered as a liaison to entrepreneurs and banks. His office and those of the Central Bureau were repeated on a smaller scale at provincial, district, and local levels and finally reached the lowest level in the form of cells and blocks, corresponding to the street cells and street blocks, within the enterprises.[6]

The Führer principle was ideologically justified by assuming that all former members of the trade unions shared an equality of will as comrades of the people, and by assuming popular confidence in the leaders. R. Muchow, organizing director of the Action Committee for the Protection of German Labor, spoke on 15 May 1933 of the "Victory of German Labor."[7] He stopped short of demanding that former trade union members become National Socialists, but a substantial majority of German white-collar workers nonetheless recognized this "victory of German labor" as the victory of their social views, that is, as the victory of those employees in the Weimar Republic who did not want to become members of the lower classes.

Appendix A: The Development of the Salaried Employees, 1907–25

On the basis of the 1925 census the Afa-Bund calculated the stratification of salaried employees according to occupation, sex, and economic specialization (see table A.1).

Commercial employees, that is, all non-technical white-collar workers employed in business, were the largest group. Office employees in state bureaus, self-administrative bodies, associations representing special industrial interests, law firms and notaries, and so forth have been treated separately. Both groups comprised nearly three-fourths of all salaried employees. The number of technical employees nearly equaled that of the office personnel. (Unlike the official census, the Afa-Bund included master miners in this group.) This group embraced technical personnel of every description and training, including university graduate engineers, architects, and chemists. Foremen, however, were mentioned separately. Again unlike the official census, the Afa-Bund included in this category such individuals as textile foremen. The classification of these men as salaried employees was sharply disputed.

The group labeled "others" almost equaled the combined figures for technicians and foremen. It was composed of various types of employees, such as nurses, social workers, pharmacists, estate overseers, actors, vaudeville performers, musicians, ship captains, teachers, physicians, editors, and so forth.

The number of female employees was more than half that of males. The characteristic importance of female help in white-collar occupations stood out especially among commercial employees, where there were no fewer than two female workers for every three men. There were, however, hardly any forewomen. Among technical employees, only 4 percent were female, most of them in the textile industry and chemical laboratories.

The main body of salaried employees was engaged in the fields of commerce and communications. 1.53 million white-collar workers, or 44 percent of the total, were employed in commerce as compared with 1.35 million industrial

Table A.1: Occupational Stratification of Salaried Employees, 1925

Occupational Groups	Total		Male		Female	
	In 1,000	%	In 1,000	%	In 1,000	%
Commercial Employees Of these:	2,290	65	1,370	60	920	77
Sales Personnel[a]	(800)	—	—	—	—	—
Office Employees	280	8	176	7	104	8
Technical Employees (engineers, chemists, architects, etc.)	270	8	260	11	10	1
Foremen	220	6	220	10	—	—
Others	440	13	274	12	166	14
Total Of these:	3,500	100	2,300	100	1,200	100
Stenographers, }[b] Typists	—	—	—	—	480–572	—
Executive Employees	145					

SOURCE: Afa-Bund, ed., *Die Angestellten in der Wirtschaft*, pp. 31, 37, 38, 40, 41.

[a]See T. Geiger, "Soziale Gliederung der deutschen Arbeitnehmer," ASS 69(1933);187.

[b]According to the estimate of the Verband der weiblichen Handels- und Büroangestellten (F. Glass and G. Kische, *Die wirtschaftlichen und sozialen Verhältnisse der berufstätigen Frauen* (Berlin, 1930), 56% of all female employees were stenographers. The estimate of the Zentralverband der Angestellten places the number at 40% (S. Suhr, *Die weiblichen Angestellten*).

employees, or 38 percent of the total. The remainder of 0.49 million, or 14 percent, were employed in government or public health, and so forth, and 130,000, or 4 percent, were in agriculture and forestry. Women were more numerous in commerce than in industry, which provided the principal field of activity for men. Only 335,000 women worked in industry as compared with 1,015,000 men, while commerce employed 612,000 women and 918,000 men. More than one-half of the women (51 percent) but only 40 percent of the men worked in commerce and communication. Not much more than one-quarter (28 percent) of the women, but nearly one-half (44 percent) of the men worked in industry. The number of female employees in government (241,000) nearly reached that of the males (249,000). Finally, the number of women in agriculture was far behind that of men.

Although most salaried employees were still in commerce, their number in this branch of the economy had advanced more slowly between 1907 and 1925 than it had in industry. The number of commercial employees had merely doubled while that of industrial employees tripled. With astonishing rapidity, many new fields of endeavor had opened in industry, especially for women, whose numbers increased five and one half times. Table A.2 indicates this development.

Inasmuch as girls and women primarily held the lowest jobs while men occupied the higher positions, the much stronger increase of female employees provides indirect proof that white-collar expansion was connected with a broadening of the social pyramid. The average level of the salaried employees had declined and their proletarianization had progressed. Table A.2 (lines 7–9) shows this development more precisely.

The social transformation of German society between 1907 and 1925 is reflected in the percentage figures of table A.2, calculated by the Afa-Bund.

Apart from the independent class, where development was severely retarded, only manual labor grew more slowly between 1907 and 1925 than the entire body of gainfully employed. In other words, its share in the total number of

Table A.2: Social Transformation of the Population and the Labor Force, 1907–25

	% of Increase			Number of Persons in 1925 (in thousands)
	Total	Male	Female	
1. Total Population	14	11	16	62,410
2. Total Gainfully Employed	27	23	35	32,009
3. Independents (including those in home industry, executive employees, and civil servants)[a]	7	6	11	5,013
4. Contributing Household Members	44	34	48	5,437
5. Civil Servants (non-executives)	c. 40	—	—	1,450
6. Laborers (excluding home workers and domestic help)	24	24	24	14,434
7. Salaried Employees (other than executives)	133	104	224	3,500
8. Employees in Industry and Handicraft	146	108	458	1,350
9. Employees in Commerce and Communication	86	35	167	1,530

SOURCE: Afa-Bund, ed., *Die Angestellten in der Wirtschaft*, p. 26.

[a]It is difficult to understand why the Afa-Bund did not segregate those running a small shop in home industry (so-called afr-persons), the directors, managers, and executive civil servants (a 3-persons) from the category of "independents." These were, according to the census, 0.9% and 0.8%, respectively, of the gainfully employed, or 298,000 and, respectively, 266,000 persons. (*Statistik des Deutschen Reichs*, vol. 402, part 2 (Berlin, 1927), p. 218. The total number of independents in table A.2 is reduced by subtracting these two groups by 565,000 to 4.448 million.

gainfully employed diminished. The increase in the number of employed derived from the expansion of other social strata and, with respect to the rapidity of this expansion, salaried employees surpassed all other sections of the population. In eighteen years it increased by two million people. Its proportionate share of gainfully employed rose from 6 percent to 10.9 percent. Every tenth wage earner was a white-collar worker, while one in four was a laborer. In industry, to be sure, the figures were not quite so drastic, with a ratio of 1:6, as in commerce, where the white-collar worker was the typical wage earner. Whereas in 1907 the number of salaried employees per every thousand manual workers fluctuated between 56 and 202 from industry to industry, in 1925 the corresponding figures were 89 and 382.

The number of salaried employees increased more rapidly in industry than in commerce. The preponderance of commercial employees had diminished considerably since 1907. It is possible that the time will again come when the number of industrial employees will match or even surpass those in commerce. It should be noted in this regard, however, that a retrogressive development took place after 1925. The number of salaried employees in industry and commerce diminished from 1.35 million in 1925 to 1.3 million in 1933, but increased in commerce and communications from 1.53 million to 1.78 million during the same period. According to the *Statistisches Jahrbuch für das Deutsche Reich* (1934), the total number of employees increased by more than 500,000 to 4.033 million between 1925 and 1933 (pp. 18–19).

The various types of white-collar workers developed along different lines. The number of foremen increased very little after 1907, from 193,000 to 220,000. This indicates a relative diminution of the group. Compared to blue-collar workers as well as to other employee groups, it lost in numerical weight. Technical employees also showed a relative retrogression, despite an absolute increase from 99,000 to 215,000. From 18 percent, they fell to 15.8 percent of the employee class. The proportion of commercial employees in trade increased from 46.7 percent to 63.7 percent. With an increase from 256,000 to 900,000 persons, this category grew to three and a half times its size in 1907.

Between 1907 and 1925 the various groups of salaried employees in industry and handicraft grew (in percent of 1907) as follows: foremen, 14 percent; technicians, 117 percent; commercial white-collar workers, 252 percent.

Appendix B: Two Letters by Theodor Geiger

Professor Dr. Theodor Geiger
Technische Hochschule Braunschweig

Braunschweig, 8-21-33
Hildebrandstrasse 45 II
Telephone: 7246

My dear Dr. Speier:

Your MS. arrived from Enke yesterday at noon. Yesterday afternoon, I read the first part, this forenoon the second part. When I came up from the beach I met the mailman who gave me your letter. I would have written to you today anyway, with my impressions fresh in mind.

Coming to the point: I am very much taken by your work—without conditions, without restrictions. As far as the content is concerned, yours is the first study which has told me more about the salaried employees than I already knew. Regarding its form, I regard your work as a masterpiece. And I mean by "form" the methodical order of ideas and the literary quality, but also the measured political-psychological balance of presentation, which is so important today.

Thematically, the work not only fits into the new series, but is especially needed, for Walther and I agree that we must especially devote ourselves to a detailed examination of stratification and its restructuring. To be sure, we shall also be concerned with problems which, at first glance, appear to belong to an entirely different category. For example, you will be astonished that the first volume to be published is to be my *Eugenics*. The common denominator for this and other such heterogeneous subjects that are seemingly alien to our discipline is the concept of "folk policy" (*Volkspolitik*), by which I mean all measures that consciously serve to steer and change the regimen and structure of the *Volk*. I would like to cultivate sociology inasmuch as it offers an empirical basis for such efforts.

The editorship was unexpectedly offered to me. At first, I was quite skeptical, now I am enjoying it. Enke demanded a man of the NSDAP as co-editor. I have won over Walther, who is also decisively committed to empirical sociology.

163

Rumpf will not be the third editor after all. Walther and I will do the job without him. Today, when it is difficult to reach agreement on many issues, this will be an advantage.

As to the prospects for your work, they depend not only on me. Several months ago, Martin, at that time still boss of the enterprise, wrote to me complaining that Enke was recoiling from the ticklish subject. My reply, which discussed many fundamental questions, was sent on by Martin to Enke, who was persuaded by it to continue the series after he had already decided to sacrifice it. In this reply, I had written about your work and suggested that one cannot blame a publisher if he is especially cautious in dealing with such a subject today. Evidently, von Martin understood this to mean that I was advising against publication. I had no reason to believe Enke would have an opportunity to read my letter. But my remarks, along with others, created the impression in Enke's mind that I was a man who, in his relations with publishers, had his heart in the right place. It now appears very propitious that I took this fundamental position before I had read your work. I should be all the more trustworthy to the publisher when I strongly encourage him to publish the book.

Enke had already written at that time that he was requesting utmost caution in my appraisal. If a co-editor close to the NSDAP were to give his blessing and perhaps even write a brief preface, he would not object to the publication. I have met Walther in Lübeck, discussed everything with him, and in this connection also prepared him for your MS. He does not know you, was reserved, but did not express his rejection in principle. It is self-understood that I shall now encourage him *with all possible emphasis* not only to say "yes" but to write a few introductory sentences. He can do it in good conscience—in respect to what you have written. What you have not written, but have made legible with remarkable skill between the lines, need not concern him. I hope very much that everything will go well.

It is true, Enke and Walther, of course, were of the opinion that one should offer the volume, if at all, not as number two or three, but a little later. Enke of course means that one should first prove in public that one has "the right position." Later, a volume which taken separately might arouse suspicion could be published casually, as it were. I do not consider it necessary to take this precaution in the case of your work.

On the other hand, I am glad to have a finished product with which to continue the series. My *Eugenics* is at the printer and will come out in October. Further projects I shall have to suggest. Walther himself has promised me a study which will be a critical examination of the census data. He wants to show

how little the data have been evaluated sociologically, and how the outdated census methods render the sociological interpretation more difficult. But he does not expect to finish this before spring. For this reason I regard as all the more important a representative work which can be published as number two in the course of the winter.

Thus far my opinion. Now, Enke and Walther are on vacation at present. I do not know whether Walther can be approached for doing work now, and I know definitely that Enke will not make any decisions before the end of September. The question now is whether or not I shall forward your MS. at once to Walther. In deciding that, a subsidiary question requires some consideration: I have found that the second part of the MS. is much less "objectionable" than the first. That is, concerning the terminology. Perhaps it would be possible to do some repair work in this regard without compromising oneself. Trifles perhaps. One cannot fully dispense with the term "class." But people don't like to hear it. It appears to me that in many spots one could use the term "stratum" instead. Further, will you consider whether a fitting word could be substituted for "proletarianization"? Ideas are so much more easily absorbed and appreciated when they are presented in the costume of an unsuspected word. In addition, I still have a few trifles—really trifles—where I want to suggest to you that you consider the possibility of a slight change in formulation.

If you agree, I shall send you the MS. with the pertinent remarks, *before* mailing it to Walther.

Let me conclude with congratulations, not entirely free of envy, on your accomplishment. I admire especially your high-mindedness of rigorously selecting your data and of thereby renouncing the possibility of calling the attention of every Tom, Dick, and Harry to the immense study of detail on which the text is based.

Have you found new employment? What kind?

My best wishes to you and Mrs. Speier! Do not worry!

Yours,
(signed) Theodor Geiger

Professor Dr. Theodor Geiger
Technical University Braunschweig

Braunschweig, 9-27-33
Hildebrandstrasse 45 II
Telephon 7246

Prof. Dr. Speier
New York

Dear Mr. Speier,

I am very much depressed by the need to tell you that Walther has protested against the inclusion of your work in the series. I could make his reasons available to you, but abstain because I regard them as erroneous in relation to the facts and because, ultimately, only one single reason, which cannot be discussed, does matter: the tactical one.

I had not expected that. Evidently, I am so little up to date that I have not even noticed what is possible and what is not. An oppressive observation. Now, I severely reproach myself for having burdened you in the turmoil of your re-settlement with a request to polish and retouch the text. That my request was well-intentioned is no excuse and of no use to you.

Walther is returning the MS. to me, where it will await your instructions. I have written at once to Enke. Of course, it would have been futile to object to Walther's verdict. But for your sake I have informed Enke that Walther's reason appears unfair to me.

Enke knows that I am writing to you, but I asked him to take care of the official wind-up. In your interest I did this with the emphatic reminder that a binding contract exists.

I assume that my letter to Lederer no longer reached him in good time in B.P. I have therefore no reply. Rockefeller-Paris is inclined to help, but can do so only if an invitation has been issued by an American institution. I have written to Otto Nathan and to an address in London mentioned to me by Rockefeller-Paris. They have apparently become quite dubious due to saturation.

In the meantime, I have received the farewell letter, and I am striking tents. Officially, I shall resettle in Munich, but first I shall visit Copenhagen.

My address: mag. phil. Oskar Thyregod, Herløv/Kjøpenhavn. Hjortespring, Villa Solhøj.

From the bottom of my heart I wish you all the best, success, and a good adjustment. Greetings to Wertheimer, Wunderlich, and Colm. Above all, however, to Nathan.

To come back to your white-collar workers, the work must be published. Why not in Switzerland? Doesn't Hirschfeld have a branch office there? Be assured once more—although you cannot reap any benefit from it—how much it would have pleased me to have been your public sponsor and how much it grieves me to have deceived you with my optimism.

Most cordially yours,
(signed) Theodor Geiger

Notes

Abbreviations

AJS   *American Journal of Sociology*
ASG   *Archiv für Sozialgeschichte*
ASS   *Archiv für Sozialwissenschaft und Sozialpolitik*
HB   *Handbuch* (handbook)
Hwb   *Handwörterbuch* (dictionary)
Jb   *Jahrbuch* (yearbook)
PVS   *Politische Vierteljahrsschrift*
Schm. Jb   *Schmoller's Jahrbuch*
VfZG   *Vierteljahrshefte für Zeitgeschichte*
VjH   *Vierteljahrshefte*
ZfGS   *Zeitschrift für die gesamte Staatswissenschaft*
Zs   *Zeitschrift*

Preface

1. These papers are reprinted in H. Speier, *Social Order and the Risks of War*, chs. 2–4, pp. 19–52.
2. L. Erdmann, "Nation, Gewerkschaften und Sozialismus," p. 129. After the occupation of trade union headquarters on 2 May 1933, Erdmann refused to work for the Nazis. On 1 September 1939 he was arrested for "preventive" reasons and taken to the concentration camp at Sachsenhausen. On 18 September he died there as a result of brutal mistreatment. Cf. A. Leber, ed., *Das Gewissen steht auf*, pp. 78–79.
3. L. Erdmann, "Nation, Gewerkschaften und Sozialismus," p. 146.
4. Ibid., p. 157.
5. Ibid., p. 161.
6. Cf. H. Speier, "Verbürgerlichung des Proletariats?"; abbreviated translation in H. Speier, *Social Order and The Risks of War*, ch. 5.
7. Cf. H. Speier, "Das Proletariat und seine Kritiker," pp. 289–304.

Introduction

1. Like the socialists, the workers were held in low esteem. An especially shocking illustration is the remark made by Major von Caprivi, first general staff officer of the Seventh Army Corps and aide-de-camp to the emperor, about the death of Ludwig Frank, who, as a wartime volunteer, had fallen in the first battle on 3 September 1914. Frank had been a Social Democratic member of the Reichstag since 1907. Caprivi referred to his death as a propaganda trick by the Social Democrats. K. Riezler, *Tagebücher, Aufsätze, Dokumente*, p. 208. Riezler himself was very critical of the political and moral qualities of the German elites and was not prejudiced toward the Social Democrats. After the split in the Social Democratic representation in the Reichstag on 24 March 1916, he wrote an article in which he made guarded but favorable predictions about the influence of socialism on German political life. He did so in the interest of power politics exercised by the masses. Ibid., pp. 541–48. Yet, in spite of all this, he referred in his diary to the trade union leaders with benevolent condescension (3 April 1915, and p. 365, 7 July 1916).
2. J. Jahn, *Das grosse Schlagwort*, p. 62.
3. F. Baumann, *Der Nutzen des Heerwesens für die deutsche Volkswirtschaft*, p. 26, cited by H. Fick, *Der deutsche Militarismus der Vorkriegszeit*, pp. 80ff.
4. Best summary: E. Lederer, "Die Umschichtung des Proletariats," pp. 129ff.
5. W. Eschmann, "Die Angestellten," p. 463.
6. J. Schumpeter, "Das soziale Antlitz des deutschen Reiches," p. 224.
7. O. Süssengut, "Die Angestellten als Stand und Klasse."
8. A. E. Günther, "Die Angestellten."
9. C. Dreyfuss, *Beruf und Ideologie der Angestellten*, pp. 64ff.
10. S. Kracauer, *Die Angestellten*, pp. 96ff.
11. J. Jahn, "Der soziologische Sinn der Gehaltspolitik," p. 99.
12. M. Weber, *Economy and Society*, p. 930.
13. Ibid., pp. 305–06.
14. Ibid., p. 927. The German original (1923) has "social order," the English translation has "status order."
15. Ibid., pp. 926–27.

Chapter I

1. T. Fontane, *Frau Jenny Treibel*, p. 298.
2. According to the survey of the Commission for Labor Statistics, in the fall of 1892 45.1 percent of male salespersons and 34.3 percent of salesgirls (of a total of 16,845) enjoyed free room and board.
3. F. Urbschat, *Das Seelenleben des kaufmännisch tätigen Jugendlichen*, p. 54.
4. From letters written by unemployed white-collar workers to the GdA, which the association was good enough to let me read.
5. G. Messarius, "Der Mittelbetrieb in der nationalen Wirtschaft."
6. H. Hamm, "Die wirtschaftlichen und sozialen Berufsmerkmale der kaufmännischen Angestellten," p. 42. This distribution is important from a political standpoint as

well. The distribution of districts for the election of delegates to the Employee Insurance Institute gave an undue advantage to the rural districts over the cities. The governing body of the Reich Institute for Employee Insurance (Reichsanstalt für Angestelltenversicherung) was elected indirectly by these delegates. When the representatives of the Allgemeiner freier Angestelltenbund demanded the introduction of direct election of the governing body, they were opposed by a solid front of the delegates of middle-class associations and representatives of the employers.

7. G. Fürst, "Die Angestellten in Klein-, Mittel- und Grossbetrieben," pp. 48ff; based on the census of 1925.

8. In his address to the session of the Reichskuratorium für Wirtschaftlichkeit (National Rationalization Board) on 27 and 28 February 1931, "The Individual and Rationalization," K. Bott of the DHV pointed to this development. He stated that the commercial employee was still active in small and medium-sized establishments "as he has been pictured idealistically"; he is more of a "complete individual" than his colleague in giant enterprises. Report of the Reichskuratorium für Wirtschaftlichkeit, p. 17.

9. K. S. Bader, *Der Kampf gegen Grossbetriebe im Einzelhandel.*

10. DWV, ed., *Der Werkmeister im Tarifvertrag,* pt. 2, p. 11.

11. K. Heinig, *Volkswirtschaftliche Rundschau.*

12. H. Buschmann, "Neue soziale und wirtschaftliche Probleme der Werkmeister," p. 8.

13. In the studies and reports on "The Social Aspects of Rationalization" published by the International Labor Office, (series B, Economic Conditions, no. 18, [Geneva, 1931], p. 356), it was emphasized that the conception of the role of the foreman in industry organized on a scientific basis had undergone a decided change. "The main work of the foreman is concerned with production and his aim must necessarily be to get the maximum of production that is reasonably possible. . . . His main function is to make other people do their jobs well. . . . Some of these estimates evaluate the non-technical or human side of the foreman's job as worth 80 percent of the whole." One can state without exaggeration that the ratio between the technical and non-technical work of the foreman in industry has been reversed in the course of half a century. The Christian-national Deutscher Werkmeister-Bund (DWB, German Foremen's League) takes a different view of this change. It claims that "not only a will to create, but also a mastery of the vast and complicated techniques" is demanded of the present-day foreman. Materials and productivity in giant enterprises are subject to his calculations[!] His direction leads the work of many to a successful completion. . . . Foremen are truly entitled to class themselves as skilled and executive [!] employees." DWB, ed., *10 Jahre Deutscher Werkmeister-Bund, 1919–1929,* p. 82.

14. H. Buschmann, "Wirtschaft, Sozialpolitik und Verband," pp. 23ff.

15. C. H. A. Geck, *Die sozialen Arbeitsverhältnisse im Wandel der Zeit,* pp. 119ff.

16. DWV, ed., *Schriften des DWV,* no. 33, p. 24.

17. Cf. for example G. Baum, *Werkmeisterrecht,* p. 16, about the distinction between foreman and section boss: "Too wide a definition of the concept of foreman would unnecessarily lower the social rank of the profession of foremen *(Werkmeisterstand)."*

18. DWV, ed., *Festschrift zum 25-jährigen Bestehen des DWV.*

19. This fact must be borne in mind in evaluating the comparatively low unemployment figures for foremen. If unemployed foremen found positions as workers, they were lost to the statistics concerning them.

20. G. Fürst, "Die Altersgliederung der Angestellten nach den Ergebnissen der Berufszählung 1925," p. 65.

21. Cf. GdA, ed., *Die wirtschaftliche und soziale Lage der Angestellten*, p. 76. See also the remarks of H. Lufft, "Kulturvitalität im Angestelltenstand." Regarding the significance of age for the attitude of the white-collar worker in industry, W. Müller says in his *Rationelle Menschenführung*, p. 23: "We believe that a mature man has more experience than the adolescent; the former usually has a family to support and will, for this reason, do anything to satisfy his superior, in order to retain his position."

22. Afa-Bund, ed., *Die Angestellten in der Wirtschaft*, p. 78. The politically neutralizing influence of small vegetable gardens *(Schrebergärten)* is well known. Compare the remarks of an official in a Christian trade union: "I have observed time and again that . . . radicalism disappears as soon as private property is acquired. . . . I often make very interesting studies in our garden clubs. No matter how great the political contrasts, whether communist or socialist, cabbages and strawberries, radishes and gooseberries give the members a common interest." Cited by T. Brauer, "Der Gewerkschaftssekretär," pp. 121ff.

23. DWV, ed., *Geschäftsbericht für 1924*, p. 59.

24. From 1861 to 1874 the number of steam engines in Prussia increased from 7,000 to 34,000, their capacity from 143,000 to 958,000 horsepower. The share of German dyestuffs on the world market, still insignificant toward the end of the sixties, amounted to 50 percent a decade later and 90 percent toward the turn of the century. The production of ingots increased between 1869 and 1879 from 161,000 to 478,000 tons. Cf. D. S. Landes, *The Unbound Prometheus*, Mass., pp. 221, 276, 257.

25. Butab, ed., *25 Jahre Technikergewerkschaft: 10 Jahre Butab*, p. 13.

26. Cf. C. H. A. Geck, *Die sozialen Arbeitsverhältnisse im Wandel der Zeit*, p. 55.

27. Butab, ed., *25 Jahre Technikergewerkschaft*, p. 17. In the same year, 1884, the DWV, the German Foremen's Union, was founded. Like the DTV and the commercial employees' organizations of the time, the growth of this foremen's group is due, in large measure, to provisions for self-help among the members.

28. Butab, ed., "Der Diplomingenieur als Arbeitnehmer," p. 16.

29. Butab, ed., *25 Jahre Technikergewerkschaft*, p. 44.

30. W. Mertens, "Zur Bewegung der technischen Privatbeamten," pp. 649–713.

31. W. D. von Witzleben, "Der Tarifvertrag für die Angestellten der Berliner Metallindustrie," p. 25.

32. K. D. Bracher, *Die deutsche Diktatur*, pp. 179ff.

33. B. Brell, *Das psychologische Berufsbild des Handlungsgehilfen*, pp. 27ff.

34. F. Nordsieck, *Die schaubildliche Erfassung und Untersuchung der Organisation*, p. 14. See also E. Walb in C. Eckert, *Rothschilds Taschenbuch für Kaufleute*, vol. 2, p. 26.

35. For an early statement about the especially large distance between the domestic (frequently proletarian) and occupational milieu of saleswomen, cf. K. Mende, "Münchener jugendliche Ladnerinnen zu Hause und im Beruf," p. 213.

36. Even the activity of the traveling salesman, who, it would seem, had to approach his customers individually, was not altogether free from rationalization. Psychological experts on the treatment of personnel have established widely applicable rules, worked out a system of negotiations and tactics in argumentation, and built a so-called "sociology of the average human being." F. Giese, *Methoden der Wirtschaftspsychologie*, pp. 239ff. They formulated standards of conduct, based upon allegedly typical behavior, which were to lead to a wished-for attitude. They abstracted reason from experience—the former, they claimed, being a part of the latter—and with it they inoculated the traveling salesman. The standard of following the path of least resistance in order to make a sale was replaced by the exact enumeration of those points which, in a fixed sequence, were to be touched upon during conversations with the customer. They also standardized refutations to expected objections and, finally, set down the verbatim text of the sales talk which the salesman had to memorize before he could begin his actual work. As a result, any salesman without inherent capabilities could rise on the ladder of success with these aids alone. But the rationalization of that which the layman believed to be exempt from rationalization forever was basically possible, and that is the point. Inasmuch as the consumer had neither the expedient of a standardized refusal at his disposal, nor studied inaccessibility, this sales psychology, widely practiced in America, would make him a pliable subject of science. He has within his power, however, a very excellent weapon: it is he who pays. This realization should make him at times immune to the proselytizing poison of this applied science.
37. H. Dominik, *Das Schaltwerk: Fabrikhochbau und Hallenbau der Siemens Schuckert Werke A.-G.*, p. 24.
38. VwA, ed., *40 Jahre VwA 1889–1929*, p. 18.
39. H. Fuykschot, "Die Rückwirkungen der Verwendung von Büromaschinen," p. 147.
40. F. Syrup, ed., *HB des Arbeiterschutzes und der Betriebssicherheit*, vol. 3, sec. 21 p. 507.
41. Afa-Bund, ed., *Erhebung über das Arbeiten an Schreibmaschinen*, p. 22.
42. S. Suhr, *Die weiblichen Angestellten*, p. 25.
43. E. Walther, "Die Handels- und Büroangestellte," p. 14.
44. W. D. von Witzleben, "Der Tarifvertrag für die Angestellten der Berliner Metallindustrie," p. 26.
45. M. Brendgen, "Die Adremaprägerin."
46. See the expert account of a vocational counselor, L. Walbrodt, "Die Rationalisierung in Büro und Handel." This instance should show the pertinence of the following questions raised by W. Deiters, "Die Buchungsmaschine als soziales Problem": "Should the bookkeeping machine cause a change in status of commercial employees? Should a semiskilled assistant clerk force his way into the commercial profession?"
47. E. Wald, "Antiproletarische Sozialpolitik," p. 263.
48. O. Aust, *Die Reform der öffentlichen Verwaltung in Deutschland*, pp. 98ff. Concerning the question of bureaucracy and especially the similarities between official and private bureaucracy, compare, in addition to Max Weber's standard discussion, H. Bente, *Organisierte Unwirtschaftlichkeit*, and O. von der Gablentz, "Industriebürokratie," pp. 539–72.

49. GdA, ed., *Die Angestellten im Behördendienst.*
50. *Reichsverband der Zivildienstberechtigten* 38, no. 9 (5 May 1932). The sum total of the percentages cited in the text is 97, not 100.

Chapter II

1. G. Fürst, "Die Angestellten nach dem Familienstand," pp. 106–09; also H. Lufft, "Kulturvitalität im Angestelltenstand."
2. That one must be careful in generalizing on the basis of these figures, which at any rate are typical of the GdA, can be seen in table 2.2.
3. GdA, ed., *Die wirtschaftliche und soziale Lage der Angestellten,* p. 43.
4. The percentage of independent tradesmen (29 percent) was very high there. The report contained an exceedingly high percentage of technicians in the building trades, while the members of Butib surveyed by Jaeckel were to a large extent industrial technicians. Cf. R. Jaeckel, *Statistik über die Lage der technischen Privatbeamten in Grossberlin*; A. Günther, *Die deutschen Techniker*; DHV, ed., *Die wirtschaftliche Lage der deutschen Handlungsgehilfen.*
5. One-fifth of the GdA membership did not give any information about their social origin. Presumably there were many who were ashamed of their lowly birth.
6. K. Stehr, "Der Zentralverband der Angestellten."
7. This corresponds to the result of an interesting little survey by H. Hamm, *Die wirtschaftlichen und sozialen Berufsmerkmale der kaufmännischen Angestellten,* p. 43, who compared the voting proportions of the three organizations at the elections of 1927 for the Employee Insurance Institute by Berlin election districts. He found that the DHV proportion was largest in the "pronounced middle-class residential districts" and the smallest in those that were "typically proletarian." Exactly reverse conditions applied to the ZdA; the GdA was in the middle:

	DHV	GdA	ZdA
Middle-class residential districts	28%	22%	15%
Proletarian districts	21%	24%	30%

8. According to the GdA, large cities "offer to the ambitious woman from the working class a welcome field of activity; it is welcome, too, because she is attracted by the bustling life of the metropolis" (*Die wirtschaftliche und soziale Lage der Angestellten,* p. 45.) This explanation is probably incorrect and certainly hastily drawn. It cannot be regarded as a foregone conclusion that salaried women coming from the working class welcomed the standardized tasks which, according to the GdA, were their principal field of activity. In addition, it is doubtful whether the lures of the big city were a factor, since most of the female employees of proletarian origin were already children of the big cities.
9. Cf. notes a and c in table 2.1; and 4 and 5 in table 2.2.
10. GdA, ed., *Die kommende Angestelltengeneration,* p. 22.

Chapter III

1. K. Wiedenfeld, *Kapitalismus und Beamtentum*, pp. 31f.
2. An example: "The twelve-year-old schoolboy H. W. from Hannover owns 5 pfennig; he buys for that five postal cards, which he sells on the street for 10 pfennig. From the proceeds he buys jumping jacks which he embellishes and sells: he gets 25 pfennig. For that he buys tin-mice, for which he gets the total of 50 pfennig. These he invests in two other articles, on which he earns another 50 pfennig." Cited by R. Weiland, *Die Kinder der Arbeitslosen*, p. 27.
3. *Die Arbeitsmarktlage für Angestellte*, supplement to the *Reichsarbeitsmarktanzeiger*, 21 July 1932.
4. During the sessions of a subcommittee of the Committee for Social Policy of the National Economic Council, with regard to a change in employer-employee relations, it was learned "that various insurance companies employed up to 30,000 representatives as so-called agents, and that, through non-payment of salary taxes, insurance premiums, etc., the companies effected enormous savings, while, on the other hand, the strictest control and discipline of the work prevented every freedom of movement on the part of these 'agents' " (GdA-Archiv, ed., *Die Angestelltenbewegung 1928–31*, p. 165).
5. DHV, ed., *DHV-Jahrbuch 1921*, p. 93.
6. J. Silbermann, *Die Angestellten als Stand*, p. 14.
7. W. Deiters, "Die Berufsgliederung der Kaufmannsgehilfen," esp. p. 254.
8. *Die Handels- und Büroangestellte*, March 1926, p. 3.
9. *Mitteilungen des internationalen Bundes christlicher Angestelltenverbände*, 1929, pp. 130f.
10. "The most important social result of the intense concentration and consolidation of business, which is asserting itself in some (although few) branches of the economy, is that possibilities of promotion to independent executive positions are being restricted for this very class of salaried employees" (K. Wiedenfeld, *Kapitalismus und Beamtentum*, p. 29).
11. H. Bente, *Organisierte Unwirtschaftlichkeit*. I know of several cases during the crisis in which auspicious business deals were not concluded because rivalries between different departments could not be overcome. The responsible gentlemen of the different departments could not agree which department should be credited with the expected profit.
12. See, for example, "Das Problem der Personal-Auslese," *Spannung: Die AEG Umschau*, January 1930. One passage reads as follows: "Many persons have been wrongly steered from the start. They occupy positions in which their performance is just fair. In another job they might, with the special knowledge at their command, which they have no occasion to show or to develop, be able to perform extremely well. Many do not succeed because they run up against a wall. This wall may be that this man's department does not present further possibilities and nobody learns that a valuable person is working there unrecognized in obscurity. But this wall can also be a superior who, perhaps, puts a spoke in the wheel at times so as not to obscure his own brightness, at others because he is interested in keeping a good man in the

background in order not to lose him or again because his judgment of the employee is incorrect."

For an enlightening presentation of the widespread anxieties and intrigues in the modern office see the American novel by J. Heller, *Something Happened*, pp. 13–67. The presentation begins: "In the office in which I work there are five people of whom I am afraid. Each of these five people is afraid of four people (excluding overlaps), for a total of twenty, and each of these twenty people is afraid of six people, making a total of one hundred and twenty people who are feared by at least one person. Each of these one hundred and twenty people is afraid of the other one hundred and nineteen, and all of these one hundred and forty-five people are afraid of the twelve men at the top who helped found and build the company and now own and direct it."

13. "Der Instruktorinnenberuf als Aufstiegsmöglichkeit."
14. A. Fröhlich, *Die mittleren Technikerberufe*, p. 36.
15. O. von der Gablentz and G. Mennicke, *Deutsche Berufskunde*, p. 147.
16. F. Zahn, "Wirtschaftsaufbau Deutschlands," p. 996; J. Nothaas, *Sozialer Auf- und Abstieg im deutschen Volk*, p. 93.

Chapter IV

1. DHV, ed., *Die Gehaltslage der Kaufmannsgehilfen*, p. 52; GdA (ed.), *Die wirtschaftliche und soziale Lage der Angestellten*, p. 18.
2. A functionary of the GdA informed me that this could not always be avoided.
3. The GdA regarded as standardized work, "for example, that of the cataloguers, file clerks, typists without stenography." The DHV considered it to be performed by "typists (no stenography), file clerks, tellers, etc." On the other hand, stenographers were placed in category 2 of the GdA, while, if they were capable of typing more than 150 syllables a minute, the DHV placed them in category 3. The office clerk, "the second salesman, the second shipping clerk who prepares the order transmitted to him for shipment," the second payroll clerk "who prepares the payroll ledger and the salary payments," and the bookkeeper "operating simple commercial bookkeeping machines" were classed in group 2. Incidentally, "second salesman" was a classification which included such salespeople "who, without any special preparatory training, sell price-marked articles or display them to customers." The bookkeeper on an Elliot-Fisher machine performed "skilled commercial work." There should be no doubt that the above-mentioned employees perform subordinate functions.

Besides these points, disputable with regard to terminology, a perusal of the DHV occupational statistics, which present a good picture of the manifold occupational grooves in commerce, shows that, among employees performing the same type of function, improbable relations of the various qualifications exist. Thus, there were about 13,000 first and 22,000 second bookkeepers, as against only 3,000 assistant bookkeepers; the number of first payroll clerks was greater than that of second clerks, and that of first correspondents almost double that of seconds; the number of first shipping clerks exceeded that of seconds; there were more registrars than assistant registrars and just as many second as first calculators, etc.

The number of non-commissioned officers can hardly be greater than that of privates. There are several likely reasons for the improbabilities of the DHV statistics. First, its survey was not representative of the entire body of male commercial employees. Only 5.61 percent of employees included were untrained, whereas, according to the GdA survey, 12 percent of the male employees had not served an apprenticeship. Moreover, the number of executive employees (executives, clerks with power of attorney, department heads, branch managers in the DHV was disproportionately high. Second, in places where only *one* bookkeeper, stock clerk, or shipping clerk, etc., was employed, he was probably designated as first bookkeeper, first stock clerk, or first shipping clerk, etc.

4. M. Rössiger, *Der Angestellte von 1930*, p. 48, where all employees of group 3 and about one-half to two-thirds of group 4 are included in the middle strata.
5. *Wirtschaft und Statistik*, 13, no. 8, (1933).
6. T. Geiger, *Die soziale Schichtung des deutschen Volkes*, p. 54.
7. W. Deiters, "Die Angestellten."
8. S. Suhr, *Die weiblichen Angestellten*, p. 9.
9. "Was wir wollen," p. 37.
10. According to L. Preller, *Sozialpolitik in der Weimarer Republik*, p. 161. Preller's table is based on the GdA survey.

Chapter V

1. G. Dehn, *Proletarische Jugend*, p. 77.
2. K. Leichter, *So leben wir . . . 1320 Industriearbeiterinnen berichten über ihr Leben*, pp. 61f.
3. M. Weber, *Wirtschaft und Gesellschaft*, p. 635.
4. *Statistisches Jahrbuch für das Deutsche Reich*, 1932, p. 321–22.
5. The official statistic demonstrates that differences in life styles of blue- and white-collar workers extend to their choice of food. For example, in the highest income groups expenditures for butter amounted to 5.7 percent among blue-collar workers, and to 9.7 percent among white-collar workers. Conversely, the expenditures for other fats and meat were higher for the blue-collar workers than for white-collar workers. Cf. *Statistisches Jahrbuch für das Deutsche Reich*, 1932, p. 321.
6. Cf. Afa-Bund, ed., *Was verbrauchen die Angestellten?* especially the section "Der Haushalt in der Krise," pp. 75ff.
7. Cf. also O. Kahn-Freund, "Der Funktionswandel des Arbeitsrechts," p. 150.
8. *Deutsche Handelswacht*, 10 September 1930, p. 329. Cf. also C. Philippe, "Die Stellung des Angestellten im Arbeitsrecht"; "Die Bedeutung des Angestelltenstandes," *Deutsche Bergwerkszeitung*, 3 July 1932; and F. Pfirrman, "Der Fuchs predigt den Hühnern."
9. M. Weber, *Wirtschaft und Gesellschaft*, p. 611.
10. From a talk with a Berlin metalworker (1933): "The time engineer arrives and a worker produces the new piece on the most modern machine, the wage being determined by the time required. This worker conspires with the foreman and has gained favor as a climber by denunciations. He works as fast as he can. From the

time-wage that has now been determined, 10 to 20 percent is deducted because, after all, the work will be piecework. No consideration is given to the fact that only the specially selected machine had made the performance possible. And nobody asks whether the tempo can be maintained if not one piece but hundreds have to be produced. The workers learn of the calculated piece wage and declare that they can't do it for this wage, because they need more time than has been calculated. The foreman arrives, then the time calculator comes, then comes the calculator, then the engineer comes, then his assistant, then also the time controller, etc. All of them stand together for a while whispering. Finally someone says that the firm can pay only such and such an amount. If this is not enough, the new order must be returned— and that's all. Then the workers finally say O.K., the time controller leaves, the calculator disappears, the engineer takes leave with his assistant, etc. But who does the work? We, the workers!"

11. F. Muschiol, *Borsig-Zeitung*, 7 July 1929.Cf. almost the same verbatim: R. Woldt, *Das grossindustrielle Beamtentum*, p. 21; also prior to World War I: A. Levenstein, *Die Arbeiterfrage*, p. 22. For postwar views about blue- and white-collar workers in the shop, see *Der deutsche Metallarbeiter*, 1929, nos. 48–52; 1930, nos. 1–5; *Borsig-Zeitung*, 1929, nos. 3–4; 1930, nos. 1–2; *Der Regulator*, 1930, nos. 8–12.
12. *Der deutsche Metallarbeiter*, 1930, no. 1.
13. Written 1929 (cf. note 14 below). In 1933 the salaried employees were no longer protected in this regard.
14. *Borsig-Zeitung*, 1929, nos. 5–6.
15. "Beamte, Angestellte und Arbeiter in der Wirtschaftskrise," p. 297.
16. *Der deutsche Metallarbeiter*, 7 December 1929.
17. L. Preller, *Sozialpolitik in der Weimarer Republik*, p. 167.
18. Cf. also F. Croner, "Die Angestelltenbewegung seit der Währungsstabilisierung," 103ff., sec. 4.
19. I know of an American case in which the vice president of an enterprise occasionally wrote to meritorious employees an unexpected letter in which he expressed gratification with the performance of the recipient. Contrary to the usual memorandum, this letter was delivered to the employee in a sealed envelope. It was not typed, but written by hand and, exclusively for these letters, he used special green ink. It was considered a great distinction in the office to receive "a green letter."
20. Afa-Bund, ed., *Die Praxis der Betriebsräte im Aufsichtsrat*, p. 16.
21. For a very extensive description of such measures and arrangements, cf. C. Dreyfuss, *Beruf und Ideologie der Angestellten*. Regarding the propagandistic treatment of the chances for promotion, cf. C. Eckert, *Rothschilds Taschenbuch für Kaufleute*, p. 14. A short compendium of the psychotechnical recommendations is F. Giese, "Menschenbehandlung beim Büropersonal"; cf. also Giese's more moderate remarks in his book, *Methoden der Wirtschaftspsychologie*. Cost-free praise and cost-free honoring as means of distinction of course are not confined to economic enterprises. They also play a great role in education, in military organizations, in the civilian bureaucracy, in family life, in clubs, in the church, and in science, etc. Public honoring and shaming serve to discipline and improve performance in the most different social structures. S. and B. Webb have referred to the especially important role of these

methods in Soviet Russia; cf. their *Soviet Communism*, p. 749. Cf. also H. Speier, "Freedom and Social Planning," Speier, *Social Order and the Risks of War*, pp. 15f.

22. H. Potthoff, *Privatangestellte und politisches Leben*.
23. Cf. H. Kaelble, *Industrielle Interessenpolitik in der Wilhelminischen Gesellschaft*, pp. 66ff.; J. Kocka, *Unternehmensverwaltung und Angestelltenschaft am Beispiel Siemens 1847 bis 1914*, pp. 536–44.
24. G. Stresemann's speech of 16 May 1908, cited by H. Kaelble, *Industrielle Interessenpolitik*, p. 76.
25. *Deutsche Industriezeitung*, 1911, p. 627.
26. Verhandlungen, Mitteilungen und Berichte des CVDI, 126, January 1913, p. 113, cited by H. Kaelble, *Industrielle Interessenpolitik*, p. 106, note 329.
27. H. Kaelble, *Industrielle Interessenpolitik*, p. 108; cf. also E. Lederer, "Die Unternehmerorganisationen im Kriege," pp. 277–97.
28. *Rechenschaftsbericht des DHV 1926*, p. 98.

Chapter VI

1. Thus, the DHV pointed out in its polemics against Vela, the association of executive employees: "It is sensible for salaried employees who advance to executive positions to remain in the associations which they joined at the beginning of their professional careers." (*Rechenschaftsbericht*, 1928, p. 269). J. Silbermann, a functionary of the VwA, did not classify the "other managers" of the census, including the directors, as "independents" but as salaried employees. (*Die Angestellten als Stand*, p. 20).
2. P. Bröcker, *Die Arbeitnehmerbewegung*, p. 98; M. Rössiger, *Der Angestellte von 1930*, p. 15.
3. Cf. F. Croner, "Der Begriff der Angestellten in der neueren Rechtssprechung," p. 188. The concept of the salaried employees according to the 1911 insurance law for salaried employees does not coincide with that of the 1929 law on shop councils; cf. E. Lederer and J. Marschak, "Der neue Mittelstand," pp. 120–41, note 2.
4. DHV, ed., *Die Gehaltslage der Kaufmannsgehilfen*, p. 9.
5. Concerning the DHV view of technical employees, cf. also O. Thiel, *Die Sozialpolitik der Kaufmannsgehilfen*, p. 4: "The GdA organizes not only male and female salaried employees of every kind but also certain groups of higher workers, male and female, whom we cannot recognize as salaried employees." Technical employees reversed the bias: "Unfortunately, it is often forgotten that the production of goods precedes their distribution." Butab, ed., *Der Techniker im Tarifvertrag*, p. 8.
6. W. D. von Witzleben, "Der Tarifvertrag für die Angestellten der Berliner Metallindustrie," p. 27.
7. I. Silbermann, *Die Angestellten als Stand*, p. 5.
8. Departing from its usual stress on professional consciousness, the DHV reproached the bank clerks—i.e., white-collar workers with a truly pronounced professional pride—that their attitude was outdated: "The old social isolation of the bank clerks from the majority of other commercial clerks has favored this attitude. But this attitude is especially misplaced in banking, because there the enormous number of dismissals during the past years, which has forced tens of thousands of bank clerks into other

enterprises, has clearly demonstrated that they can prevail only as members of the big family of commercial clerks." *Rechenschaftsbericht des DHV für 1928*, p. 88.

9. W. Sombart, "Beruf," *Hwb der Soziologie*, p. 31.

10. H. Schäfer, "Die leitenden Angestellten: Ein neuer sozialer Typus."

11. The following information on the number of job applications submitted by unemployed executives taken from *Rechenschaftsbericht der Vela 1929*, pp. 246–47, may complement the picture: 1–50 applications were submitted by 186 unemployed executives; 50–100 by 111; 100–200 by 87; 200–300 by 43; 300–600 by 44; 600–1,000 by 9; and 1000–1,500 by 13. Twenty-one persons said they had sent "hundreds" or "innumerable" applications. In 12 cases no reply was received; in 117 cases less than 10 percent of the written applications were answered, in 89 cases 10–20 percent, in 56 cases 20–30 percent. The remainder received replies more frequently.

12. A. Zimmermann, *Der Deutschnationale Handlungsgehilfen-Verband*, p. 95.

13. According to the report of the factory inspector; cf. the statistic in: GdH, ed., *Die kommende Angestelltengeneration*, pp. 11–18.

14. *Der GdA-Führer*, 1931, p. 120 Cf. also J. Jahn, "Das Sozialbewusstsein der Angestellten," pp. 246–47.

15. F. Croner, "Die Angestellten seit der Währungsstabilisierung," pp. 103–46. For a recent, much more detailed Marxist analysis of white-collar workers, cf. U. Kadritzke, *Angestellte: Die geduldigen Arbeiter*. The book combines a praiseworthy presentation of copious data with the demand that the reader translate the author's views, which are hidden in a doctrinaire jargon, into intelligible German. They defy translation into English. For example, Kadritzke writes about insurance for salaried employees: "Die spezifische, durchaus schon taktisch konzipierte 'Borniertheit' der Bourgeoisie konstituiert in der Gründung einer besonderen, die rechtliche Exklusivstellung ergänzenden Angestelltenversicherung ein Moment der 'Angestelltenmentalität', das, obgleich seine objektive gesellschaftliche Basis schon zu schwinden beginnt, die Formen der folgenden Klassenauseinandersetzungen doch *folgenreich bestimmen kann*" (p. 226).

16. C. Dreyfuss in *Beruf und Ideologie der Angestellten* recognized this fact, which constitutes the methodological merit of his book. Dreyfuss endeavored to prove in detail that the entrepreneurs created ever anew the *illusion* of prestige through the carefully calculated creation of an artificial hierarchy in the firm. Although this explanation does not suffice to explain the phenomenon of social esteem, it is more productive than the Marxian assumption of "false consciousness."

17. Cf. J. Jahn, *Das Sozialbewusstsein der Angestellten*.

18. C. Nörpel, "Grenzen des Arbeitsrechts." Cf. also in the same journal the discussion following this article.

19. Afa-Bund, ed., *Protokoll des 4. Afa-Gewerkschaftskongresses*, p. 151.

Chapter VII

1. H. Speier, "Das Proletariat und seine Kritiker," p. 295.

2. A. L. Schlözer, *Theorie der Statistik*, p. 134. On the transvaluation of social esteem, cf. also H. Speier, "Militarism in the Eighteenth Century," *Social Order and the*

Risks of War., esp. the sections "Society vs the State" and "The Devaluation of Courage," pp. 241–52.

3. Cf. M. Weber's definition of social order, cit. above p. 8.

4. On the concept of "relative deprivation," now often used in American sociology, see H. Speier, "Social Stratification," in M. Ascoli and F. Lehmann, eds., *Political and Economic Democracy*, pp. 264–65.

5. The function of education (2.a and 2.b) is discussed in chap. 9, and nationalism (3.a and 3.b) in chap. 10.

Chapter VIII

1. Regarding the hierarchy in the office cf. G. Briefs, "Betriebssoziologie," in *Hwb der Soziologie*, pp. 441ff.; C. H. A. Geck, *Die sozialen Arbeitsverhältnisse im Wandel der Zeit*, p. 51; C. Dreyfuss, *Beruf und Ideologie der Angestellten*, pp. 11ff.; J. Silbermann, *Die Angestellten als Stand*, pp. 12ff.

2. To offer an extreme example from a large firm known to me in 1932, a subordinate correspondent consoled a typist who had complained about the routine character of her work as follows: "You can advance." "How?" "If you prove to be efficient, you will be permitted to type the opening of replies on your own initiative rather than by dictation." This meant that she would be permitted to type on her own: "Gentlemen, we acknowledge with thanks the receipt of your letter dated. . ."

3. It is well known that the differences in rank among executive employees are reflected in income, size and furnishings of the office, use of a company car, and the like. In addition, of special importance are ease and frequency of access to persons of higher rank and greater power. A modern, grotesque example taken from the higher American bureaucracy of the White House—not different in principle from the bureaucracy in private business—is given by T. H. White in his book about President Nixon's administration. White writes that familiarity with "the political topography" makes it possible "to judge the importance of people" by the location of their office. Then he tells the following anecdote about Daniel P. Moynihan, later U.S. Ambassador to the United Nations and, still later, U.S. Senator from New York: "In his rivalry with Arthur Burns in the first year of the Nixon administration, Moynihan opted for a tiny office in the basement of the White House West Wing, next to Kissinger's, while Burns opted for a large suite of offices for himself and staff across the street in the Executive Office Building. Moynihan, whose wisdom is at once profound and practical, had made the better choice—'Why, it meant I could piss standing next to Haldeman in the same toilet,' he said one day, explaining the strategic geography of the White House." (T. H. White, *Breach of Faith*, pp. 113–14).

4. Also not in the large firms of retail trade. Cf. the instructive functional analysis of a department store with about 700 employees by H. Schröer, *Die betriebliche Ausbildung des Verkaufspersonals im Einzelhandel*, pp. 14ff.; cf. also F. Nordsieck, *Die schaubildliche Erfassung und Untersuchung der Organisation*, p. 80; and F. Nordsieck, "Die Arbeitsaufgaben und ihre Verteilung," *Hb des Einzelhandels*.

5. E. Kannwitz, "Aus dem Berufsleben eines technischen Vorkalkulators."

6. F. Giese, *Methoden der Wirtschaftspsychologie*, p. 276.

7. Reported by C. Höfchen, in H. Potthoff, ed. *Die sozialen Probleme des Betriebs*, p. 290.

8. This basic fact can also be found in international affairs. A highly renowned British statesman, asked about the possibilities of securing peace, proposed on the wireless that diplomats be the first sent to the front if war broke out.

Chapter IX

1. E. Jünger, *Der Arbeiter*, pp. 120, 105.
2. H. Freyer, *Revolution von rechts*, p. 71.
3. Cit. by H. Speier, "Das Proletariat *und seine Kritiker*," p. 289.
4. Cf. I. Hamel, *Völkischer Verband und nationale Gewerkschaft*, p. 225.
5. A. Winnig, *Vom Proletariat zum Arbeitertum*, p. 58.
6. A. Zimmermann, *Der Deutschnationale Handlungsgehilfen-Verband*, p. 93.
7. DHV, ed., *Stoffsammlung für die Bildungsarbeit des DHV: Schule und Erziehung*, p. 10.
8. DHV, ed., *Rechenschaftsbericht des DHV für 1926*, p. 11.
9. Cf. *Deutsche Handelswacht*, 25 June 1928.
10. M. Habermann, *Stand und Staat* (Hamburg, 1931).
11. This well-known transformation of the middle strata is discussed in the spirit of the DHV by A. Fraenkel, "Die zwei wirtschaftlichen Weltprobleme." The author tries to develop and prove the thesis "that a society formed by culture cannot originate and preserve itself without a middle class" (p. 373). In the *Zentralarchiv des DHV* (June/September 1929) the article is judged to be "the best scientific assessment of the salaried employees in our sense that is available from a scientific source."
12. Cf. B. Mewes, *Die erwerbstätige Jugend*; V. Engelhardt, "Die Bildungsinteressen in den einzelnen Berufen"; F. Grosse, *Bildungsinteressen des grossstädtischen Proletariats*; F. Urbschat, *Das Seelenleben der kaufmännisch tätigen Jugendlichen*; R. Dinse, *Das Freizeitleben der Grossstadtjugend*.
13. GdA, ed., *Die wirtschaftliche und soziale Lage der Angestellten*, p. 49.
14. DHV, ed., *Rechenschaftsbericht des DHV für 1926*, p. 11.
15. T. Fontane, *Briefe an seine Familie*, vol. 2, p. 174 (letter to his son Theodor of May 9, 1888). Cf. also H. Speier, "Zur Soziologie der bürgerlichen Intelligenz in Deutschland," pp. 58–72.
16. Cf. F. Goldschmidt, *Die soziale Lage und die Bildung des Kaufmannsgehilfen*.
17. In 1892 of every 100,000 inhabitants 25 were students of commercial continuation schools in Prussia, 91 in Saxony.
18. E. Engelhard, "Die Angestellten," p. 583.
19. H. von Treitschke, *Politik*, vol. 2, p. 400.
20. Cf. E. Kehr, "Zur Genesis des kgl. preussischen Reserveoffiziers," pp. 492–502. According to a decision of the Ministry of War on 18 February 1914, Social Democrats were excluded from one-year service. What belated effects arrogance about one's education continue to have is illustrated by the following grotesque story, told by an eyewitness of the event. At a demonstration of radical left-wing students in Berlin at the beginning of the 1960s, a policeman refused to be provoked into manhandling

the demonstrators. But then one of the students had the good idea to address the policeman as "you elementary school pupil," whereupon the policeman struck the student.

21. Marx recognized this as early as 1875. Cf. *Das Kapital*, vol. 3 pp. 311–12.

22. GdA, ed., *Der GdA-Führer*, 1931, no. 8.

23. Cf. Abundant information about the importance and scope of the examinations can be found in GdA, ed., *Die kommende Angestelltengeneration*, pp. 133–43: In 1931, 31 chambers of commerce (of about 130) administered such examinations. They were voluntary but sometimes held by agreement incorporated into the contracts on apprenticeship (in Upper Silesia in 10 percent of the cases). The fees for the examinations amounted to RM 5–15. Special preparatory courses [!] took place in five localities; four of these cost between RM 10 and 15. Only a fraction of the apprentices took these examinations. "One might assume that they are the best, but the results of the examinations show that this is not the case. They are, rather, apprentices urged by the boss to participate, or careerists." The examinations appear not to have had any tangible results: "It has been reported that one Chamber of Commerce . . . every year reminds its member firms that they ought to hire only applicants who have a certificate of examination. The Association of Food Retail-Traders have resolved to hire only such applicants." A functionary of the GdA told me that applicants who failed the examination "have a better chance of being hired, because they offer to work below the standard wage."

24. At its twenty-ninth convention on 16 June 1930 the DWV passed a resolution containing the following statement: "In consequence of rationalization, foremen face new professional problems. This is especially true of professional training. The guiding principle must be: professional claims only on the basis of professional work, professional promotion only on the basis of professional accomplishments." Regarding the attitude of the DWV toward the question of education, especially toward the efforts of entrepreneurs who focus on the problem of "human engineering," cf. DWV, ed., *Geschäftsbericht für 1928–29*, pp. 158–96.

25. O. Suhr, "Angestelltenbildung," *Hwb des deutschen Volksbildungswesens*.

26. M. M. von Weber, cited in *25 Jahre technische Gewerkschaft: 10 Jahre Butab*, p. 11.

27. Cf. "Vorbildung und Leistung schöpferischer Technik in Beispielen: 353 kurze Lebensabrisse," *Der Ingenieurstand*, 1926; K. Matschoss, "Berufskundliche Untersuchung des Buches 'Männer der Technik'," pp. 120ff.; cf. also the discussion and bibliography in E. Jung, *Die unsterbliche Ingenieurfrage*, pp. 11ff.

28. According to A. Günther's survey (prior to World War I), the proportion of employed technicians who had nine years of schooling *(Einjährige)* fluctuated between 10 percent (in the building trades) and 16.3 percent (among civil servants); in industry it was 15.5 percent. A. Günther, *Die deutschen Techniker*, p. 63.

29. In Wurttemberg from 1837 to 1885 civil servants had to take a special course of studies in public finance and administration. Regarding the competition between jurists and technicians cf. W. Franz, *Das Technikerproblem*; and C. Eckert, ed., *Der Eintritt der erfahrungswissenschaftlichen Intelligenz in die Verwaltung*. The paper by O. Schleicher in this book contains a comprehensive historical presentation of the problem in the literature.

30. A more detailed presentation of this process would have to give an account of the following: the emergence of new types of schools (*Realgymnasium, Realschule,* etc.), changes in the requirements of education preparatory to study at a university, the origin and spread of new types of higher educational institutions (for the practical needs of mining, agriculture, commerce, and industry), and the development of student organizations at institutions of higher learning. For a few hints cf. F. Schulze and P. Scymank, *Das deutsche Studententum,* pp. 300ff.

Chapter X

1. M. R. Lepsius, *Extremer Nationalismus,* p. 14. Lepsius surpasses the views presented in the text by comparisons with both the functions of nationalism in other German social strata and extremist movements in other countries. Especially important are Lepsius's suggestions that the nationalism of the German middle class had nothing to do "with a special concentration of authoritarian personalities in the middle class" (p. 14). According to an investigation by Martin Trow in a small Vermont town, among the followers of Senator McCarthy "authoritarian personalities were [also] not represented above the average" (cit. p. 16).
2. *Deutsche Werkmeister Zeitung,* 22 August 1919.
3. G. Briefs, "Betriebssoziologie," in *Hwb der Soziologie,* p. 47.
4. "Das Meisterproblem," *Betriebsräte-Zeitung,* 1922, no. 2.
5. A. von Berger, *Der leitende Wirtschaftsbeamte,* pp. 121ff.
6. M. Habermann, *Stand und Staat,* p. 20.
7. *Stand und Staat,* 5 May 1931.
8. *Liederbuch für deutschnationale Handlungsgehilfen,* 21st ed. (1927), pp. 18ff.
9. *Stand und Staat,* August 1932.
10. Cf. on this subject H. Speier, "Risk, Security and Modern Hero Worship," Speier, *Social Order and the Risks of War,* pp. 112–30.
11. H. A. Turner, Jr. *Faschismus und Kapitalismus in Deutschland,* p. 168.
12. From the voluminous literature cf. E. Nolte, *Der Faschismus in seiner Epoche;* F. Stern, *Kulturpessimismus als politische Gefahr,* K. von Klemperer, *Konservative Bewegungen,* A. Mohler, *Die konservative Revolution in Deutschland;* H. Lebovics, *Social Conservatism and the Middle Classes in Germany.*
13. Cf. R. Heberle, *From Democracy to Nazism.* Also, the Hitler Youth was strongest in Austria and northern Germany (Hannover, Schleswig-Holstein, Lower Saxony) and weakest in the Catholic parts (Rhineland, the Saar, Bavaria.) The Hitler Youth was at first unable to "conquer" the traditional bulwarks of the left (Berlin, the Ruhr, Hamburg). In January 1932, when the NSDAP was the strongest political party in Germany, the Hitler Youth had fewer than 1,000 members in Berlin. Cf. W. Z. Laqueur, *Young Germany,* p. 193.
14. Cf. especially S. M. Lipset, *Political Man,* p. 141, table 1. Lipset compared the votes for the individual parties (or group of parties) in percentages of the total votes cast in the elections for the Reichstag since 1928. He presented the following confirmation of the statement (made in the text) that Catholic, Social Democratic, and Communist loyalties were stable. From 1928 to the second election in 1932, the percentage of DNVP voters dwindled from 14.2 to 8.5, i.e., by 40 percent, that of

the DVP voters from 8.7 to 1.8, i.e., by 79 percent and that of the DDP voters from 4.8 to 0.95, i.e., by 80 percent. By contrast, the percentage of Nazi votes increased from 2.6 to 33.1, i.e., by 1,277 percent. Only the Center Party, with a gain of 5 percent, and SPD and KPD together, with a loss of 8 percent remained relatively stable. (The SPD alone suffered a loss in its share of the votes, from 29.8 percent in 1928 to 20.4 percent in 1932, whereas the corresponding percentages for the KPD increased from 10.6 to 16.85.) On the basis of these and other figures, Lipset advanced his thesis that German National Socialism was "extremism of the middle." For criticism of this thesis, cf. H. A. Winkler, *Mittelstand, Demokratie und Nationalsozialismus*, p. 180.

15. Cf. L. E. Jones, "The Crisis of White-Collar Interest Politics: Deutschnationaler Handlungsgehilfen-Verband und Deutsche Volkspartei in the World Economic Crisis," in H. Mommsen et al., eds., *Industrielles System und politische Entwicklung in der Weimarer Republik*, pp. 811–23.
16. A. Krebs, *Tendenzen und Gestalten der NSDAP*, pp. 27–28.
17. Cf. ibid., pp. 30–32.
18. Cited by I. Hamel, *Völkischer Verband und nationale Gewerkschaft*, p. 248.
19. Cf. ibid., p. 212.
20. G. L. Mosse, *The Crisis of German Ideology*, p. 261.
21. After 30 January 1933 Bechly had to resign his office, and Habermann was sharply attacked by Nazi members of the DHV even after his loss of office. As an active member of the illegal opposition, he worked with Wilhelm Leuschner and Jakob Kaiser on plans for a unified trade union after Hitler's downfall. In 1936–37 he participated in the drafting of memoranda for General von Fritsch on the brutal treatment of workers and Jews. After 1939 he was in contact with the circle around Oster and, later, with Goerdeler and Beck. After 20 July, he was arrested and perished miserably. I have had no access to the biographical study by A. Krebs on Max Habermann. But cf. I. Hamel, *Völkischer Verband und nationale Gewerkschaft*, pp. 121–23; A. Krebs, *Tendenzen und Gestalten der NSDAP*, pp. 27–39; H. Brüning, *Memoiren 1918–1934*, pp. 516, 518; R. Pechel, *Deutscher Widerstand*, pp. 208ff.; P. Hoffmann, *Widerstand, Staatsstreich, Attentat*, pp. 52, 135, 431, 461; E. Nebgen, *Jakob Kaiser*, p. 128.
22. In a letter to his daughter of 1 April 1895 the old Fontane characterized Bismarck as "this mixture of superman and sly dog, of a founder of States and a stable-owner refusing to pay his taxes . . . of hero and cry-baby." Cf. T. Fontane, *Briefe an seine Familie*, vol. 2, p. 309.
23. Cf. I. Hamel, *Völkischer Verband und nationale Gewerkschaft*, p. 136.
24. G. L. Mosse, *The Crisis of German Ideology*, p. 258.
25. L. E. Jones, "The Dying Middle," p. 816, note 21.
26. According to information given by the GdA to the author in 1932.
27. H. Gerth, "The Nazi Party: Its Leadership and Composition," p. 527, table 1. Cf. also E. Doblin and C. Pohly, "The Social Composition of the Nazi Leadership," pp. 42–49; and D. Lerner et al., *The Nazi Elite*. The importance of the middle classes in the Nazi movement before Hitler's assumption of power was clearly recognized prior to 1933; cf. H. D. Lasswell, "The Psychology of Hitlerism as a Response of the Lower Middle Classes to Continuing Insecurity" (1933), reprinted in Lasswell,

The Analysis of Political Behavior, pp. 235–45. Regarding the "new middle class" cf. C. Mierendorff, "Gesicht und Charakter der nationalsozialistischen Bewegung," pp. 489–504; T. Geiger, "Panik im Mittelstand," pp. 637–54; T. Geiger, *Die soziale Schichtung des deutschen Volkes*, p. 120f; H. Neisser, "Sozialstatistische Analyse der Wahlergebnisse," pp. 654–59. In his book *Die deutschen Reichstagswahlen 1871– 1930 und die Wandlungen der Volksgliederung*, A. Dix advanced the proposition that the electoral success of the NSDAP could in part be attributed to young first voters. Dix was "the only non-Nazi journalist" (S. Neumann) who had predicted that the NSDAP would have a hundred deputies in the Reichstag by 1930; his prediction was based on the age stratification and its change since 1928. In the modern literature cf. especially H. A. Turner, Jr., *Faschismus und Kapitalismus in Deutschland*; D. Schoenbaum, *Hitler's Social Revolution*; A. F. K. Organski, "Fascism and Modernization," in S. J. Woolf, ed., *The Nature of Fascism*, pp. 19–41; G. Germani, "Fascism and Class," in ibid., pp. 65–96; J. Kocka, "Zur Problematik der deutschen Angestellten 1914–1933," in H. Mommsen et al., eds., *Industrielles System und politische Entwicklung in der Weimarer Republik*, pp. 792–811; the monographs by W. Schäfer and A. Weber cited in notes 28 and 29 below; S. M. Lipset, *Political Man* (despite its simplistic thesis that Hitler was "a centrist extremist"; S. A. Pratt, "The Social Basis of Nazism and Communism in Germany"; U. Kadritzke, *Angestellte: Die geduldigen Arbeiter*, pp. 365–81.

28. W. Schäfer, *NSDAP: Entwicklung und Struktur der Staatspartei des Dritten Reiches*; p. 17.

29. A. Weber, "Soziale Merkmale der NSDAP-Wähler," pp. 68ff.

30. Cf. ibid., p. 134. Unfortunately little is known about the number of white-collar workers who became and remained members of the NSDAP prior to 1933. Nor do we know how many who left were matched or exceeded by new entries. Schäfer mentions (p. 17) that the "inner movement of members" in the NSDAP between 1930 and 1933 amounted to no less then 156.5 percent, i.e., one and a half times as much as its actual membership at the time the party came to power. It might be mentioned that the fluctuation of KPD members was also very large. According to a report by O. Pjatnizki at the 11th EKKI Plenary Session of the Comintern, the KPD had 133,000 paying members in January 1930 and 180,000 at the end of December. During that year, however, 143,000 new members joined the KPD. Of these only 47,200 remained in the party, whereas 95,300 members left the party during the course of the year. Cf. O. Pjatnizki, *Brennende Fragen*, vol. 2, p. 40. Presumably, the quota of "inner movement of members" was higher in the parties of the extreme right and left than in the parties of the middle. During visits to the homes of unemployed families in Berlin in 1932, I gained the impression that young unemployed persons changed over easily from Red Front to the SA. Often this change seemed to be caused by better supply of free beer and the like. The increase of unemployed and decrease of employed workers in the KPD were very large during the economic crisis. According to Pjatnizki, the percentage of employed workers in the KPD decreased from 62.3 to 20–22 between 1928 and 1931. Cf. ibid., p. 25.

31. A. Schopenhauer, "Aphorismen zur Lebensweisheit," in *Sämtliche Werke*, ed. Frischeisen-Köhler, vol. 6, p. 348. Schopenhauer polemicized against the "German brethren and democrats" of his time. The sociopolitical function of nationalism is subject to

historical change, which is true also of the nationalistic inclinations of individual social strata.

32. H. Freyer, *Revolution von rechts*, p. 37.
33. Ibid., p. 44.
34. Ibid., pp. 52–53.
35. H. Freyer's pamphlet was published at a time when the electoral successes of the Nazis deprived even sober observers of the political landscape in Germany of their judgment. Thus, Sigmund Neumann wrote in 1932 (a year before he emigrated from Germany) that the National Socialists were "of tremendous value as a critique of what exists at present . . . even if they were not to develop beyond their negations." Cf. S. Neumann, *Die deutschen Parteien*, p. 74. The book was widely read at the time and republished as late as 1965. For a contemporary critique cf. H. Speier in *Zs für Sozialforschung* 1(1932):452–53.

Chapter XI

1. Cited by W. Stiller, *Der Verein für Handlungs-Commis von 1858*, p. 247.
2. I. Reif, "Der VDH zu Leipzig," p. 102.
3. S. Aufhäuser, *Eine unromantische Betrachtung zum Geshichtsbild der Angestelltenverbände*, p. 17.
4. To be regarded as a precursor was the Freie Organisation junger Kaufleute in Berlin (1884–87), which was newly founded in 1889 as Freie Vereinigung junger Kaufleute.
5. S. Aufhäuser, *Eine unromantische Betrachtung*, p. 14.
6. E. Lederer, *Die Privatangestellten in der modernen Wirtschaftsentwicklung*, p. 173, note.
7. I. Hamel, *Völkischer Verband und nationale Gewerkschaft*, p. 53.
8. Cited in ibid., p. 55.
9. P. Bröcker in *Deutsche Handelswacht*, 1928, p. 42 (in a memorial article for A. Stöcker).
10. During the same period of industrialization, similar anti-semitic middle-class movements aroused attention in other European capitals (Vienna, Paris, etc.) Cf. M. Spahn, "Die christlich-soziale Bewegung."
11. P. Bröcker, in *Deutsche Handelswacht*, 1928, p. 25.
12. DHV, ed., *Die Deutschnationale Handlungsgehilfen Bewegung und die politischen Parteien*, 57 (1911):29.
13. Cf. the polemics from a Social Democratic vantage point against this proposed Bund der Kaufmännischen Angestellten by R. Woldt, *Das grossindustrielle Beamtentum*, pp. 89ff. and *Protokoll des 8. Kongresses der Gewerkschaften Deutschlands*, p. 359.
14. J. Kocka, *Klassengesellschaft im Krieg 1914–1918*, pp. 76–82; and J. Kocka, "Zur Problematik der deutschen Angestellten," in H. Mommsen et al., eds., *Industrielles System und politische Entwicklung in der Weimarer Republik*, pp. 793–95.
15. Cf. the table in J. Kocka, *Klassengesellschaft*, p. 83. To be sure, the figures presented by Kocka show the growth of membership in the last year of war to be relatively larger in the middle-class Arbeitsgemeinschaft than in the Afa organizations in 1917–18. The DHV had the relatively and absolutely biggest increase. But also, during the last year of the war the Verein für Handlungskommis von 1858 and the Leipziger

Verband Deutscher Handlungsgehilfen gained (absolutely and relatively) more members than any Afa-Bund organization.

16. E. Lederer, "Sozialpolitische Chronik," in *ASS*, 44(1917):320; I. Hamel, *Völkischer Verband und nationale Gewerkschaft*, p. 169.
17. I. Hamel, *Völkischer Verband und nationale Gewerkschaft*, p. 170.
18. *Erste Reichstagung der kaufmännischen Angestellten Deutschlands* (1918), pp. 43, 45.
19. J. Kocka, *Klassengesellschaft*, pp. 77–78.
20. Cited by A. Rosenberg, *Die Entstehung der deutschen Republik*, p. 194.

Chapter XII

1. GdA, ed., *Jahresbericht*, 1919–20, p. 6
2. Very precise was K. Milde's observation regarding the unionization of academic technicians, in as much as they had not been members of Butib: "After all, it was no longer a question of 'wanting to' but 'having to' [organize]." (*Sozialpolitische Schriften des Bundes angestellter Akademiker technisch-naturwissenschaftlicher Berufe*. 1st series, no. 1, p. 9). As regards the executive employees, who at that time founded Vela in order to keep their social distance from other white-collar workers, cf. the remarks by Dr. Müffelmann in his "Die Gewerkschaftsbewegung der leitenden Angestellten." Müffelmann pointed out that collective bargaining agreements were a road to the autonomous creation of new law. But insofar as "the creators of this new law are only the trade unions, the executive employees today would have to form a professional organization of their own, if they had not as yet, unless they wanted to relinquish their legal position in the process of production" (p. 13).
3. E. Lederer, "Sozialpolitische Chronik," 591.
4. Deputy Koenen (USPD), in E. Heilfron, ed., *Die deutsche Nationalversammlung im Jahre 1919*, vol. 6, p. 4336.
5. Cf. the new formulation of paragraph 2, sec. 2 of the DHV constitution—based on a resolution by management and the board of directors—on 25 May 1919; cf. I. Hamel, *Völkischer Verband und nationale Gewerkschaft*, pp. 174–75.
6. E. Lederer, "Sozialpolitische Chronik," *ASS* 47(1920):590.
7. *Deutsche Handelswacht*, 10 June 1919, cit. by I. Hamel, *Völkischer Verband und nationale Gewerkschaft*, p. 117.
8. GdA-Archiv, ed., *Epochen der Angestelltenbewegung, 1774–1930*, p. 197.
9. Ibid., p. 198.
10. On the significance of the right of co-determination, cf. ibid., pp. 201ff.
11. *Deutsche Handelswacht*, 10 June 1919, cit. by I. Hamel, *Völkischer Verband und nationale Gewerkschaft*, p. 177.
12. In October 1920 Lederer was still quite skeptical regarding the attitude of the DHV toward strikes. He regarded the recognition of the strike by the DHV as "more theoretical" and cited examples of DHV functionaries "accepting all the arguments made by the entrepreneurial press against strikes without any reservations"; in dubious cases they appeared in fact "to tilt rather toward rejection of the strike and thus toward a conflict with the striking organizations." Cf. Lederer, "Sozialpolitische Chronik," *ASS* 47(1920):597.

13. W. Lambach, *Sozialisierung und kaufmännische Angestellte*, p. 28.
14. H. Bechly, *Der nationale Gedanke nach der Revolution*, p. 43; cit. by I. Hamel, *Völkischer Verband und nationale Gewerkschaft*, p. 180.
15. F. Mantel, "Die Vollsozialisierung der Angestellten."
16. K. Renner, "Die Geltung der Ingenieurarbeit in Wirtschaft und Gesellschaft," p. 15.
17. *Deutsche Handelswacht*, 10 April 1919.
18. W. Lambach, *Sozialisierung und kaufmännische Angestellte*, p. 45.
19. Cf. I. Hamel, *Völkischer Verband und nationale Gewerkschaft*, p. 181.
20. Cf. E. Lederer, "Sozialpolitische Chronik," ASS 47(1920):616, note 86-c.
21. Cf. G. Werner, "Der Weg zur Sozialisierung des Kohlenbergbaus."
22. Cf. *Deutsche Werkmeisterzeitung*, 12 November 1920, which also contains a warning against "bureaucratization."
23. M. Habermann, *Die Sozialisierung der Kohle*, p. 16.
24. Cf., for example, C. Köhler, "Die Sozialisierung und die Angestellten," p. 8; F. Mantel in *Verbandsblätter*, 1920, no. 6; and A. Heinrichsbauer, in *Verbandsblätter*, 1919, no. 8.
25. E. Frommholz, *Die Sozialisierung des Kohlenbergbaus*, p. 31.
26. Cf. E. Fraenkel, "10 Jahre Betriebsrätegesetz," p. 117. Fraenkel discusses the origin of the law and the development of its application in sociological perspective.
27. W. zur Megede, *Volkswirtschaftliche und soziale Auswirkungen des Betriebsrätegesetzes*, pp. 10–11, note.
28. G. Schneider, *Die Angestellten im demokratischen Volksstaat*, p. 31.
29. For data cf. Afa-Bund, ed., *Die Praxis der Betriebsräte im Aufsichtsrat*.
30. *Verbandsblätter*, 1919, no. 8, p. 115.
31. G. Schneider, *Die Angestellten im demokratischen Volksstaat*, p. 27; *Die Deutsche Nationalversammlung*, vol. 6, p. 4379.
32. *Die Deutsche Nationalversammlung*, p. 4370.
33. GdA-Archiv, ed., *Epochen der Angestelltenbewegung 1774–1930*, pp. 209f.
34. Cf. the articles by v. Brost in *Der Deutsche*, 10 September 1921 and 14 March 1922.
35. *Der Arbeitgeber*, 1 August 1922, p. 253.
36. Cf. the following articles in *Soziale Praxis*, 1927: O. Thiel (DHV), "Für oder gegen Ersatzkassen in der Arbeitslosenversicherung," pp. 493ff.; F. R. Spliedt (ADGB), "Ersatzkassen in der AV," p. 545f; W. Bösche (GdA), "Für oder gegen Ersatzkassen in der AV," pp. 630ff.
37. Cf. for example *Protokoll des 4. Verhandlungstags des ZdA*, pp. 96ff.
38. Cf. I. Hamel, *Völkischer Verband und nationale Gewerkschaft*, p. 190–91.
39. As has already been mentioned, the list of authors of the Hanseatische Verlagsanstalt contained the names of many writers who contributed to the "debourgeoisement" of the German people and thus prepared the way for National Socialism.
40. After the break with Hugenberg, a DNVP polemicist said in 1933 that the DHV exercized such far reaching political influence "as no other economic concern, including the almighty I.G.-Farben." Cf. Anon., *Der DHV als national-politischer Störenfried*.
41. Cit. by I. Hamel, *Völkischer Verband und nationale Gewerkschaft*, p. 177.

42. For a recent detailed discussion of the views on embourgeoisement held at the time by Theodor Geiger and myself cf. Birgit Mahnkopf, *Verbürgerlichung* (Frankfurt and New York, 1985), ch. 6: "Die Kontroverse zwischen H. Speier und Th. Geiger," pp. 97–123.

Chapter XIII

1. Especially in the mining industry, the number of independent organizations was fairly large owing to the characteristic nature of the enterprises in that branch of the economy. The proportion of agents, captains, and other merchant marine officers, academic employees, and agricultural employees who were not members of free trade unions was especially high. The various reasons for this are so evident that they need no elaboration.
2. DWV, ed., *Der Werkmeister im Tarifvertrag*, vol. 1, p. 555.
3. Afa-Bund, ed., *Die Angestelltenbewegung 1928–1931*, pp. 410ff.
4. A. Erkelenz, "Um die Einheit der Gewerkschaftsbewegung."
5. Cf. "Entwertung des Menschen"; P. G. Gundlach, "Staat, Gesellschaft und Wirtschaft in der individualistischen Ära unter katholischer Sicht," in J. van den Velden, ed., *Die berufsständische Ordnung*, p. 43.

Chapter XIV

1. Concerning objections to the concordat, cf. H. Brüning, *Memoiren 1918–1934*, pp. 670–72.
2. Regarding the following cf. H.-G. Schumann, *Nationalsozialismus und Gewerk-schaftsbewegung*, pp. 53–60.
3. Ibid., p. 57.
4. Cf. A. Erkelenz, "Um die Einheit der Gewerkschaftsbewegung."
5. The *Bankbeamten-Zeitung* of 6 June 1933 said: "Details are not yet known, but it can be said that the old constitution of the DBV will continue to apply to membership fees, unemployment benefits, and survivor and dowry payments" (p. 66).
6. Concerning the organization of the DAF, cf. W. Müller, *Das soziale Leben in Deutschland*, ill. 6.
7. *Arbeitertum*, 15 May 1933.

Bibliography

1. Publications of White-Collar Workers' Organizations

Afa-Bund, ed. *Die Angestelltenbewegung 1921–1925*. Berlin, 1925.
———. *Die Angestelltenbewegung 1925–1928*. Berlin, 1928.
———. *Die Angestelltenbewegung 1928–1931*. Berlin, 1931.
———. *Die Angestellten in der Wirtschaft: Eine Auswertung der amtlichen Berufszählung von 1925*. Berlin, 1928.
———. *Erhebung über das Arbeiten an Schreibmaschinen*. Berlin, 1931.
———. *Der Haushalt der Kaufmannsgehilfen*. Berlin, 1927.
———. *Die Praxis der Betriebsräte im Aufsichtsrat*. Berlin, 1930.
———. *Protokoll des 4. Afa-Gewerkschaftskongresses*. Berlin, 1931.
———. *Tarifverträge der freien Angestelltenverbände*. Berlin, 1933.
———. *Was verbrauchen die Angestellten?* Berlin, 1931.
Berufszählung 1925. Statistik des Deutschen Reichs. vol. 402. Berlin, 1927.
Butab, ed. *Der Techniker im Tarifvertrag*. Berlin, 1924.
———. *25 Jahre Technikergewerkschaft: 10 Jahre Butab, Jubiläumsschrift 1929*. Berlin, 1929.
DHV, ed. *Die Gehaltslage der Kaufmannsgehilfen*. Hamburg, 1931.
———. *Der Tarifvertrag der Kaufmannsgehilfen*. Hamburg, 1931.
———. *DHV-Jahrbuch 1921*. Hamburg, 1922.
———. *Rechenschaftsbericht 1926, 1928*. Hamburg, 1927, 1929.
———. *Die wirtschaftliche Lage der deutschen Handlungsgehilfen*. Hamburg, 1910.
DWB, ed. *10 Jahre Deutscher Werkmeister-Bund, 1919–1929*. Essen, n.d.
DWV, ed. *Festschrift zum 25-jährigen Bestehen des DWV*. Düsseldorf, 1919.
———. *Geschäftsbericht für 1928–1929*. Düsseldorf, 1929.
———. *Der Werkmeister im Tarifvertrag*. Düsseldorf, 1930.
GdA, ed. *Die Angestellten im Behördendienst*. October 1930.
———. *Jahresberichte 1919–20, 1922–23*. Berlin, 1921, 1924.
———. *Die kommende Angestelltengeneration*. Berlin, 1933.
———. *Die wirtschaftliche und soziale Lage der Angestellten; Ergebnisse und Erkenntnisse aus der grossen Erhebung des GdA*. Berlin, 1931.
GdA-Archiv, ed. *Epochen der Angestelltenbewegung 1774–1930*. Berlin, 1930.
———. *Die Angestelltenbewegung 1928–31*, Berlin, 1932.

Internationales Arbeitsamt, ed. *Die sozialen Auswirkungen der Rationalisierung*, Studien und Berichte, Series B, no. 19, (Geneva, 1932).
Mitteilungen des internationalen Bundes christlicher Angestellten-Verbände: Kongressbericht des IV. Internationalen Kongresses, 1929, no. 4.
Vela, ed. *Rechenschaftsbericht der Vela 1929*. Berlin, 1929.
VwA, ed. *40 Jahre VwA, 1889–1929; Jubiläumsschrift*. Berlin, 1929.
ZdA, ed. *Protokoll des 4. Verhandlungstags des ZdA*. Berlin, 1930.

2. General Literature on the History and Sociology of White-Collar Workers in the Weimar Republic.

Allen, W. S. *The Nazi Seizure of Power*. Chicago, 1965.
Aman, J., and P. Lange. *Angestelltengewerkschaften und Presse*. Berlin, 1928.
Anon. *Die Arbeitsmarktlage für Angestellte*. Supplement to the *Reichsarbeitsmarktanzeiger*, 21 July 1932.
———. "Beamte, Angestellte und Arbeiter in der Wirtschaftskrise." *Zentralblatt der Christlichen Gewerkschaften*, 10 October 1930.
———. "Die Bedeutung des Angestelltenstandes." *Deutsche Bergwerkszeitung*, 3 July 1932.
———. "Der DHV als national-politischer Störenfried." Special edition of Zs *Soziale Erneuerung*. Ed. P. Bang et al., 1933.
———. "Entwertung des Menschen." *Das neue Ufer. Germania*, 30 July 1932.
———. "Forderungen zur Wirtschafts- und Sozialpolitik." *GdA-Schriften*, no. 45. Berlin, 1928.
———. "Der Instruktorinnenberuf als Aufstiegsmöglichkeit." *Die Handels- und Büroangestellte*, 1930, no. 8.
———. Das Problem der Personalauslese." *Spannung: Die AEG-Umschau*, January 1930.
Aufhäuser, S. *Weltkrieg und Angestelltenbewegung*. Berlin, 1918.
———. *Ideologie und Taktik der Angestelltenbewegung*. Berlin, 1931.
———. *Eine unromantische Betrachtung zum Geschichtsbild der Angestelltenverbände*. Berlin, 1960.
Aust, O. *Die Reform der öffentlichen Verwaltung in Deutschland*. Berlin, 1928.
Bader, K. S. *Der Kampf gegen Grossbetriebe im Einzelhandel*. Jena, 1932.
Baum, G. *Werkmeisterrecht*. Düsseldorf, 1928.
Baum, M. *Drei Klassen von Lohnarbeiterinnen in Industrie und Handel der Stadt Karlsruhe*. Karlsruhe, 1906.
Bechly, H. *Die deutschnationale Handlungsgehilfenbewegung und die politischen Parteien*. Hamburg, 1911.
———. *Die Führerfrage im neuen Deutschland*. Hamburg, 1932.
———. *Der nationale Gedanke nach der Revolution*. Hamburg, 1919.
———. *Volk, Staat und Wirtschaft*. Hamburg, 1924.
Beckert, F. *Das Berufsbildungswesen der Angestelltenverbände*. Hamburg, 1931.
Behringer, F. *Herkunft, Vorbildung und Berufsausbildung der Kaufmannsgehilfen*. Berlin, 1928.

Bendix, R. *Herrschaft und Industriearbeit*, Frankfurt, 1960.

———, and S. M. Lipset, eds. *Class, Status and Power: Social Stratification in Comparative Perspective*. New York, 1953.

Bennecke, H. *Wirtschaftliche Depression und politischer Radikalismus*. Munich, 1968.

Bente, H. *Organisierte Unwirtschaftlichkeit*. Jena, 1929.

Berger, A. von. *Der leitende Wirtschaftsbeamte*. Vienna, 1926.

Bergsträsser, L. *Die preussische Wahlrechtsfrage im Kriege und die Entstehung der Osterbotschaft 1917*. Tübingen, 1929.

Bode, W. "Der Beruf der Stenotypistin." *Jb der Frauenarbeit* 6(1930).

Bohnstedt, W. "Zur Lage der deutschen Angestellten," *Sozialrechtliches Jb* 3(1932);87–98.

Bohnstengel, P. "Die revolutionäre Angestelltenbewegung." *Der Rote Aufbau*, 1932.

Bolte, K. M., ed. *Beruf und Gesellschaft in Deutschland*. Opladen, 1969.

Borchardt, R. *Deutsche Literatur im Kampfe um ihr Recht*. Munich, 1931.

Bracher, K. -D. *Die Auflösung der Weimarer Republik*. Villingen, 1964.

———. *Die deutsche Diktatur*. Cologne, 1969.

———, W. Sauer, and G. Schulz. *Die nationalsozialistische Machtergreifung*. Cologne/Opladen, 1962.

Brauer, T. "Der Gewerkschaftssekretär." *Sozialrechtliches Jb* 2(1931).

Brell, B. *Das psychologische Berufsbild der Handlungsgehilfen*. Berlin, 1933.

Brendgen, M. "Die Adremaprägerin." *Jugend und Beruf*, 1930, no. 4.

Briefs, G. "Proletariat." In A. Vierkandt, ed. *Hwb der Soziologie*. Stuttgart, 1931. Pp. 441–58.

Bröcker, P. *Die Arbeitnehmerbewegung*. Hamburg, 1919.

Brost, G. *Die Einflüsse der Sozialpolitik auf den Berufsweg des Kaufmannsgehilfen*. Hamburg, 1928.

Broszat, M. "Die völkische Ideologie und der Nationalsozialismus." *Deutsche Rundschau* 84(1958):53–68.

Brüning, H. *Memoiren 1918–1934*. Stuttgart, 1970.

Bry, G. *Wages in Germany, 1871–1945*. Princeton, 1960.

Buschmann, H. "Neue soziale und wirtschaftliche Probleme der Werkmeister." *Schriften des DWV*, no. 45. Düsseldorf, 1930.

———. "Wirtschaft, Sozialpolitik und Verband." *Schriften des DWV*, no. 38, 1925.

Clemenz, M. *Gesellschaftliche Ursprünge des Faschismus*. Frankfurt, 1972.

Conze, W., and H. Raupach, eds. *Die Staats- und Wirtschaftskrise des deutschen Reiches 1929/1933*. Stuttgart, 1967.

Coyner, S. J. "Class Patterns of Family Income and Expenditure during the Weimar Republic: German White Collar Employees as Harbingers of Modern Society." diss., Rutgers University. New Brunswick, N.J., 1975.

Croner, F. *Die Angestellten in der modernen Gesellschaft*. Frankfurt, 1954.

———. "Die Angestelltenbewegung seit der Währungsstabilisierung." *ASS* 60(1928):103ff.

———. "Der Begriff des Angestellten in der neueren Rechtssprechung." *Afa-Bundeszeitung*, 1931, p. 188.

———. *Grundzüge freigewerkschaftlicher Sozialpolitik*. Berlin, 1930.

Crozier, M. *The World of the Office Worker*. New York, 1973.

Dahrendorf, R. *Class and Class Conflict in Industrial Society.* Stanford, 1959.
———. "Demokratie und Sozialstruktur in Deutschland." In *Gesellschaft und Freiheit.* Munich, 1963. Pp. 260–99.
———. *Gesellschaft und Demokratie in Deutschland.* Munich, 1965.
Dederke, K. H. *Reich und Republik: Deutschland 1917–1933.* Munich/Stuttgart, 1969.
Dehn, G. *Proletarische Jugend.* Berlin, 1929.
Deiters, W. "Die Angestellten." *Sozialwissenschaftliche Rundschau.* Supplement to *Ärztliche Mitteilungen,* 15 August 1931.
———. "Die Berufsgliederung der Kaufmannsgehilfen." *Der Kaufmann in Wirtschaft und Recht,* June 1930, pp. 249–58.
———. "Die Buchungsmaschine als soziales Problem." *Der Kaufmann in Wirtschaft und Recht,* April 1927, pp. 159–66.
Dinse, R. *Das Freizeitleben der Großstadtjugend.* Eberswalde, 1932.
Dix, A. *Die deutschen Reichstagswahlen 1871–1930 und die Wandlungen der Volksgliederung.* Tübingen, 1930.
Doblin, E., and C. Pohly. "The Social Composition of the Nazi Leadership." *AJS* 51(1945–46):42–49.
Dohn, L. *Politik und Interesse.* Meisenheim, 1970.
Dominik, H. *Das Schaltwerk: Fabrikhochbau und Hallenbau der Siemens-Schuckert Werke A.G.* Berlin, 1929.
Dreyfuss, C. *Beruf und Ideologie der Angestellten.* Munich, 1933.
Eckert, C., ed. *Der Eintritt der erfahrungswissenschaftlichen Intelligenz in die Verwaltung.* Stuttgart, 1919.
———, ed. *Rothschilds Taschenbuch für Kaufleute.* 2 vols. Leipzig, 1927.
Eliasberg, W. "Wirtschaft und Vertrauen: Beiträge zur Psychologie der älteren Angestellten." *Schm. Jb* 52(1928):61–70.
Engelhard, K. "Die Angestellten." *Kölner VjH für Soziologie* 10(1931);479–520.
Engelhardt, V. "Die Bildungsinteressen in den einzelnen Berufen." *Freie Volksbildung,* 1926.
Erdmann, G. *Die deutschen Arbeitgeberverbände im sozialgeschichtlichen Wandel der Zeit.* Neuwied, 1966.
Erdmann, L. "Nation, Gewerkschaften und Sozialismus." *Die Arbeit* 10(1933):129–61.
Erkelenz, A. "Um die Einheit der deutschen Gewerkschaftsbewegung." *Kölner VjH für Sozialpolitik,* 1932, no. 2.
Eschenburg, T. *Die improvisierte Demokratie: Gesammelte Aufsätze zur Weimarer Republik.* Munich, 1963.
Eschmann, W. "Die Angestellten." *Die Tat,* 1930.
Eulenburg, F. "Die sozialen Wirkungen der Währungsverhältnisse." *Jb für Nationalökonomie und Statistik,* 1924, pp. 748–94.
Eyck, E. *Geschichte der Weimarer Republik.* 2 vols. Erlenbach/Zürich, 1954–56.
Fallada, H. *Kleiner Mann, was nun?.* Berlin, 1932.
Fedisch, R. *Berufsständische Gehaltpolitik.* Hamburg, 1930.
Feldman, G. D., et al. "Die Massenbewegung der Arbeiterschaft in Deutschland am Ende des Ersten Weltkrieges (1917–1920)." *PVS* 13(1972):84–105.
Fick, H. *Der deutsche Militarismus der Vorkriegszeit.* Potsdam, 1932.

Fischer, F. W. "Die Angestellten, ihre Bewegung und ihre Ideologien." Diss., Heidelberg, 1932.

Fischer, W. *Deutsche Wirtschaftspolitik 1918–1945.* Opladen, 1968.

Flick, P. "Zur Analyse des Bankberufs." *Zs für angewandte Psychologie* 35(1930).

Fontane, T. *Briefe an seine Familie.* 2 vols. Berlin, 1924.

————. *Frau Jenny Treibel* (1892). In *Sämtliche Werke: Romane, Erzählungen, Gedichte.* Vol. 4. Munich, 1963.

Fraenkel, A. "Die zwei wirtschaftlichen Weltprobleme." *Schm. Jb* 49(1925):355–80, 653–706.

Fraenkel, E. "10 Jahre Betriebsrätegesetz." *Die Gesellschaft* 7(February 1930):117–29.

Franz, W. *Das Technikerproblem: Grundsätzliches zur Frage künftiger Auslese für den höheren Verwaltungsdienst.* Berlin, 1929.

Freyer, H. *Revolution von rechts.* Jena, 1931.

Fritsch, T. *Handbuch der Judenfrage.* Hamburg, 1932.

Fröhlich, A. *Die mittleren technischen Berufe.* Berlin, 1929.

Frommholz, E. *Die Sozialisierung des Kohlenbergbaus: Materialschrift für die Geschäftsführer des GdA.* Berlin, 1920.

Funk, W. "Die Lage der kaufmännischen Angestellten im deutschen Bankbetriebe." Diss., Giessen, 1927.

Fürst, G. "Die Altersgliederung der Angestellten nach den Ergebnissen der Berufszählung 1925." *Afa-Bundeszeitung,* 1929, pp. 64–65.

————. "Die Angestellten in Klein-, Mittel- und Grossbetrieben." *Afa-Bundeszeitung,* 1929, pp. 48–51.

————. "Die Angestellten nach dem Familienstand." *Afa-Bundeszeitung,* 1929, pp. 106–08.

————. "Die Angestelltenfamilien und ihre Zusammensetzung." *Afa-Bundeszeitung,* 1930, pp. 152–54.

Fuykschot, H. "Die Rückwirkungen der Verwendung von Büromaschinen." In *Mitteilungen des internationalen Bundes christlicher Angestelltengewerkschaften.* Munich, 1929.

Gablentz, O. von der, and G. Mennicke. eds. *Deutsche Berufskunde.* Leipzig, 1930.

————. "Industrie-Bürokratie." *Schm. Jb* 50(1926):539–72.

Gay, P. *Die Republik der Aussenseiter: Geist und Kultur in der Weimarer Zeit 1918–1933.* Frankfurt, 1970.

Geck, C. H. A. *Die sozialen Arbeitsverhältnisse im Wandel der Zeit.* Berlin, 1931.

Geiger, H. "Die Stosskraft der Angestellten." *Die Tat,* 1930.

Geiger, T. "Die gesellschaftliche Bildungsaufgabe der kaufmännischen Schule." In *Erster deutscher Handelsschultag.* Hannover, 1930.

————. "Die Mittelschichten und die Sozialdemokratie." *Die Arbeit* 8(1931):619–35.

————. "Panik im Mittelstand." *Die Arbeit* 7(1930):637–53.

————. "Soziale Gliederung der deutschen Arbeitnehmer." *ASS* 1(1933):151–88.

————. "Zur Kritik der Verbürgerlichung." *Die Arbeit* 8(1931):534–53.

————. *Die soziale Schichtung des deutschen Volkes.* Stuttgart, 1932; new ed., 1967.

Gerth, H. "The Nazi Party: Its Leadership and Composition." *AJS* 54(1940):517–41.

Giese, F. "Menschenbehandlung beim Büropersonal." *Der Werksleiter,* 1928, no. 5.

————. *Methoden der Wirtschaftspsychologie.* Berlin, 1927.

Glass, F., and D. Kische. *Die wirtschaftlichen und sozialen Verhältnisse der berufstätigen Frauen.* Berlin, 1930.

Gloy, L., and F. Schneider-Landmann, *Der DHV und die Presse.* Hamburg, 1928.

Goldschmidt, F. *Die soziale Lage und die Bildung der Kaufmannsgehilfen.* Berlin, 1894.

Grebing, H. *Aktuelle Theorien über Faschismus und Konservativismus.* Stuttgart, 1974.

————. *Der Nationalsozialismus: Ursprung und Wesen.* Munich, 1959.

Grosse, F. *Bildungsinteressen des großstädtischen Proletariats.* Breslau, 1932.

Grotkopp, W. *Die grosse Krise: Lehren aus der Überwindung der Wirtschaftskrise 1929/ 32.* Düsseldorf, 1954.

Grünberg, E. *Der Mittelstand in der kapitalistischen Gesellschaft.* Leipzig, 1932.

Grünfeld, J. "Angestellte und Arbeiter unter dem Druck der Mechanisierung." *Die Gesellschaft* 5(1928):552–68.

Gundlach, P. G. "Staat, Gesellschaft und Wirtschaft in der individualistischen Ära unter katholischer Sicht." In I. van der Velden, ed. *Die berufsständische Ordnung.* Cologne, 1932.

Günther, A. *Die deutschen Techniker, auf Grund einer Erhebung unter den Mitgliedern des DTV.* Leipzig, 1912.

Günther, A. E. "Die Angestellten." *Deutsches Volkstum,* 1930, no.1.

Günther, H. F. K. *Rassenkunde des deutschen Volkes.* Munich, 1926.

Habermann, M. *Die Sozialisierung der Kohle: Ein Gutachten der kaufmännischen Angestellten im Auftrag des DHV.* Hamburg, 1920.

————. *Stand und Staat: Eine Rede an die junge Mannschaft des DHV.* Hamburg, 1931.

Hamel, I. *Völkischer Verband und nationale Gewerkschaft: Der Deutschnationale Handlungsgehilfen-Verband 1893–1933.* Frankfurt, 1966.

Hamm, H. "Die wirtschaftlichen und sozialen Berufsmerkmale der kaufmännischen Angestellten." Diss., Borna/Leipzig, 1931.

Hartfield, G. *Angestellte und Angestelltengewerkschaften in Deutschland.* Berlin, 1961.

Hartwich, H. - H. *Arbeitsmarkt, Verbände und Staat: Die öffentliche Bindung unternehmerischer Funktionen in der Weimarer Republik.* Berlin, 1967.

Heberle, R. *From Democracy to Nazism: A Regional Case Study on Political Parties in Germany.* Baton Rouge, 1945.

Heilfron, E., ed. *Die deutsche Nationalversammlung im Jahre 1919.* Vol. 6. Berlin, n.d.

Heinig, K. *Volkswirtschaftliche Rundschau.* Supplement to the *Deutsche Werkmeister-Zeitung,* 1928, no. 31.

Heller, J. *Something Happened.* New York, 1974.

Hennig, E. *Thesen zur deutschen Sozial- und Wirtschaftsgeschichte 1933–1938.* Frankfurt, 1973.

Hennig, G. *Arbeitgeber, Gewerkschaften, öffentliche Meinung und Presse.* Berlin, 1930.

Henning, F. - W. *Das industrialisierte Deutschland 1914 bis 1972.* Paderborn, 1974.

Hoffmann, P. *Widerstand, Staatsstreich, Attentat: Der Kampf der Opposition gegen Hitler.* Munich, 1969.

Höfchen, C. "Der Stand angestellter Akademiker in Volk und Wirtschaft: Eine soziologische Denkschrift." *Sozialpolitische Schriften des Bundes angestellter Akademiker technisch-naturwissenschaftlicher Berufe e.V.* First series, no. 8. Berlin, 1925.

Hoske, H. "Der Gesundheitszustand der berufstätigen Jugend." *Der Deutsche*, 31 January 1932.

Hüllbüsch, U. "Gewerkschaften und Staat: Ein Beitrag zur Geschichte der Gewerkschaften zu Anfang und zu Ende der Weimarer Republik." Diss., Heidelberg, 1961.

International Labor Office. "The Social Aspects of Rationalization." Series B, Economic Conditions, no. 18. Geneva, 1931.

Jaeckel, R. *Statistik über die Lage der technischen Privatbeamten in Grossberlin.* Jena, 1908.

Jahn, J. *Das grosse Schlagwort.* Hamburg, 1932.

———. "Das Sozialbewusstsein der Angestellten." *Der Kaufmann in Wirtschaft und Recht*, 1930, pp. 241–49.

———. "Der soziologische Sinn der Gehaltspolitik." *Der Kaufmann in Wirtschaft und Recht* no. 3 (1928):97–104.

Jasper, G. *Von Weimar zu Hitler 1930–1933.* Cologne/Berlin, 1968.

Jones, L. E. "The Dying Middle: Weimar Germany and the Fragmentation of Bourgeois Politics." *Central European History* 5(1972):32–54.

Jost, W. *Das Sozialleben des industriellen Betriebs.* Berlin, 1932.

Jung, E. *Die unsterbliche Ingenieurfrage.* Aussig, 1931.

Jünger, E. *Der Arbeiter.* Hamburg, 1932.

———. *In Stahlgewittern.* Berlin, 1920.

———. ed. *Krieg und Krieger.* Hamburg, 1930.

Kadritzke, U. *Angestellte: Die geduldigen Arbeiter.* Frankfurt, 1975.

Kaelble, H. *Industrielle Interessenpolitik in der Wilhelminischen Gesellschaft.* Berlin, 1967.

Kahn-Freund, O. "Der Funktionswandel des Arbeitsrechts." ASS 67(1932):146–74.

Kalveram, W. "Rationalisierung und kaufmännische Betriebsorganisation." In B. Harms, ed. *Strukturwandlung der deutschen Volkswirtschaft.* Berlin, 1928.

Kampffmeyer, P. *Unter dem Sozialistengesetz.* Berlin, 1928.

Kannwitz, E. "Aus dem Berufsleben eines technischen Vorkalkulators." *Jugend und Beruf*, March 1931.

Kater, M. H. "Zur Soziographie der frühen NSDAP." VfZG 19(1971):124–59.

Kehr, E. "Zur Genesis des kgl. preussischen Reserveoffiziers." *Die Gesellschaft*, 1928, pp. 492–502.

Kele, M. H. *Nazi and Workers: National Socialist Appeals to German Labor, 1919 to 1933.* Chapel Hill, 1972.

Kisker, I. *Die Frauenarbeit in den Kontoren einer Großstadt.* Tübingen, 1911.

Klemperer, K. von. *Konservative Bewegungen.* Munich, 1962.

Kocka, J. "The First World War and the 'Mittelstand': German Artisans and White Collar Workers." *Journal of Contemporary History* 8(1973):101–24.

———. *Klassengesellschaft im Krieg 1914–1918.* Göttingen, 1975.

———. *Unternehmensverwaltung und Angestelltenschaft am Beispiel Siemens 1847 bis 1914.* Stuttgart, 1969.

———. "Zur Problematik der deutschen Angestellten." In H. Mommsen et al., eds. *Industrielles System und politische Entwicklung in der Weimarer Republik.* Düsseldorf, 1974. Pp. 792–811.

Köhler, C. "Die Sozialisierung und die Angestellten." *Schriftenreihe Deutschlands Wiederaufbau*, no. 7. Berlin, 1919.

Köhler, M. *Die Privatbeamtenpolitik nach dem Kriege*. Bonn, 1918.

Kolb, E. *Vom Kaiserreich zur Weimarer Republik*. Cologne, 1972.

Kracauer, S. *Die Angestellten*. Frankfurt, 1930; new ed., 1971.

Krebs, A. *Tendenzen und Gestalten der NSDAP: Erinnerungen an die Frühzeit der Partei*. Stuttgart, 1959.

Kretzschmar, H. "Die technischen Akademiker und die Führerauslese." *Schriften des Bundes angestellter Akademiker technisch-naturwissenschaftlicher Berufe*. Berlin, 1930.

Kroll, G. *Von der Weltwirtschaftskrise zur Staatskonjunktur*. Berlin, 1958.

Kühnl, R. *Deutschland zwischen Demokratie und Faschismus*. Munich, 1969.

————. *Formen bürgerlicher Herrschaft: Liberalismus-Faschismus*. Hamburg, 1971.

Küstermeyer, R. *Die Mittelschichten und ihr politischer Weg*. Potsdam, 1933.

Kunze, O. *Schutz der älteren Angestellten*. Berlin, 1929.

Lakenbacher, E. "Die Erschütterung des Angestelltentums." *Der Kampf*, 1930, pp. 470–75.

————. "Wende in der Angestelltenpolitik." *Der Kampf*, 1931, pp. 394–403.

Lambach, W. *Sozialisierung und kaufmännische Angestellte*. Hamburg, 1919.

————. *Ursachen des Zusammenbruchs*. Hamburg, 1921.

Landes, D. S. *The Unbound Prometheus*. Cambridge, 1969.

Lange, P. *Die soziale Bewegung der kaufmännischen Angestellten*. Berlin, 1920.

Laqueur, W. *Weimar: A Cultural History*. New York, 1974.

————. *Young Germany: A History of the German Youth Movement*. New York, 1962.

Lasswell, H. D. "The Psychology of Hitlerism as a Response of the Lower Middle Classes to Continuing Insecurity" (1933). In Lasswell, *The Analysis of Political Behavior*. New York, 1947.

Leber, A., ed. *Das Gewissen steht auf: 64 Lebensbilder aus dem deutschen Widerstand 1933–1945*. Berlin, 1954.

Lebovics, H. *Social Conservatism and the Middle Classes in Germany*. Princeton, 1969.

Lederer, E. *Die Privatangestellten in der modernen Wirtschaftsentwicklung*. Tübingen, 1912.

————. "Sozialpolitische Chronik." *ASS* 38(1914);598–645; 39(1914)297–345; 41(1915);569–612; 42(1917);1013–46; 44(1917);309–47; 47(1920);218–69; 47(1920);585–619.

————. "Die Umschichtung des Proletariats: Vortrag auf dem 3. Afa-Gewerkschaftskongress vom 1. -4.10. 1928 in Hamburg." *Protokoll des Kongresses*. Pp. 129ff.

————. "Zum sozialpsychischen Habitus der Gegenwart." *ASS* 39(1918/19);11ff.

————. "Die Unternehmerorganisationen im Kriege." *ASS* 41(1915):277–97.

————, and J. Marschak. "Der neue Mittelstand." In *Grundriss der Sozialökonomik*. sect. 9, pt. 1. Tübingen, 1926. Pp. 120–41.

Leichter, K. *So leben wir . . . 1320 Industriearbeiterinnen berichten über ihr Leben: Eine Erhebung*. Vienna, 1932.

Lepsius, M. R. *Extremer Nationalismus*. Stuttgart, 1966.

————. "Parteiensystem und Sozialstruktur: Zum Problem der Demokratisierung der deutschen Gesellschaft." In G. A. Ritter, ed. *Deutsche Parteien vor 1918*. Cologne, 1973. Pp. 57–80.

Lerner, D., et al. *The Nazi Elite*. Stanford, 1951.

Levenstein, A. *Die Arbeiterfrage*. Munich, 1912.

Liederbuch für deutschnationale Handlungsgehilfen. Hamburg, 1927.

Lipset, S. M. *Political Man*. New York, 1959.

Ludwig, K. -H. *Technik und Ingenieure im Dritten Reich*. Düsseldorf, 1974.

Lufft, H. "Kulturvitalität im Angestelltenstand." *Deutsche Arbeit*, February 1931, pp. 66–82.

Mahnkopf, B. *Verbürgerlichung*. Frankfurt and New York, 1985. Esp. "Die Kontroverse zwischen H. Speier und Th. Geiger," pp. 79–123.

Mantel, F. *Die Angestelltenbewegung in Deutschland*. Leipzig, 1921.

———. "Die Vollsozialisierung der Angestellten." *Verbandsblätter: Zs des Verbandes der deutschen Handlungsgehilfen*, 1920, no. 6.

Marx, K. *Das Kapital*. Berlin, 1975.

Massing, P. *Rehearsal for Destruction: A Study of Political Antisemitism in Imperial Germany*. New York, 1949.

Matschoss, K. "Berufskundliche Untersuchung des Buches 'Männer der Technik.' " *Der Ingenieurstand*, 1925.

McKibbin, R. J. "The Myth of the Unemployed: Who Did Vote for the Nazis?" *Australian Journal for Politics and History*, 1969, pp. 25–40.

Megede, W., zur. *Volkswirtschaftliche und soziale Auswirkungen des Betriebsrätegesetzes*. Munich, 1927.

Mende, K. "Münchener jugendliche Ladnerinnen zu Hause und im Beruf." Diss., Munich, 1912.

Merkl, P. H. "Die alten Kämpfer der NSDAP." *Sozialwissenschaftliches Jb der Politik* 2(1971):495–517.

Mertens, W. "Zur Bewegung der technischen Privatbeamten." ASS 25(1907):649–713.

Messarius, G. "Der Mittelbetrieb in der nationalen Wirtschaft." *Die Welt des Kaufmanns*, October 1932.

Mewes, B. *Die erwerbstätige Jugend*. Berlin, 1929.

Michels, R. *Umschichtungen in den herrschenden Klassen nach dem Kriege*. Stuttgart, 1934.

Mierendorff, C. "Gesicht und Charakter der nationalsozialistischen Bewegung." *Die Gesellschaft* 7(1930):489–504.

Milatz, A. *Wähler und Wahlen in der Weimarer Republik*. Bonn, 1965.

Moeller von den Bruck, A. *Das dritte Reich*. Hamburg, 1931.

Mohler, A. *Die konservative Revolution in Deutschland*. Stuttgart, 1950.

Mohr, "Die Angestellten in der deutschen Landwirtschaft." *Kölner VjH für Sozialpolitik*, 1932.

Mommsen, H., et al., eds. *Industrielles System und politische Entwicklung in der Weimarer Republik*. Düsseldorf, 1974.

Mosse, G. L. *Nazi Culture*. New York, 1966.

———. *The Crisis of German Ideology: Intellectual Origins of the Third Reich*. New York, 1964.

Dr. Müffelmann. "Die Gewerkschaftsbewegung der leitenden Angestellten." *Schriften der Vela*, no. 2. 1921.

Müller, F. "Das soziale Schicksal des alternden Arbeitsnehmers." *Sozialrechtliches Jb* 1(1930):3–80.

Müller, H. *Nivellierung und Differenzierung der Arbeitseinkommen in Deutschland seit 1925.* Berlin, 1954.

Müller, W. *Rationelle Menschenführung.* Berlin, 1930.

————. *Das soziale Leben in Deutschland.* Berlin, 1938.

Naphtali, F. *Wirtschaftsdemokratie: Ihr Wesen, Weg und Ziel.* Berlin, 1928; Frankfurt, 1969.

Nebgen, L. *Jakob Kaiser.* Stuttgart, 1967.

Neisser, H. "Sozialdemokratische Analyse der Wahlergebnisse." *Die Arbeit* 7(1930):654–59.

Nestriepke, S. *Die Gewerkschaftsbewegung.* 3 vols. Stuttgart, 1923.

Neuhaus, G. "Die berufliche und soziale Gliederung der Bevölkerung im Zeitalter des Kapitalismus." In *Grundriss der Sozialökonomik.* sect. 9, pt. 1. Tübingen, 1926. Pp. 360–459.

Neumann, F. *Behemoth: The Structure and Practice of National Socialism.* New York, 1942.

Neumann, S. *Die deutschen Parteien.* Berlin, 1932; new ed., Stuttgart, 1965.

Nolte, E. *Der Faschismus in seiner Epoche.* Munich, 1965.

————. *Die faschistischen Bewegungen.* Munich, 1973.

————, ed. *Theorien über den Faschismus.* Cologne, 1972.

Nordsieck, F. "Die Arbeitsaufgaben und ihre Verteilung." In *HB des Einzelhandels.* Stuttgart, 1932.

————. *Die schaubildliche Erfassung und Untersuchung der Organisation.* Stuttgart, 1932.

Nörpel, C. "Grenzen des Arbeitsrechts." *Die Arbeit* 8(1932).

Nothaas, J. "Sozialer Auf- und Abstieg im deutschen Volk." *Bayerisches Statistisches Landesamt. Beiträge zur Statistik Bayerns,* no. 117. Munich, 1930.

O'Lessker, K. "Who Voted for Hitler?" *AJS* 74(1968):63–69.

Orlow, D. *The History of the Nazi Party.* Vol. 1: 1919–1933. Pittsburgh, 1971.

Pachter, H. M. "The Intellectuals and the State of Weimar." *Social Research* 39(1972):228–53.

Parsons, T. "Democracy and Social Structure in Pre-Nazi Germany" (1942)." In Parsons, *Essays in Sociological Theory.* Glencoe, 1958.

Pechel, R. *Deutscher Widerstand.* Erlenbach-Zürich, 1947.

Petzina, D. "Germany and the Great Depression." *Journal of Contemporary History* 4(1969):59–74.

————. "Materialien zum sozialen und wirtschaftlichen Wandel in Deutschland seit dem Ende des 19. Jahrhunderts." *VfZG* 17(1969): 308–78.

Pfirrmann, F. "Der Fuchs predigt den Hühnern." *Afa-Bundeszeitung,* September 1932.

Philippe, C. "Die Stellung des Angestellten im Arbeitsrecht." *Magazin der Wirtschaft,* 3 July 1931, pp. 1075–79.

Pjatnizki, O. "Brennende Fragen." *Bücherei des Parteiarbeiters.* Vol. 2. Hamburg, 1931.

Potthoff, H. ed. *Die sozialen Probleme des Betriebes.* Berlin, 1925.

————. *Privatangestellte und politisches Leben.* Munich, 1911.

Pratt, S. A. "The Social Basis of Nazism and Communism in Urban Germany; A Correlation Study of the July 31, 1932, Reichstag Election in Germany." M. A. thesis, Michigan College, Dept. of Sociology and Anthropology, 1948.

Preller, L. *Sozialpolitik in der Weimarer Republik.* Stuttgart, 1949.

Reif, I. "Der VDH zu Leipzig." In *Jb der Angestelltenbewegung,* 1914.

Renner, K. "Die Geltung der Ingenieurarbeit in Wirtschaft und Gesellschaft." *Schriftenreihe des Bundes der Industrieangestellten Österreichs,* no. 3. 1924.

Riemer, S. "Mittelstand und sozialistische Politik." *Die Arbeit* 9(1932):265–72.

Riezler, K. *Tagebücher, Aufsätze, Dokumente.* Göttingen, 1972.

Rocker, R. *Johann Most: Das Leben eines Rebellen.* Berlin, 1924.

Rössiger, M. *Der Angestellte von 1930.* Berlin, 1930.

———. *Der werdende Wirtschaftsbürger.* Berlin, 1928.

Rosenberg, A. *Die Entstehung der deutschen Republik.* Berlin, 1928; Frankfurt, 1971.

———. *Geschichte der Weimarer Republik.* Frankfurt, 1971.

Sauer, W. "National Socialism: Totalitarianism or Fascism?" *AHR* 73(1967): 404–24.

Schäfer, H. "Die leitenden Angestellten: Ein neuer sozialer Typus." *Bergwerkszeitung,* 11 November 1928.

Schäfer, W. *NSDAP: Entwicklung und Struktur der Staatspartei des Dritten Reichs.* Hannover, 1956.

Schlözer, A. L. *Theorie der Statistik.* Göttingen, 1804.

Schmoller, G. *Die soziale Frage.* Munich, 1918.

———. "Was verstehen wir unter dem Mittelstand?" In *Verhandlungen des 8. Evangelischsozialen Kongresses.* Göttingen, 1897.

Schnaas, H. "Der Arbeitsmarkt der Angestellten und die Arbeitsmarktpolitik der Angestelltenorganisationen." Diss., Münster, 1929.

Schneider, G. *Die Angestellten im demokratischen Volksstaat.* Leipzig, 1920.

———. *Die Angestelltenbewegung im Lichte des Krieges und der Revolution.* Berlin, 1919.

———. *Die geistigen Grundlagen der GdA-Arbeit.* Berlin, 1930.

Schoenbaum, D. *Hitler's Social Revolution.* New York, 1968.

Schopenhauer, A. "Aphorismen zur Lebensweisheit." In *Sämtliche Werke.* Ed. M. Frischeisen-Köhler. Vol. 6. Berlin and New York, n.d. Pp. 303–477.

Schröer, H. *Die betriebliche Ausbildung des Verkaufspersonals im Einzelhandel.* Stuttgart, 1933.

Schulze, F., and P. Scymank. *Das deutsche Studententum.* Leipzig, 1910.

Schumann, H. -G. *Nationalsozialismus und Gewerkschaftsbewegung.* Hannover, 1956.

Schumpeter, J. A. "Das soziale Antlitz des deutschen Reiches" (1929). In Schumpeter, *Aufsätze zur Soziologie.* Tübingen, 1953. Pp. 214–25.

Schuon, H. *Der deutschnationale Handlungsgehilfen-Verband zu Hamburg.* Jena, 1914.

Silbermann, J. "Die soziale Herkunft der Berliner Handlungsgehilfen." *Soziale Praxis* 12(1903):1304–06.

———. "Zur Entlohnung der Frauenarbeit." *Schm. Jb* 23(1899):1401–44.

Silbermann, *Die Angestellten als Stand.* Berlin, 1932.

Sintheimer, K. *Antidemokratisches Denken in der Weimarer Republik: Die politischen Ideen des deutschen Nationalismus zwischen 1918 und 1933.* Munich, 1966.

Sohn-Rethel, A. *Ökonomie und Klassenstruktur des deutschen Faschismus: Aufzeichnungen und Analyse.* Frankfurt, 1973.

Sombart, W. "Beruf." In A. Vierkandt, ed. *Hwb der Soziologie.* Stuttgart, 1931.

Spahn, M. "Die christlich-soziale Bewegung." *Hochland* 26(1929):164–82.

Speier, H. "Betrachtungen zur Erfassung der sozialen Struktur." ASS 69(1933):705–25.
——. "Das Proletariat und seine Kritiker." Die Neue Rundschau 43(1932):289–304.
——. Social Order and the Risks of War: Papers in Political Sociology. New York, 1952; pbk., Cambridge, Mass., 1969.
——. "Social Stratification." In M. Ascoli and F. Lehmann, eds. Political and Economic Democracy. New York, 1937. Pp. 255–70.
——. "Verbürgerlichung des Proletariats?" Magazin der Wirtschaft, 27 March and 3 April 1931.
——. "Zur Soziologie der bürgerlichen Intelligenz in Deutschland." Die Gesellschaft, 1929, pp. 58–72.
Stapel, A. Der christliche Staatsmann: Eine Theologie des Nationalismus. Hamburg, 1932.
Stapel, W. Die Fiktionen der Weimarer Verfassung: Versuch einer Unterscheidung der formalen und der funktionalen Demokratie. Hamburg, 1928.
——. Volksbürgerliche Erziehung. Hamburg, 1920.
Stegmann, D. "Zwischen Repression und Manipulation: Konservative Machteliten und Arbeiter- und Angestelltenbewegung 1910–1918." ASG 12(1972):351–432.
Stehr, K. "Der Zentralverband der Angestellten." Diss., Halle, 1926.
Steinhausen, G. Der Kaufmann in der deutschen Vergangenheit. Leipzig, 1899.
Stern, F. Kulturpessimismus als politische Gefahr. Bern, 1963.
Stiller, W. Der Verein für Handlungs-Commis von 1858. Jena, 1910.
Stillich, O. "Die Herkunft der Bankbeamten." ZfGS 72(1916):401–15.
Stoecker, A. Christlich-sozial: Reden und Aufsätze. Berlin, 1890.
Strater, E. "Die soziale Stellung der Angestellten." Diss., Bonn, 1933.
Süssengut, O. "Die Angestellten als Stand und Klasse." Diss., Halle, 1927.
Suhr, O. "Angestelltenbildung." In Hwb des deutschen Volksbildungswesens. Ed. Becker. Breslau, 1932.
——. "Die Angestellten in der deutschen Wirtschaft." In Protokoll des 3. Afa-Gewerkschaftskongresses vom 1. 4. 1928. Pp. 82–107.
——. Die Lebenshaltung der Angestellten: Untersuchungen auf Grund statistischer Erhebungen des Afa-Bundes. Berlin, 1928.
Suhr, S. Die weiblichen Angestellten. Berlin, 1930.
Süss, B. Klärung der Angestelltenbewegung. Berlin, 1921.
Syrup, F., ed., HB des Arbeiterschutzes und der Betriebssicherheit. Berlin, n.d.
Thiel, O. Die Sozialpolitik der Kaufmannsgehilfen. Hamburg, 1926.
Thomas, A., E. Lederer, and O. Suhr. Angestellte und Arbeiter. Berlin, 1928.
Timm, H. Die deutsche Sozialpolitik und der Bruch der grossen Koalition im März 1930. Düsseldorf, 1952.
Tobis, H. Das Mittelstandsproblem der Nachkriegszeit und seine statistische Erfassung. Grimmen, 1930.
Tönnies, F. Der Kampf um das Sozialistengesetz 1878. Berlin, 1929.
Treitschke, H. von. Politik. 2 vols. Ed. M. Cornicelius. Leipzig, 1918.
Turner, H. A., Jr. Faschismus und Kapitalismus in Deutschland. Göttingen, 1972.
Urbschat, F. Das Seelenleben der kaufmännisch tätigen Jugendlichen. Langensalza, 1932.
Van der Velden, I., ed. Die berufsständische Ordnung. Cologne, 1932.
Victor, M. "Die Stellung der deutschen Sozialdemokratie zu den Fragen der auswärtigen Politik (1869–1914)." ASS 60(1928): 147–79.

Walbrodt, L. "Die Rationalisierung in Büro und Handel." *Jugend und Beruf,* April 1931.

Wald, E. "Antiproletarische Sozialpolitik." *Der Kaufmann in Wirtschaft und Recht,* June 1930.

Walther, E. "Die Handels- und Büroangestellte." *Schriften des Berufskundlichen Ausschusses bei der Reichsanstalt für Arbeitsvermittlung und Arbeitslosenversicherung,* no. 10. Berlin, n.d.

"Was wir wollen." 1. *Schriftenreihe des DHV,* no. 3. Hamburg, 1903.

Webb, S. and B. *Soviet Communism.* London, 1930.

Weber, A. "Soziale Merkmale der NSDAP-Wähler." Diss., Freiburg i. Br., 1969.

Weber, M. *Economy and Society.* Ed. G. Roth and C. Wittich. Berkeley, 1978.

⸺. *Wirtschaft und Gesellschaft.* Tübingen, 1925; 1972.

Weiland, R. *Die Kinder der Arbeitslosen.* Eberswalde, 1933.

Werner, G. "Der Weg der Sozialisierung des Kohlenbergbaus." *Schriften des Butab,* no. 6. Berlin, 1920.

White, T. H. *Breach of Faith.* New York, 1975.

Wiedenfeld, K. *Kapitalismus und Beamtentum.* Berlin, 1932.

Winkler, H. A. "Extremismus der Mitte? Sozialgeschichtliche Aspekte der nationalsozialistischen Machtergreifung." *VfZG* 20(1972):175–91.

⸺. *Mittelstand, Demokratie und Nationalsozialismus.* Cologne, 1972.

Winnig, A. *Vom Proletariat zum Arbeitertum.* Hamburg, 1930.

Wissdorf, A. "Die Verkäuferin im Lebensmittelhandel." *Kölner VjH für Sozialpolitik,* 1931.

Witsch, J. *Weibliche Angestellte in der schönen Literatur.* Cologne, 1933.

Witzleben, W. D. von. "Der Tarifvertrag für die Angestellten der Berliner Metallindustrie." *Schriften der Vereinigung der deutschen Arbeitgeberverbände,* no. 15. Berlin, 1926.

Woldt, R. *Das grossindustrielle Beamtentum.* Stuttgart, 1911.

⸺. "Der Werkmeister im Wirtschaftskampfe." *Schriften des DWV,* no. 34. Düsseldorf, 1920.

Woolf, S. J., ed. *The Nature of Fascism.* New York, 1968.

Zahn, F. "Wirtschaftsaufbau Deutschlands." In *Hwb der Staatswissenschaften: Ergänzungsband.* Jena, 1929. Pp. 980ff.

Zechlin, E. *Staatsstreichspläne Bismarcks und Wilhelm II. 1890–94.* Stuttgart, 1929.

Zimmermann, A. *Der Deutschnationale Handlungsgehilfen-Verband: Sein Werden, Wirken und Wollen.* Hamburg, n.d.

Index

machine operators, 27, 29–30
management, 88
managers, unemployment, 179n11
Mannheim, Karl, xix
Martin, Alfred von, xvii, 169
Marx, Karl, 90, 95
Marxist class theory of white-collar workers, 5, 7, 75ff.
Marxist theory of society, 4
May day, as Nazi holiday, 153
middle class, new, 68; old, 12; radicalization in World War I, 68; middle-class theory of white-collar workers, 5, 7, 42f., 69ff.
Mierendorff, Carl, xix
militarism, 3, 4, 32, 103ff., 109
Moeller van den Bruck, Arthur, 96
Most, Johann, 121
Muchow, R., 156, 157
Mussolini, Benito, 108

nationalism, 103ff.
nationalization of industry, debate on (1919), 133ff.
Neumann, Sigmund, xvii, 186n35
nobility, 4
Nörpel, G., 79
NSBO, 151, 152
NSDAP, xxi, 22, 110–13, 114, 139, 151–52, 184n14; and DHV, 108ff., 153ff.; and engineers, 22

October Revolution, Russian, 126
office employees, 159, 160
office machines, 26–27, 30, 120
officers, military, prestige of. See prestige
one-price-store, 24–26

Papen, Franz von, 151
Pjatnizki, O., 185n30
prestige, social, xviii, 7–8, 20; of education, 81; of managers, 86; of nationalism, 103ff.; of nobility, 4, 80; of officers, 4, 80–81; and power, 8, 86; of state service, 80
Priestley, John Boynton, 12
proletarianization, 23, 33, 52, 58, 61, 76, 83, 139
proletariat, transformation of, 5, 161
promotion, 41ff.
Protestantism, 109

Raabe, Wilhelm, 112
Rapallo Treaty (1922), 151
Renner, Karl, 132
reserve officers, 106
Rössiger, Max, 50, 51

SA, 111, 151, 153
salespeople, 11, 15, 24–26; social origin, 35, 36; social rank according to goods sold, 15
Salomon, Albert, xvii
Schäfer, Wolfgang, 113
Scharnhorst, G. J. D., 98
Schmeer, R., 156
Schneider, Gustav, 135ff.
Scholözer, A. L., 81
Schopenhauer, Arthur, 113–14
Schumann, R., 156
Schumpeter, Josef, 6
shop councils, law on, 131, 133ff.
Silbermann, J., 72, 82
social insurance for salaried employees (1911), 66ff., 123
Sombart, Werner, 74, 112
SPD, xx, 77, 105, 111, 113, 114, 124, 126, 135, 184n14, 151
Spengler, Oswald, 105
SS, 151, 153
"stab-in-the-back" legend, 82, 133ff.
Stahlhelm, 111
Stapel, Wilhelm, 107, 110, 112, 116
Stoecker, Adolf, 115, 120, 121, 122
Stöhr, Franz, 139, 156
Stresemann, Gustav, 67, 110, 151
Strasser, Gregor, 110, 157
strikes, 124, 126, 130, 187n12; strikes of white-collar workers, 119, 131–32
Suhr, Otto, xix
Suhr, Susanne, 52

textile industry, 16
Thiel, Otto, 110, 139
time keepers, 16
Tirpitz, Grossadmiral von, 112
trade unions, 109, 128, 142; recognized in Weimar constitution, 128
traveling salesmen, 42, 172n36
Traven, B., 89
Treitschke, Heinrich von, 96, 97, 98
Turner, Henry Ashby, Jr., 108
typists, 28–29

Ullmann, Hermann, 112
unemployment: of white-collar workers, 61ff.; of managers, 74
unemployment insurance, law on (1927), 137
unionization. See trade unions, commercial employees, foremen, white-collar workers
USPD, 126, 132, 135, 137

VdDI, 14
Vela, xix, 74, 78, 142